the daily lives of high school boys

1

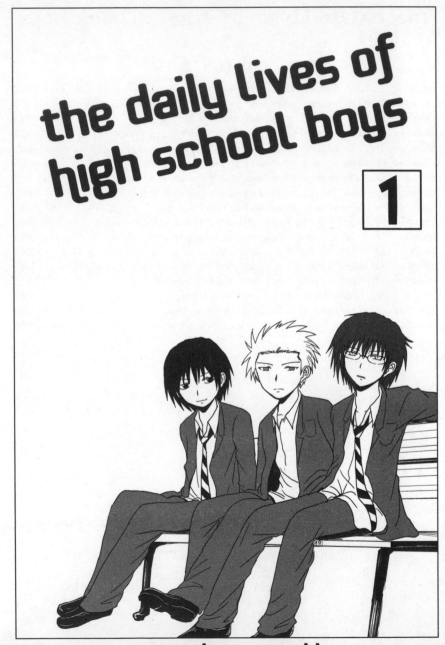

yasunobu yamauchi

the daily lives of high school boys

CONTENTS

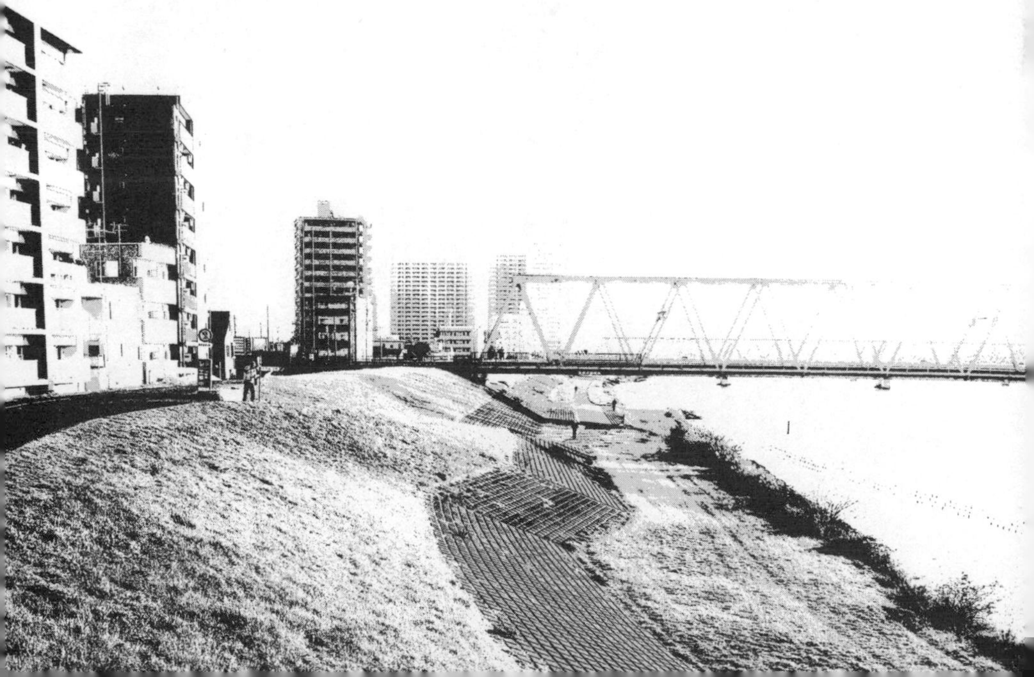

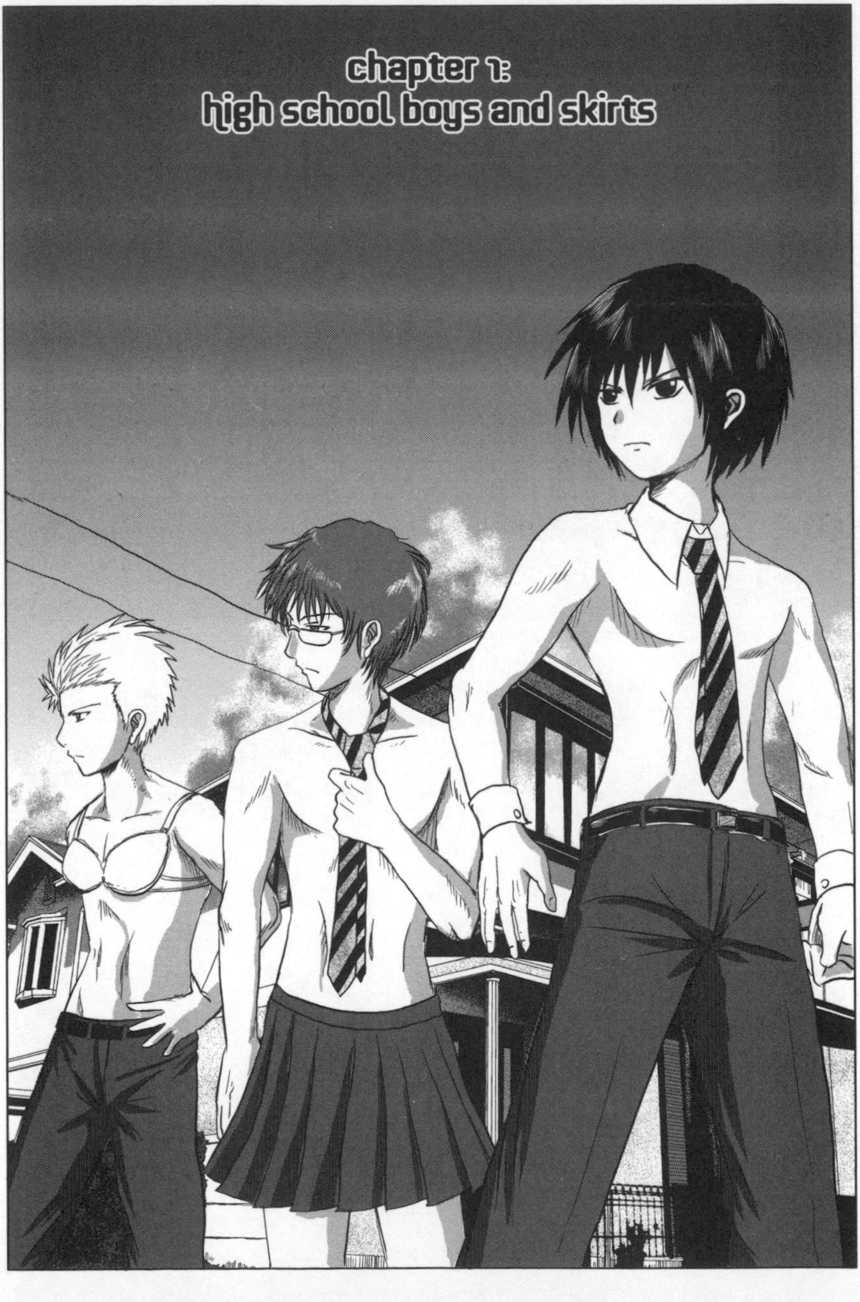
chapter 1:
high school boys and skirts

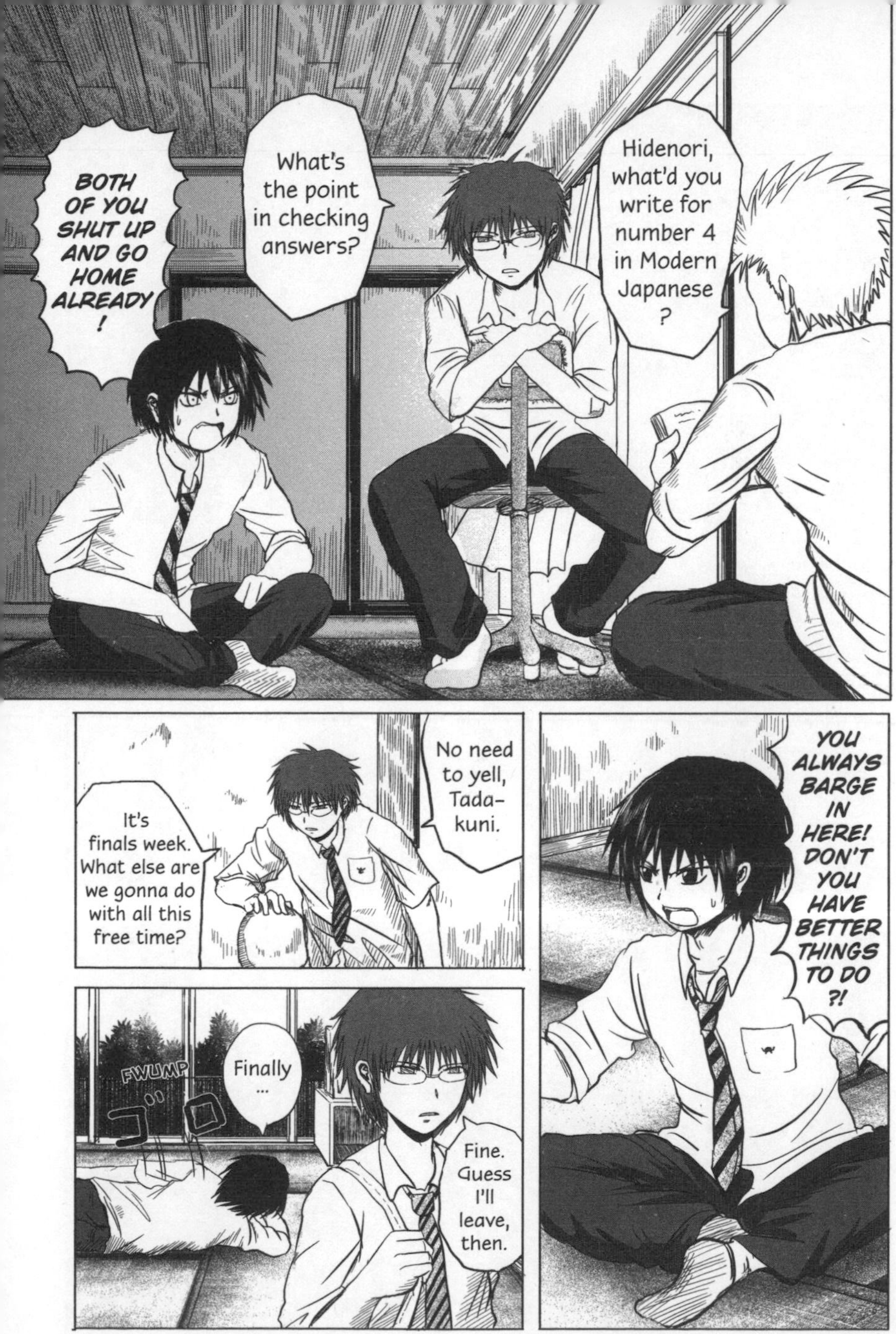

Hidenori, what'd you write for number 4 in Modern Japanese?
What's the point in checking answers?
BOTH OF YOU SHUT UP AND GO HOME ALREADY!
YOU ALWAYS BARGE IN HERE! DON'T YOU HAVE BETTER THINGS TO DO?!
No need to yell, Tada-kuni.
It's finals week. What else are we gonna do with all this free time?
Fine. Guess I'll leave, then.
Finally...
FWUMP
ゴロ

*cicadas chirping

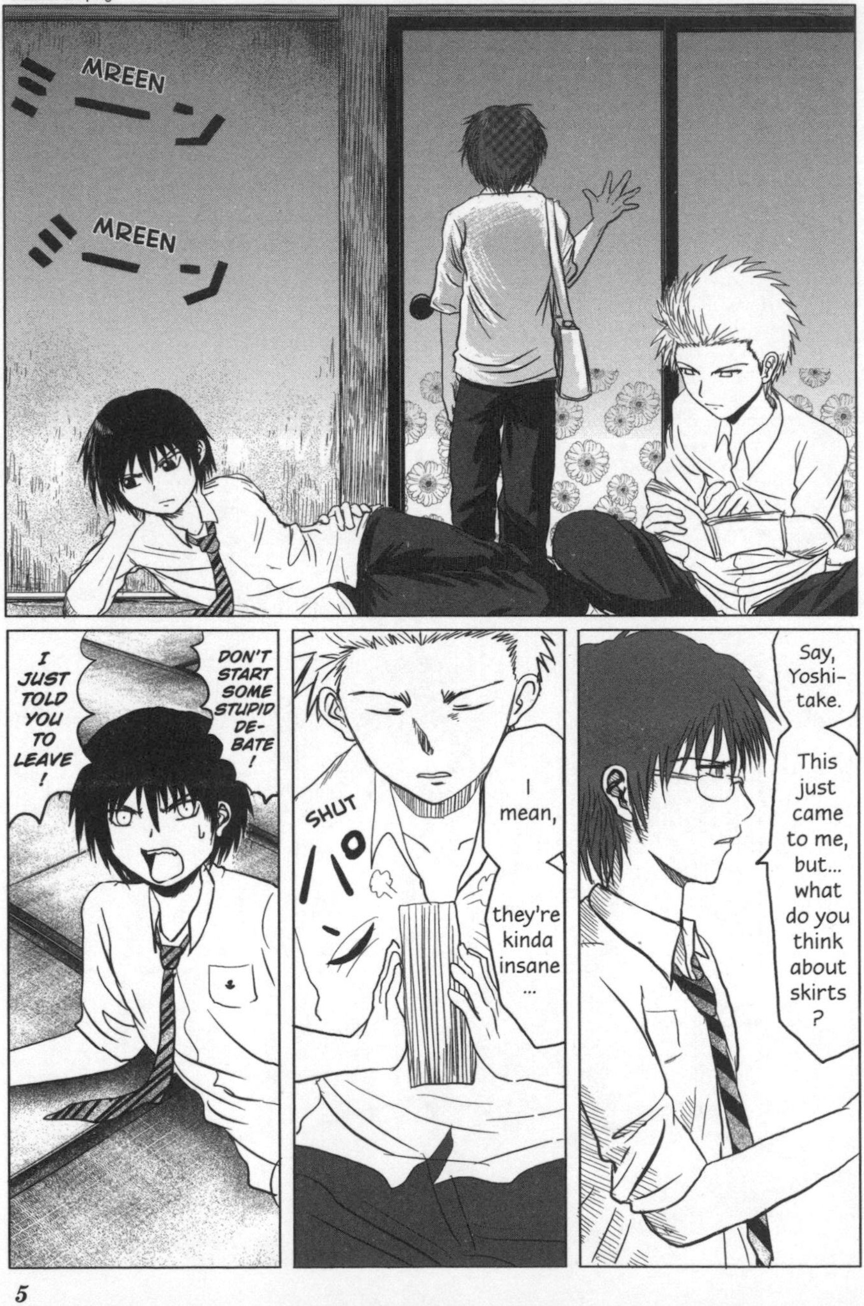
MREEN
ミーン
MREEN
ミーン
Say, Yoshi-take.
This just came to me, but... what do you think about skirts?
I mean,
they're kinda insane ...
SHUT
パン
DON'T START SOME STUPID DE-BATE!
I JUST TOLD YOU TO LEAVE!

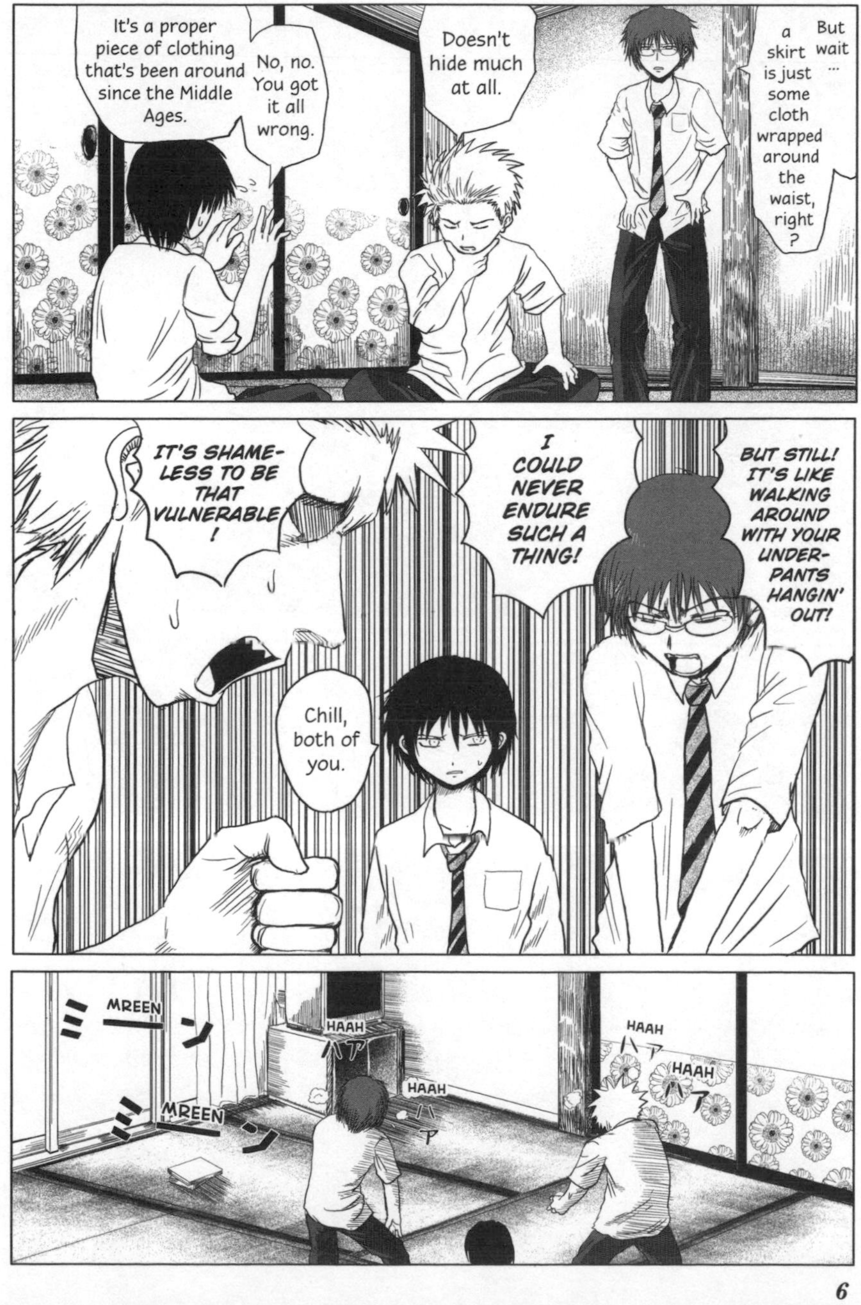
But wait … a skirt is just some cloth wrapped around the waist, right?
Doesn't hide much at all.
No, no. You got it all wrong.
It's a proper piece of clothing that's been around since the Middle Ages.
BUT STILL! IT'S LIKE WALKING AROUND WITH YOUR UNDER-PANTS HANGIN' OUT!
I COULD NEVER ENDURE SUCH A THING!
IT'S SHAME-LESS TO BE THAT VULNERABLE!
Chill, both of you.
HAAH ハア
HAAH ハア
HAAH ハア
HAAH ハア
MREEN ミーン
MREEN ミーン

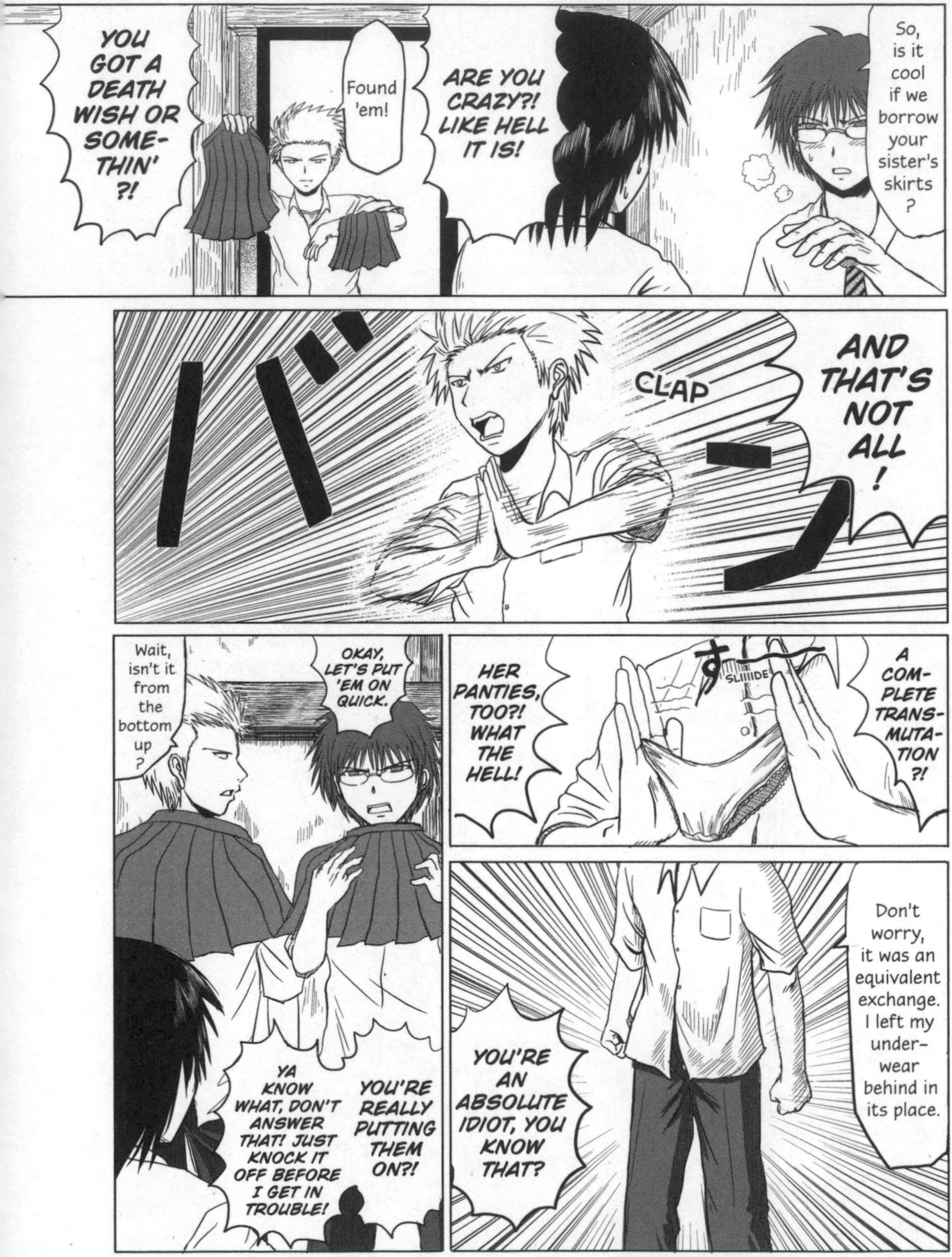

So, is it cool if we borrow your sister's skirts?
ARE YOU CRAZY?! LIKE HELL IT IS!
Found 'em!
YOU GOT A DEATH WISH OR SOMETHIN'?!
AND THAT'S NOT ALL!
CLAP
バーン
A COMPLETE TRANSMUTATION?!
す
SLIIIDE
HER PANTIES, TOO?! WHAT THE HELL!
Don't worry, it was an equivalent exchange. I left my underwear behind in its place.
YOU'RE AN ABSOLUTE IDIOT, YOU KNOW THAT?
OKAY, LET'S PUT 'EM ON QUICK.
Wait, isn't it from the bottom up?
YOU'RE REALLY PUTTING THEM ON?!
YA KNOW WHAT, DON'T ANSWER THAT! JUST KNOCK IT OFF BEFORE I GET IN TROUBLE!

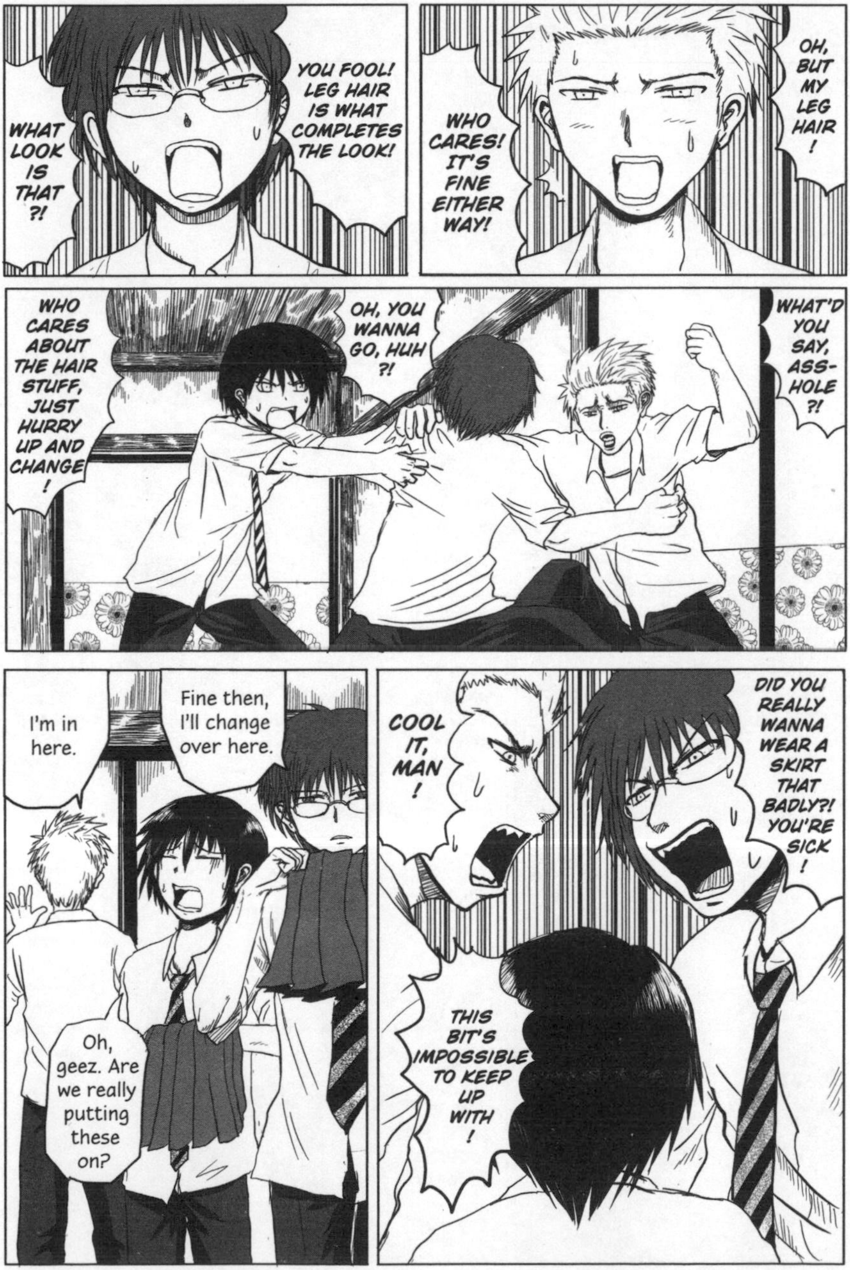
OH, BUT MY LEG HAIR!
WHO CARES! IT'S FINE EITHER WAY!
YOU FOOL! LEG HAIR IS WHAT COMPLETES THE LOOK!
WHAT LOOK IS THAT?!
WHAT'D YOU SAY, ASSHOLE?!
OH, YOU WANNA GO, HUH?!
WHO CARES ABOUT THE HAIR STUFF, JUST HURRY UP AND CHANGE!
DID YOU REALLY WANNA WEAR A SKIRT THAT BADLY?! YOU'RE SICK!
COOL IT, MAN!
THIS BIT'S IMPOSSIBLE TO KEEP UP WITH!
Fine then, I'll change over here.
I'm in here.
Oh, geez. Are we really putting these on?

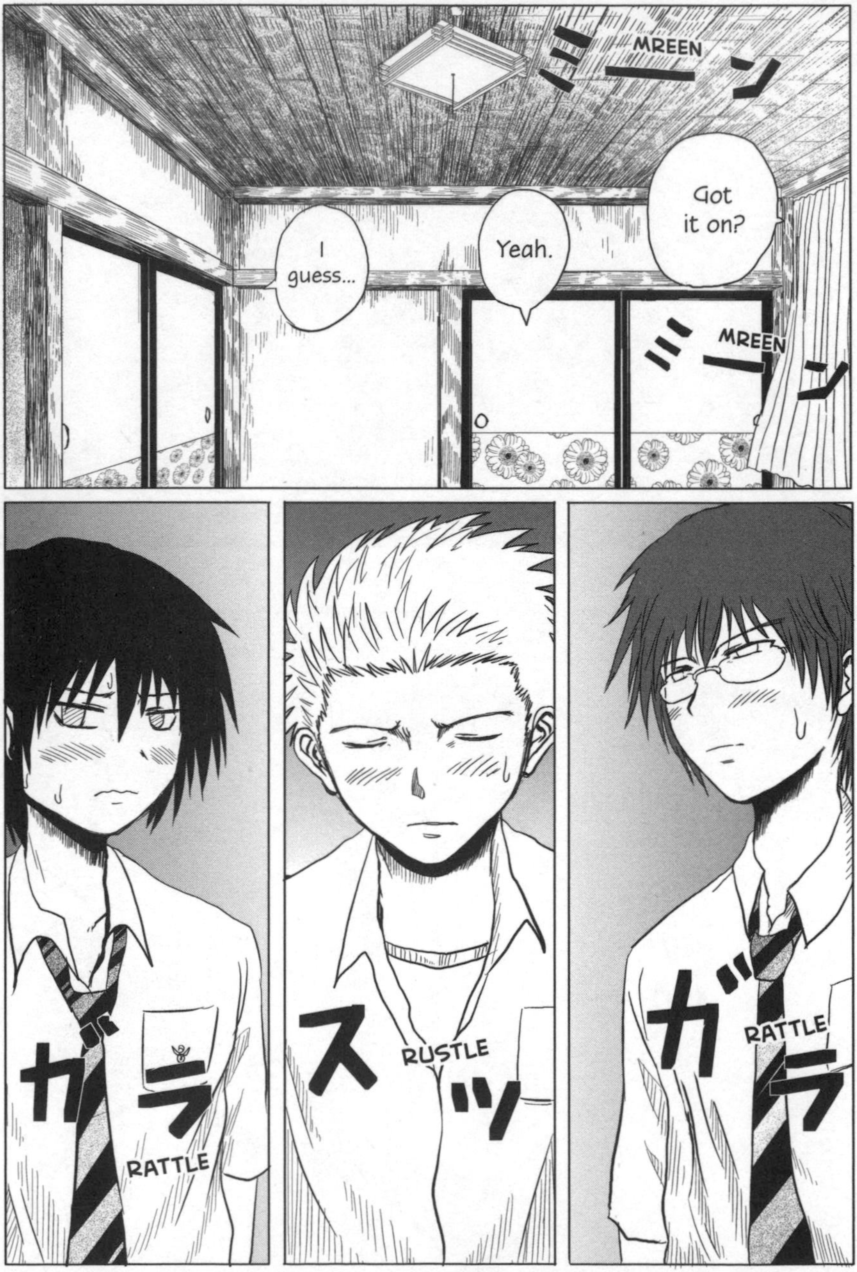
ミーン
MREEN
Got it on?
Yeah.
I guess...
ミーン
MREEN
ガラ
RATTLE
スッ
RUSTLE
ガラ
RATTLE

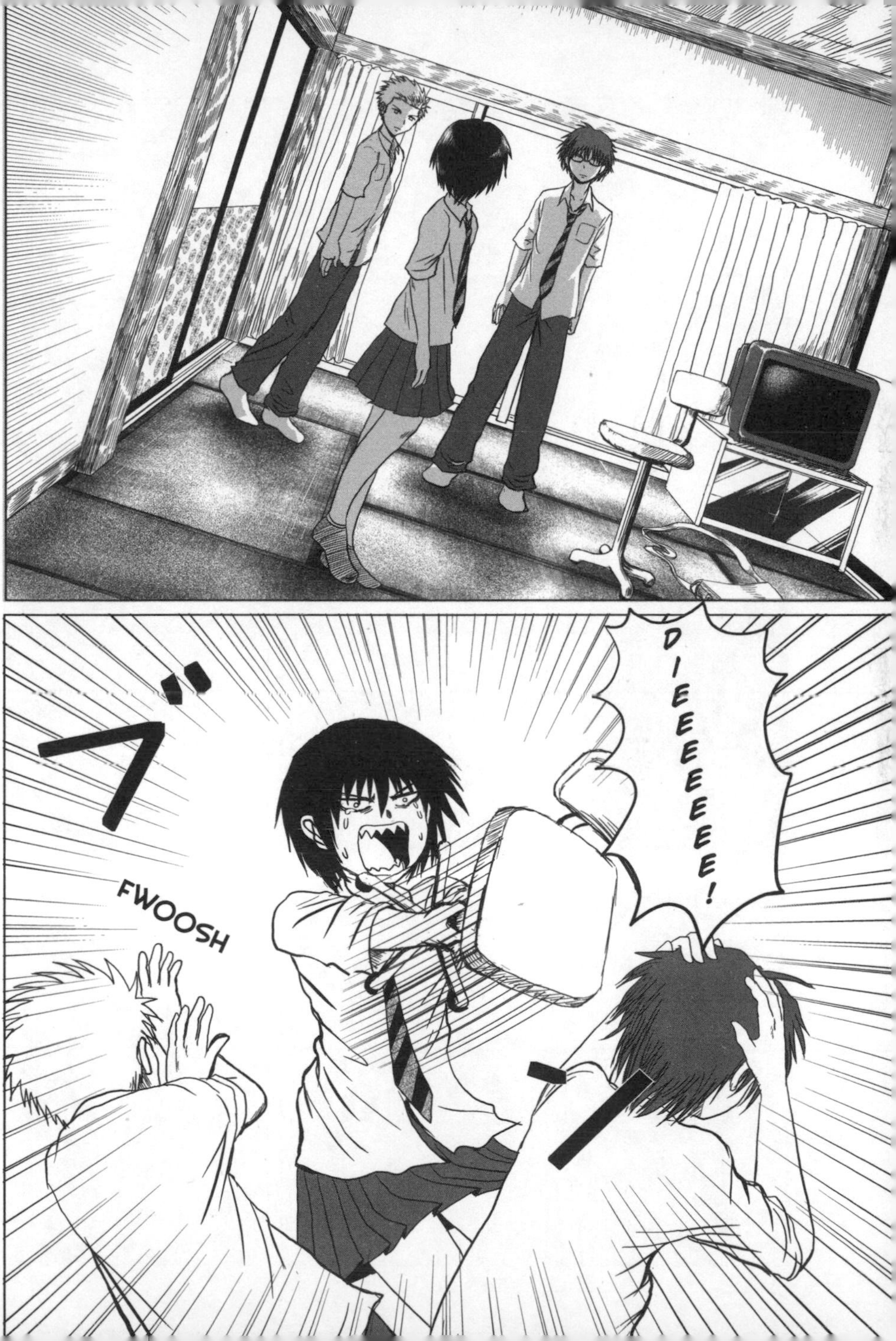
DIEEEEEEEE!
ブ
FWOOSH

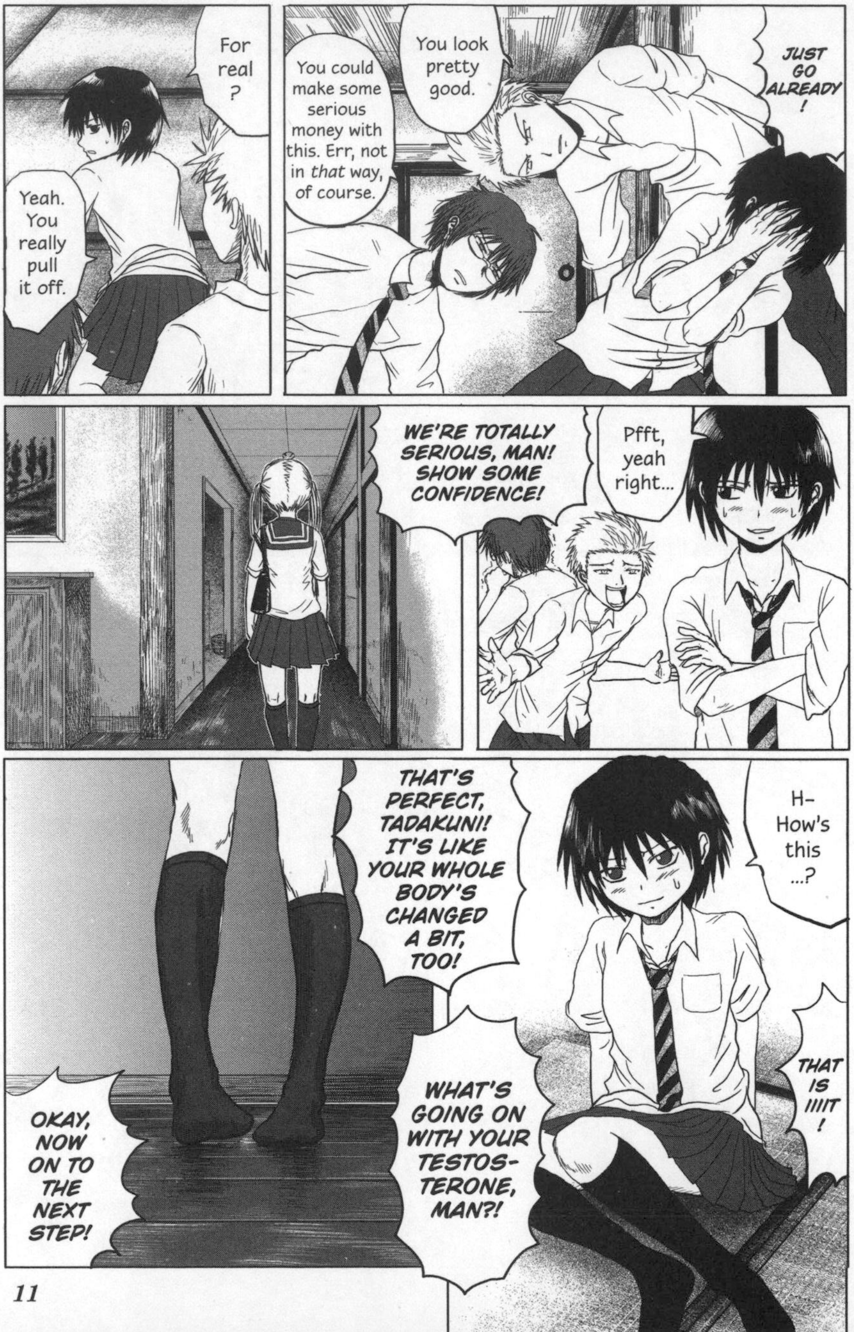
JUST GO ALREADY!
You look pretty good.
You could make some serious money with this. Err, not in *that* way, of course.
For real?
Yeah. You really pull it off.
Pfft, yeah right...
WE'RE TOTALLY SERIOUS, MAN! SHOW SOME CONFIDENCE!
H-How's this ...?
THAT'S PERFECT, TADAKUNI! IT'S LIKE YOUR WHOLE BODY'S CHANGED A BIT, TOO!
THAT IS IIIIT!
WHAT'S GOING ON WITH YOUR TESTOS-TERONE, MAN?!
OKAY, NOW ON TO THE NEXT STEP!

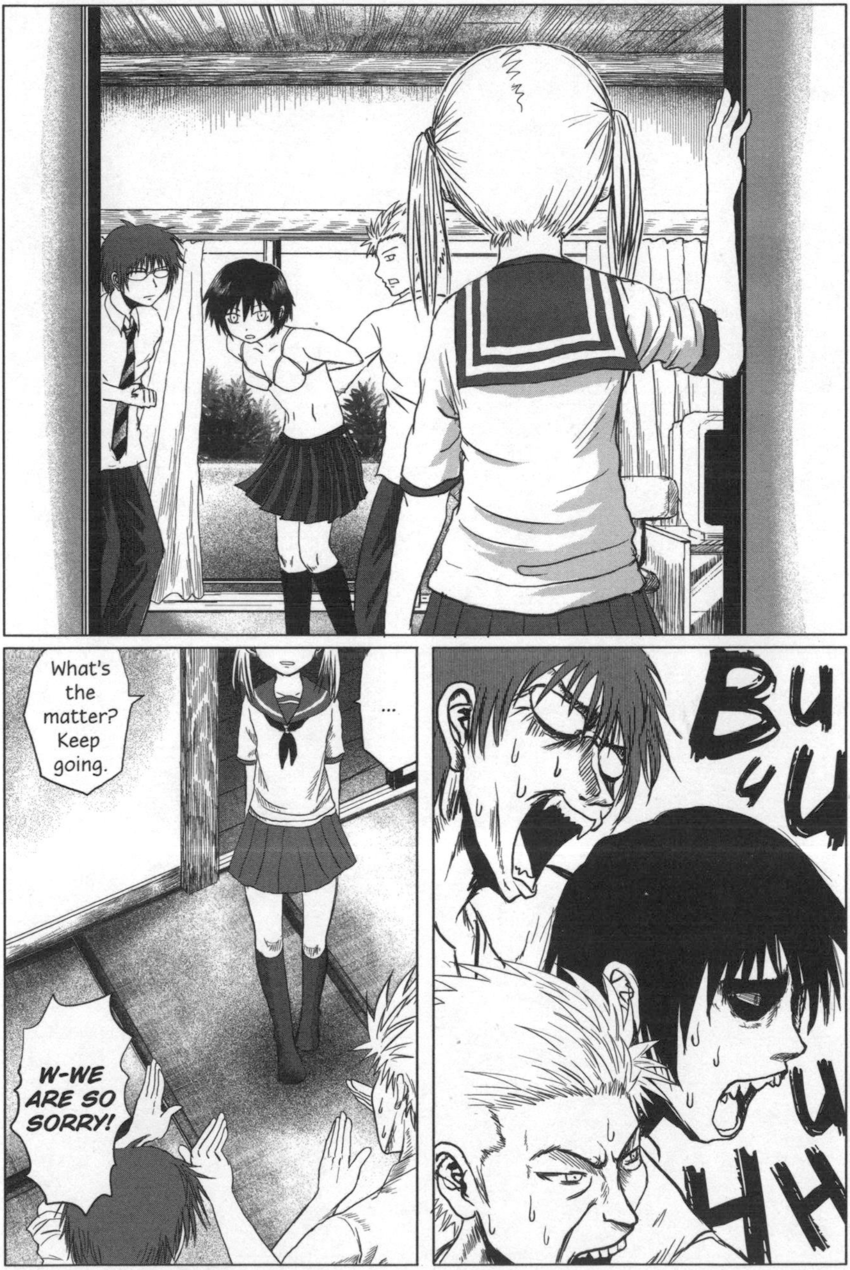
BUUUUUHH
...
What's the matter? Keep going.
W-WE ARE SO SORRY!

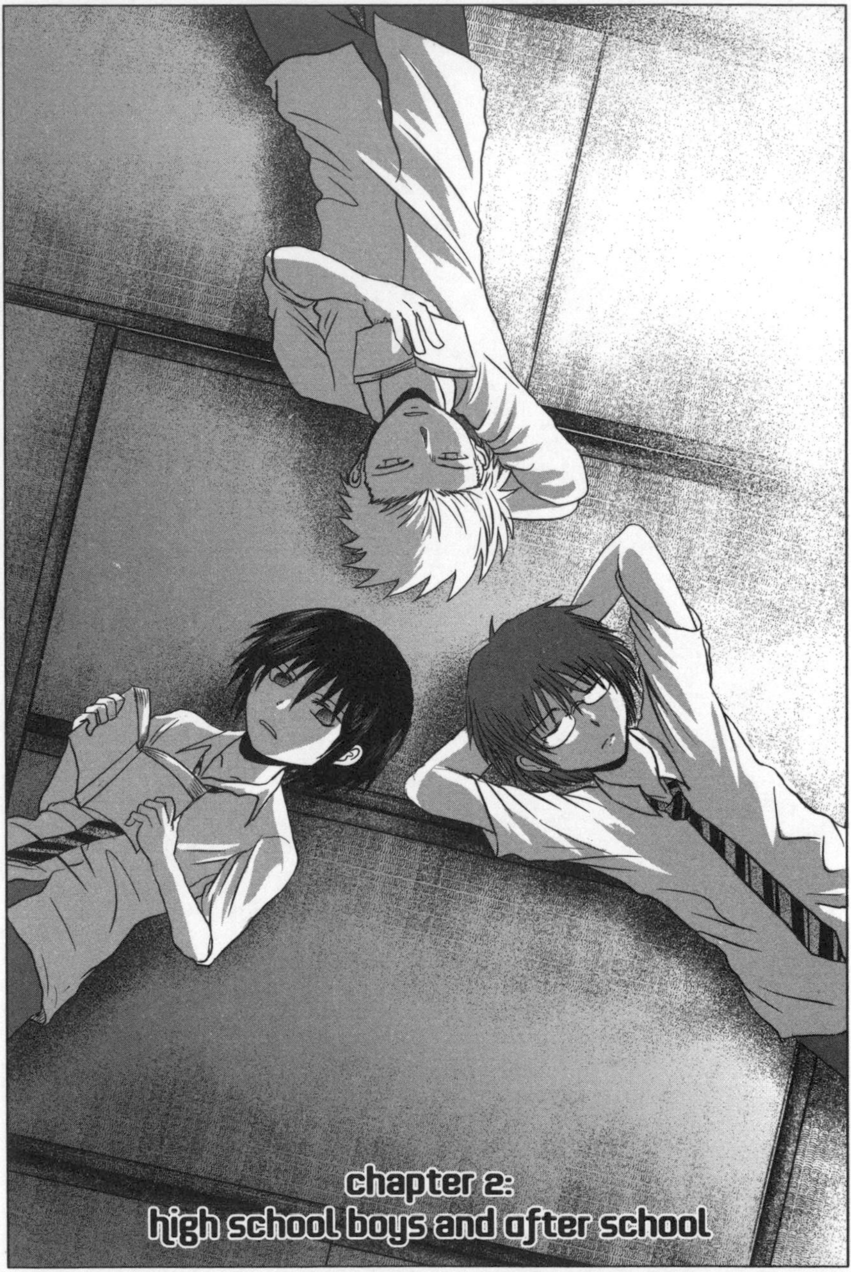
chapter 2:
high school boys and after school

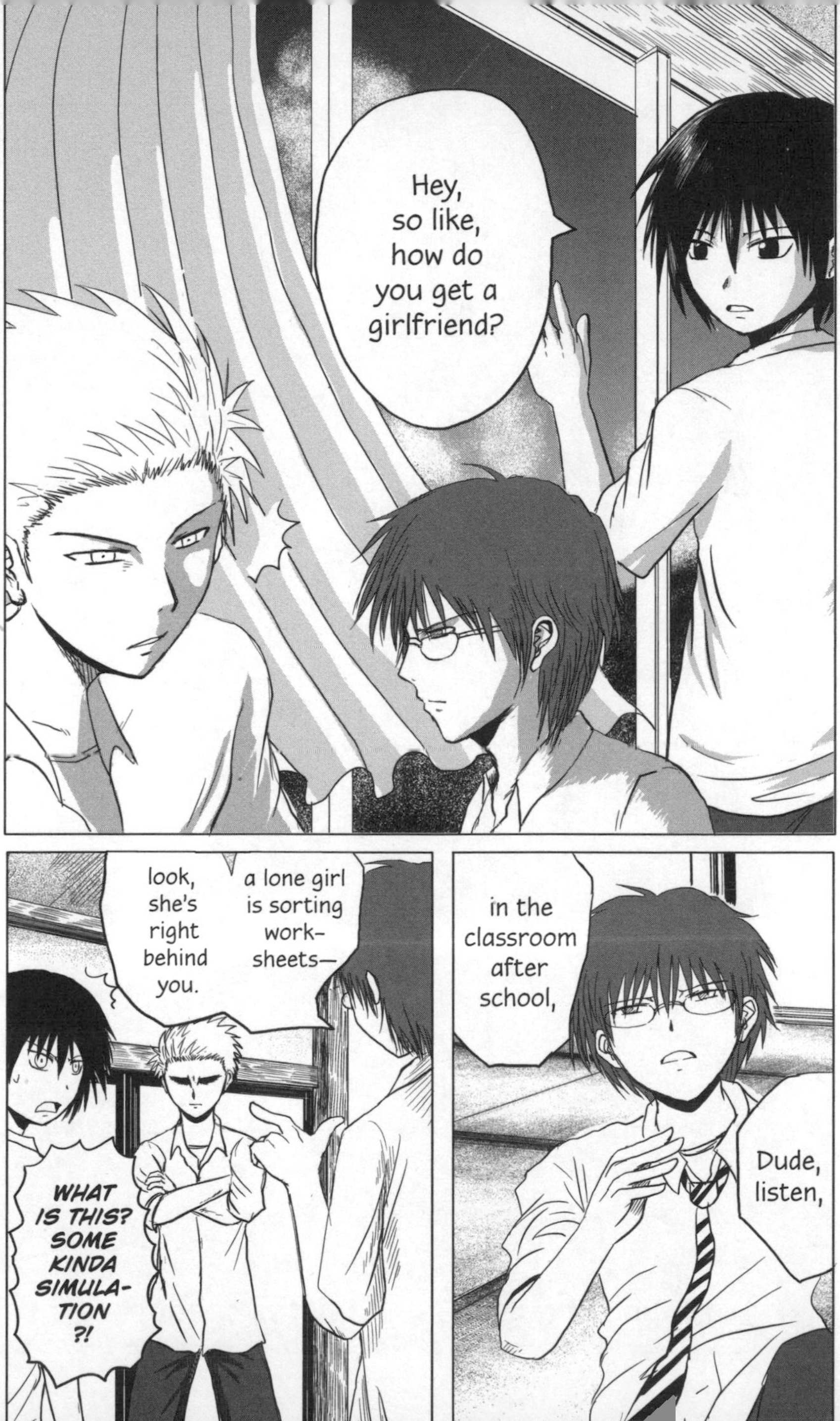
Hey, so like, how do you get a girlfriend?
Dude, listen,
in the classroom after school,
a lone girl is sorting work-sheets—
look, she's right behind you.
WHAT IS THIS? SOME KINDA SIMULA-TION ?!

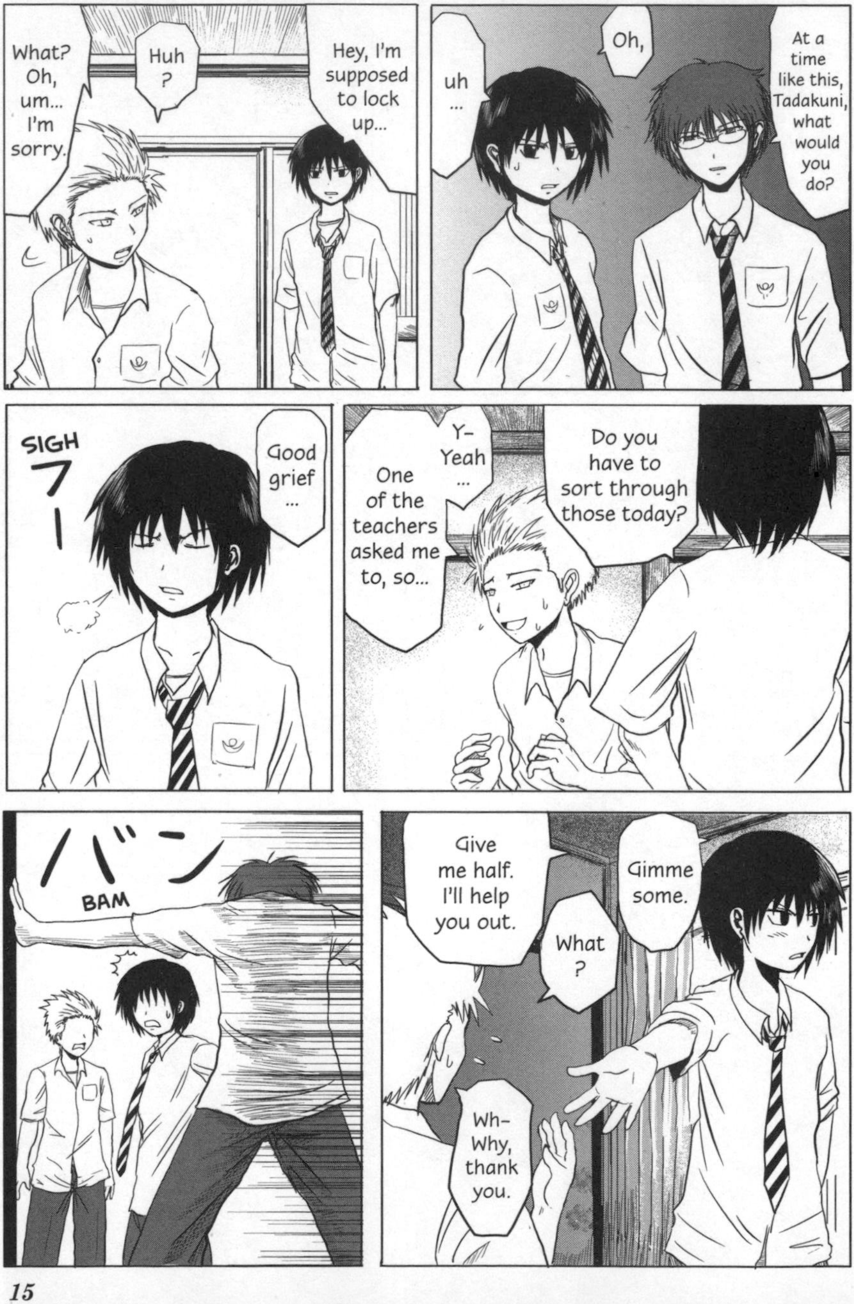
At a time like this, Tadakuni, what would you do?
Oh,
uh ...
Hey, I'm supposed to lock up...
Huh ?
What? Oh, um... I'm sorry.
Do you have to sort through those today?
Y- Yeah ...
One of the teachers asked me to, so...
Good grief ...
SIGH
フー
Gimme some.
Give me half. I'll help you out.
What ?
Wh- Why, thank you.
バン
BAM

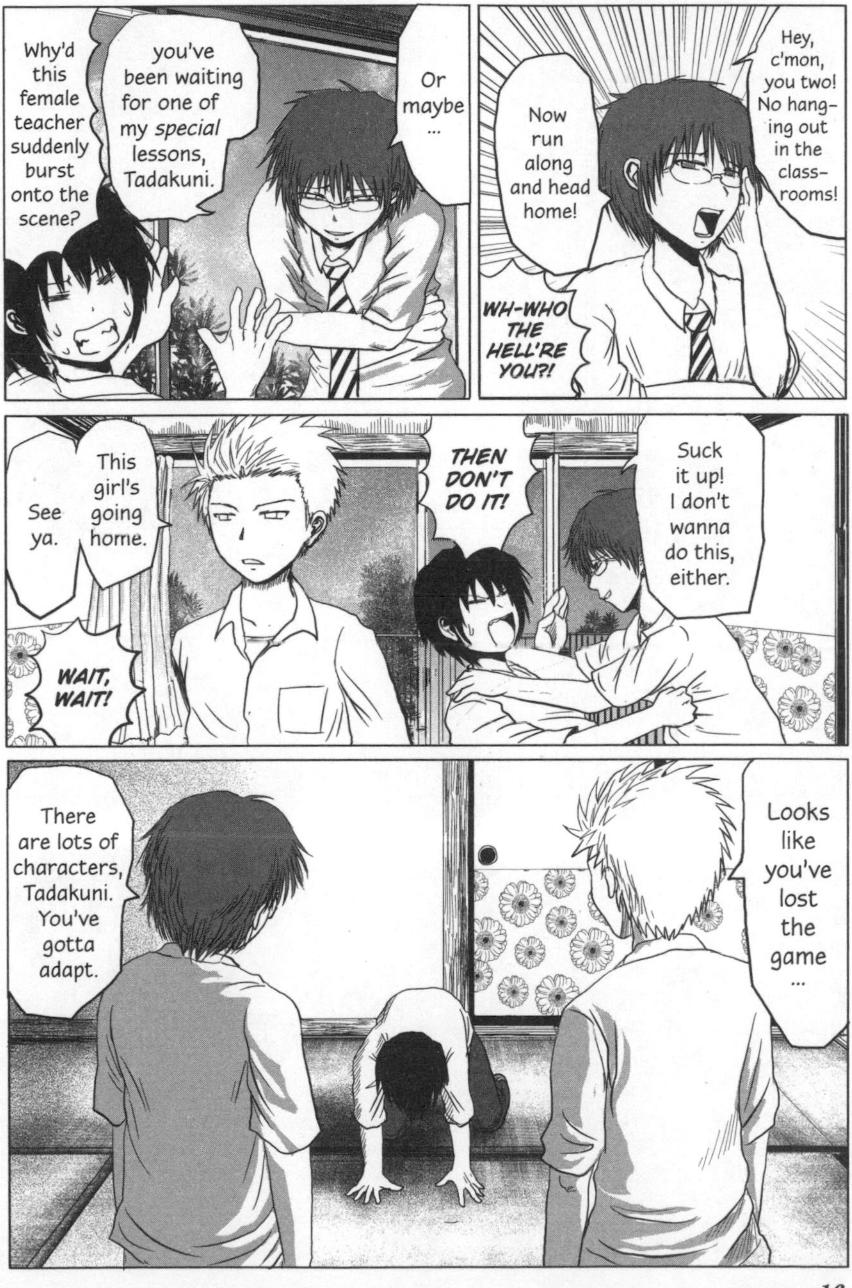
Hey, c'mon, you two! No hang-ing out in the class-rooms!
Now run along and head home!
WH-WHO THE HELL'RE YOU?!
Or maybe ...
you've been waiting for one of my *special* lessons, Tadakuni.
Why'd this female teacher suddenly burst onto the scene?
Suck it up! I don't wanna do this, either.
THEN DON'T DO IT!
This girl's going home.
See ya.
WAIT, WAIT!
Looks like you've lost the game ...
There are lots of characters, Tadakuni. You've gotta adapt.

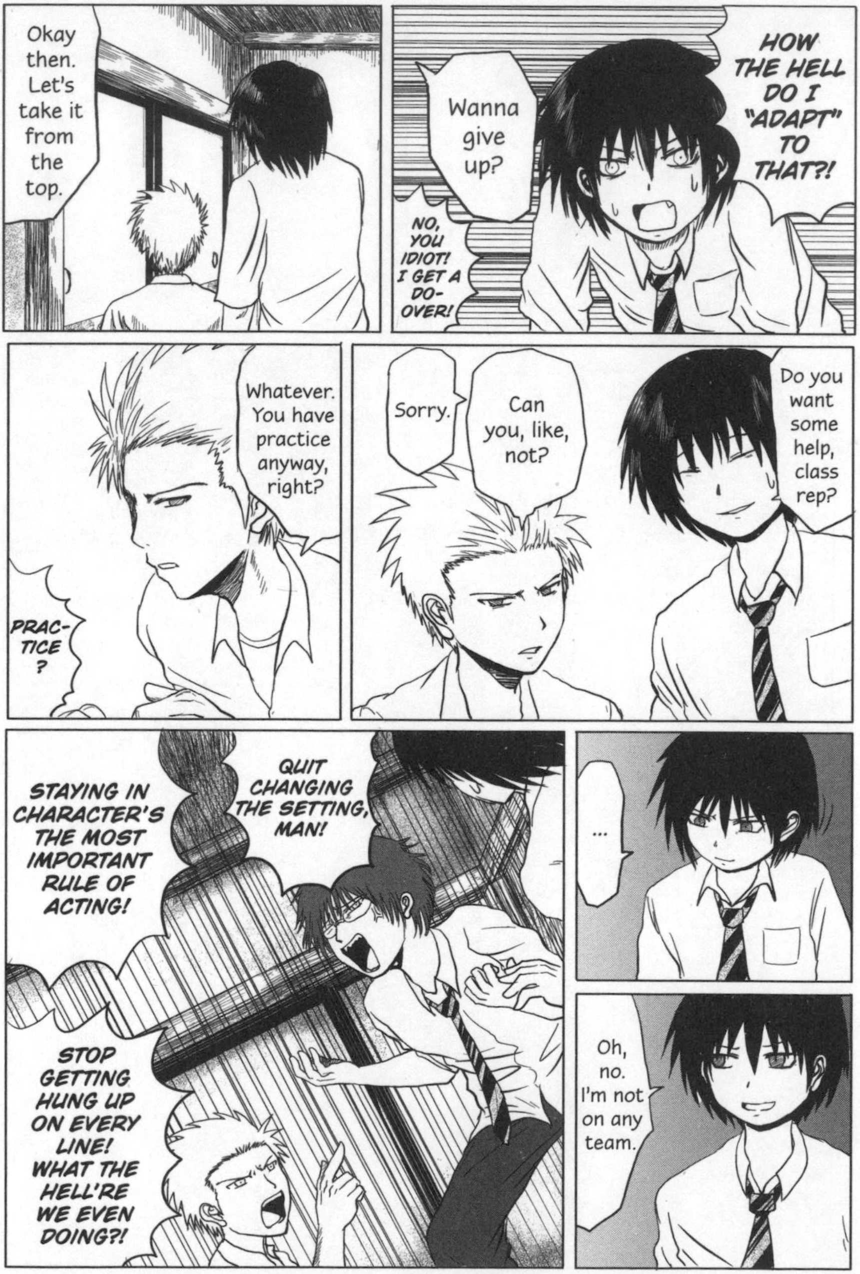
HOW THE HELL DO I "ADAPT" TO THAT?!
Wanna give up?
NO, YOU IDIOT! I GET A DO-OVER!
Okay then. Let's take it from the top.
Do you want some help, class rep?
Can you, like, not?
Sorry.
Whatever. You have practice anyway, right?
PRAC-TICE?
...
Oh, no. I'm not on any team.
QUIT CHANGING THE SETTING, MAN!
STAYING IN CHARACTER'S THE MOST IMPORTANT RULE OF ACTING!
STOP GETTING HUNG UP ON EVERY LINE! WHAT THE HELL'RE WE EVEN DOING?!

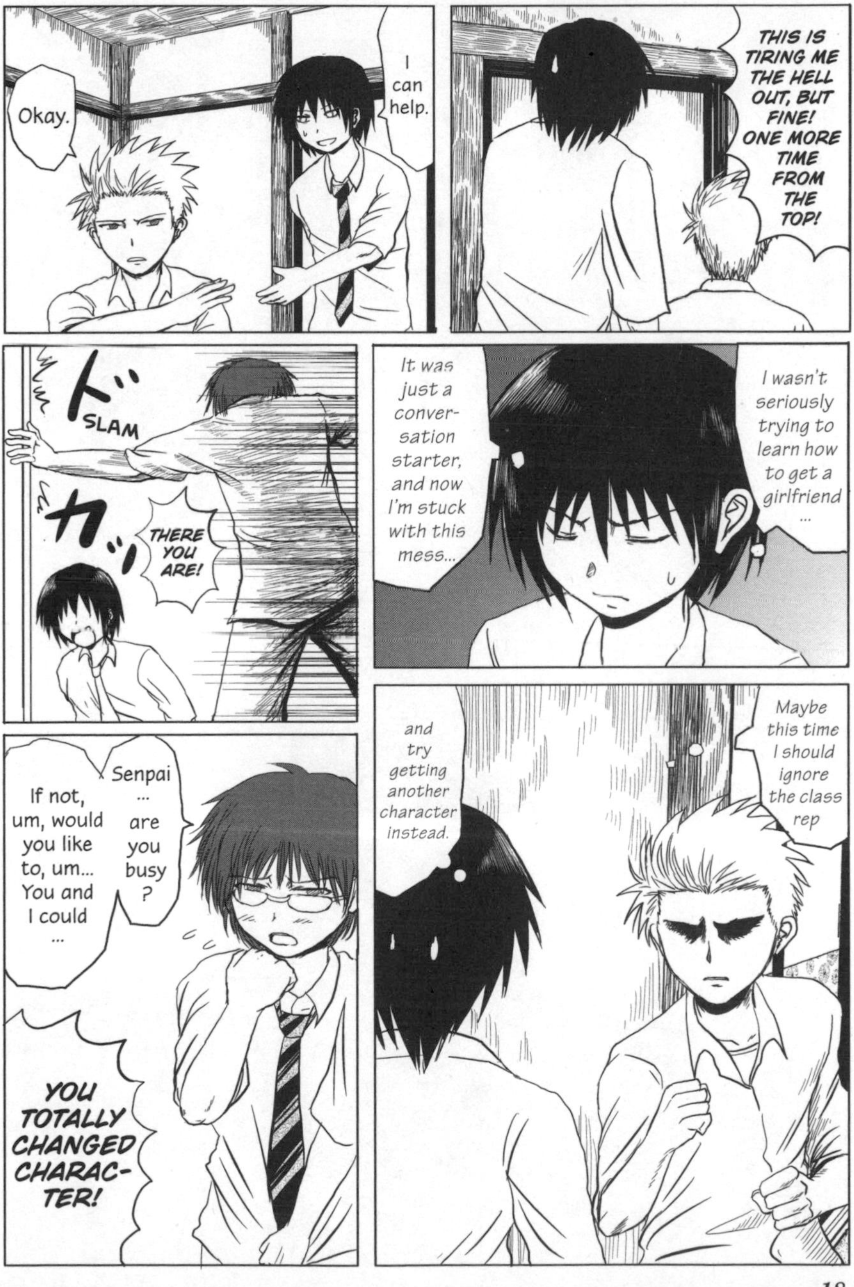
THIS IS TIRING ME THE HELL OUT, BUT FINE! ONE MORE TIME FROM THE TOP!
I can help.
Okay.
I wasn't seriously trying to learn how to get a girlfriend ...
It was just a conversation starter, and now I'm stuck with this mess...
ド
SLAM
カッ
THERE YOU ARE!
Maybe this time I should ignore the class rep
and try getting another character instead.
Senpai ... are you busy ?
If not, um, would you like to, um... You and I could ...
YOU TOTALLY CHANGED CHARACTER!

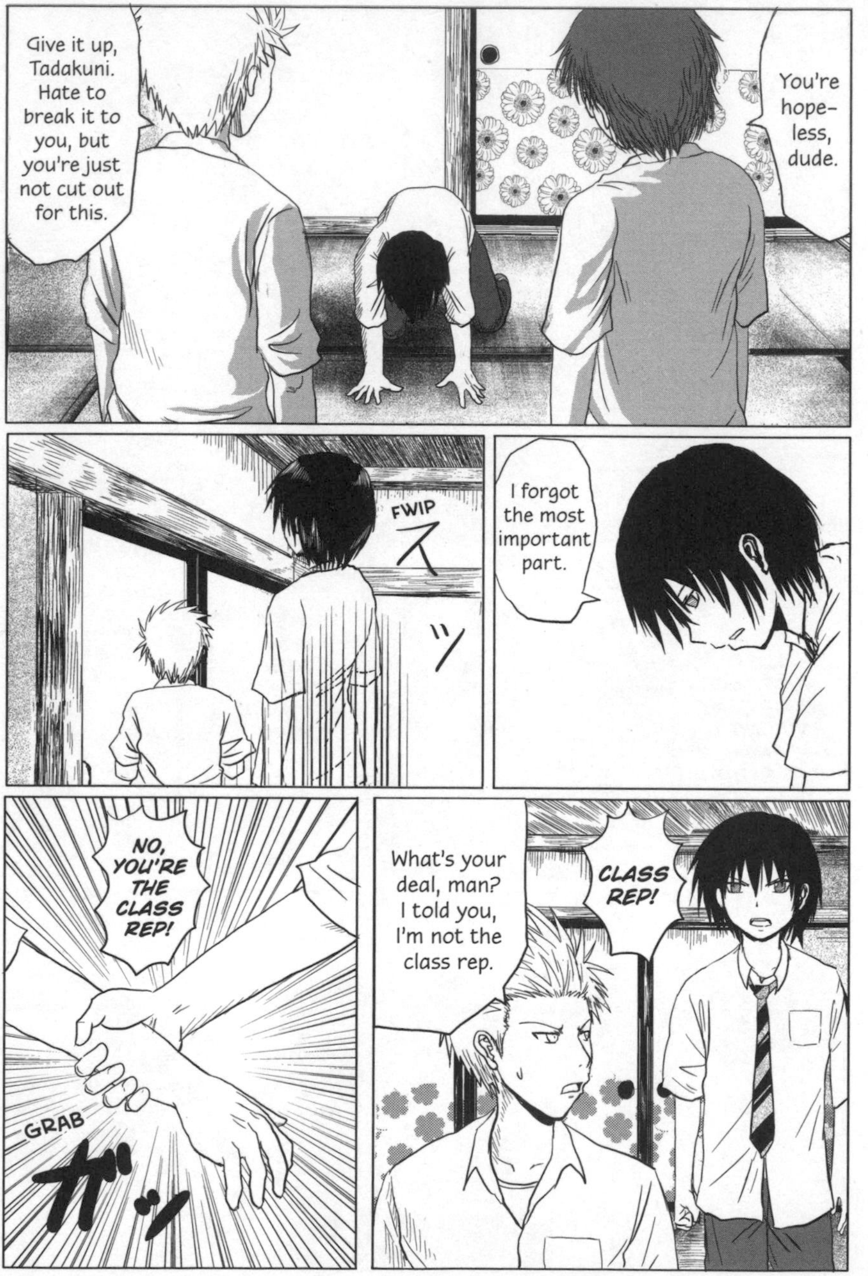
You're hope-less, dude.
Give it up, Tadakuni. Hate to break it to you, but you're just not cut out for this.
I forgot the most important part.
FWIP
CLASS REP!
What's your deal, man? I told you, I'm not the class rep.
NO, YOU'RE THE CLASS REP!
GRAB

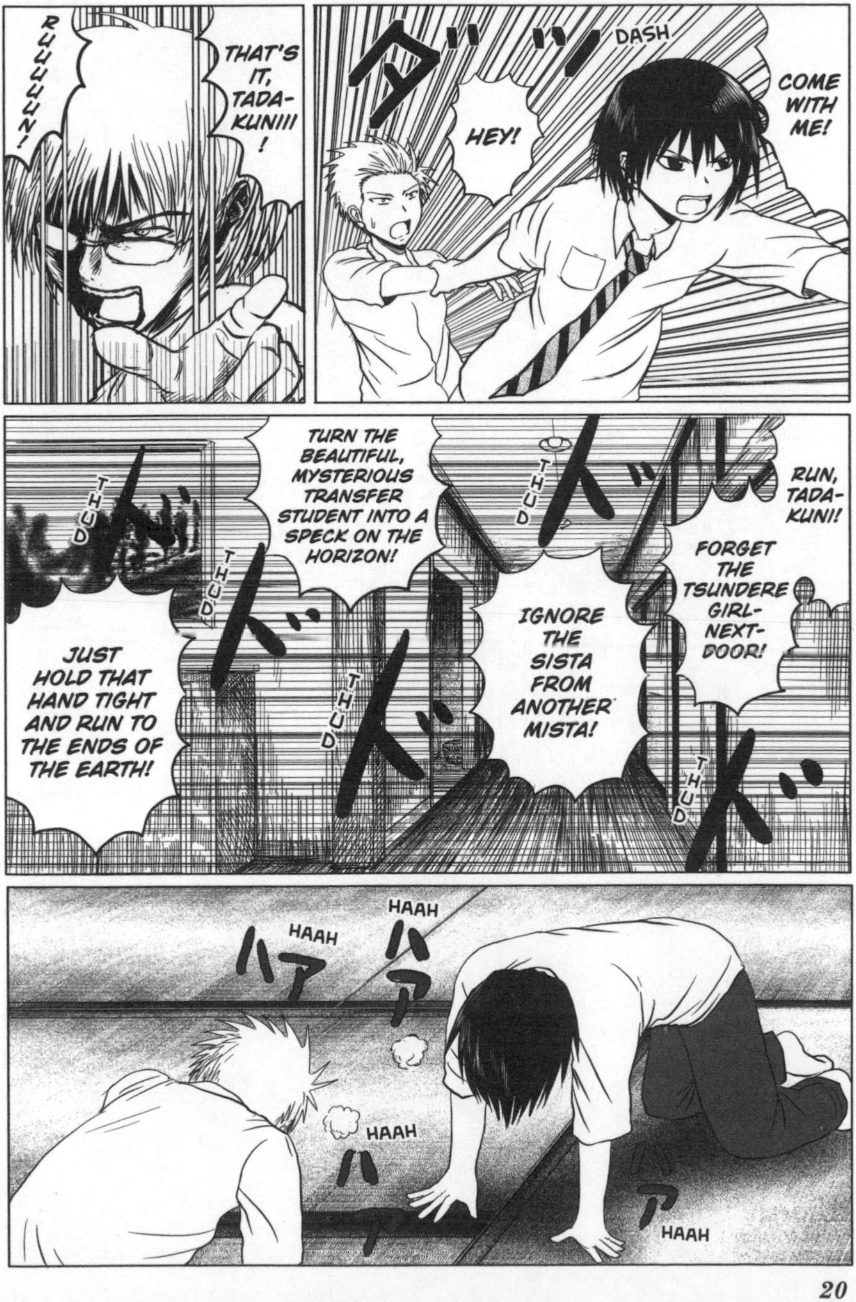
DASH
COME WITH ME!
HEY!
THAT'S IT, TADA-KUNIII!
RUUUUUN!
RUN, TADA-KUNI!
FORGET THE TSUNDERE GIRL-NEXT-DOOR!
THUD
THUD
IGNORE THE SISTA FROM ANOTHER MISTA!
THUD
TURN THE BEAUTIFUL, MYSTERIOUS TRANSFER STUDENT INTO A SPECK ON THE HORIZON!
THUD
THUD
JUST HOLD THAT HAND TIGHT AND RUN TO THE ENDS OF THE EARTH!
HAAH
HAAH
HAAH
HAAH

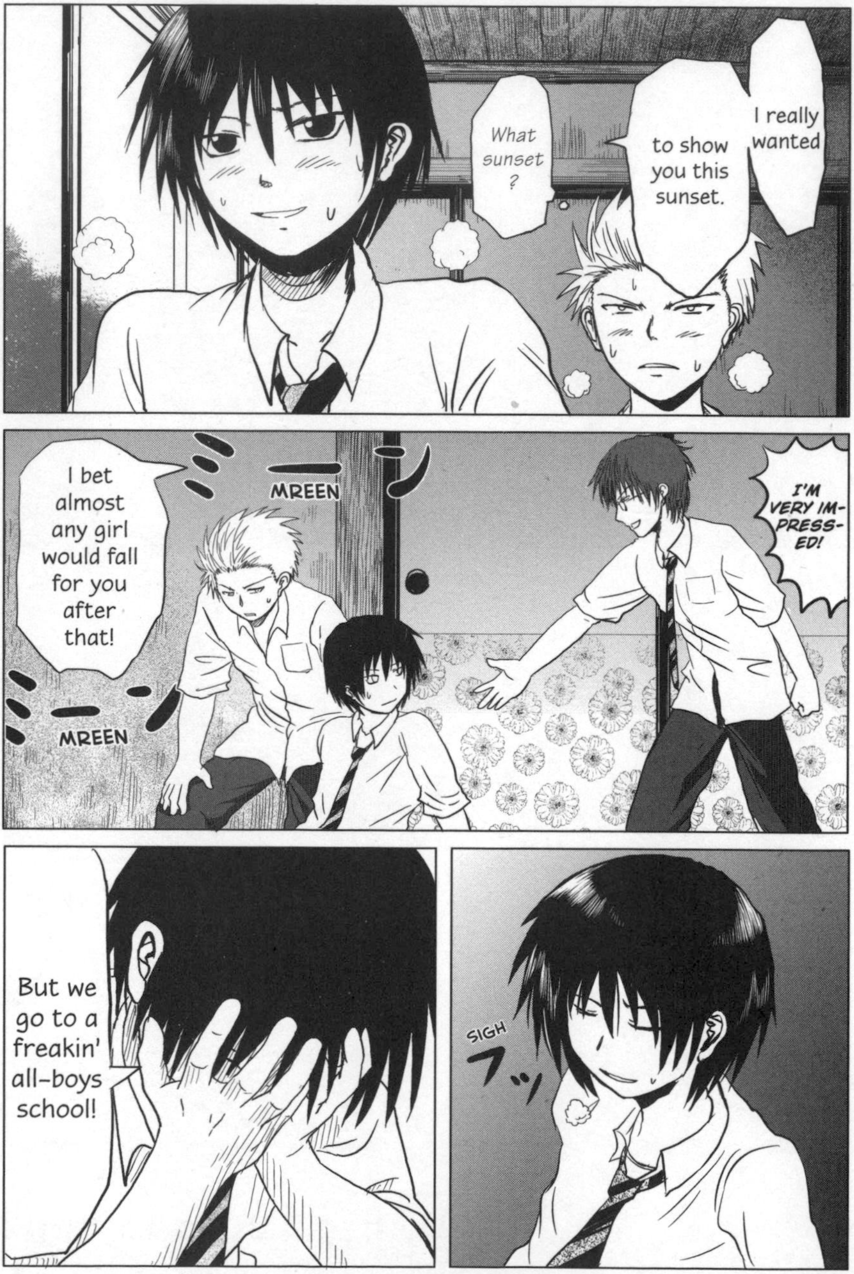
I really wanted
to show you this sunset.
What sunset?
I'M VERY IM-PRESS-ED!
MREEN
I bet almost any girl would fall for you after that!
MREEN
SIGH
But we go to a freakin' all-boys school!

the

daily

lives

of

 high school boys

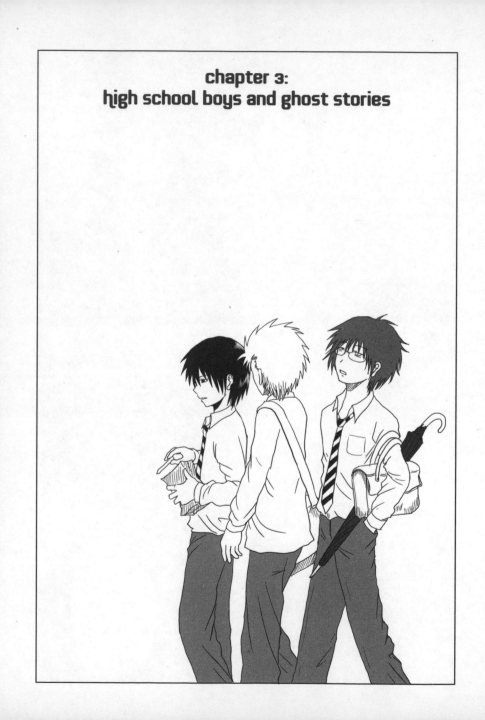

chapter 3:
high school boys and ghost stories

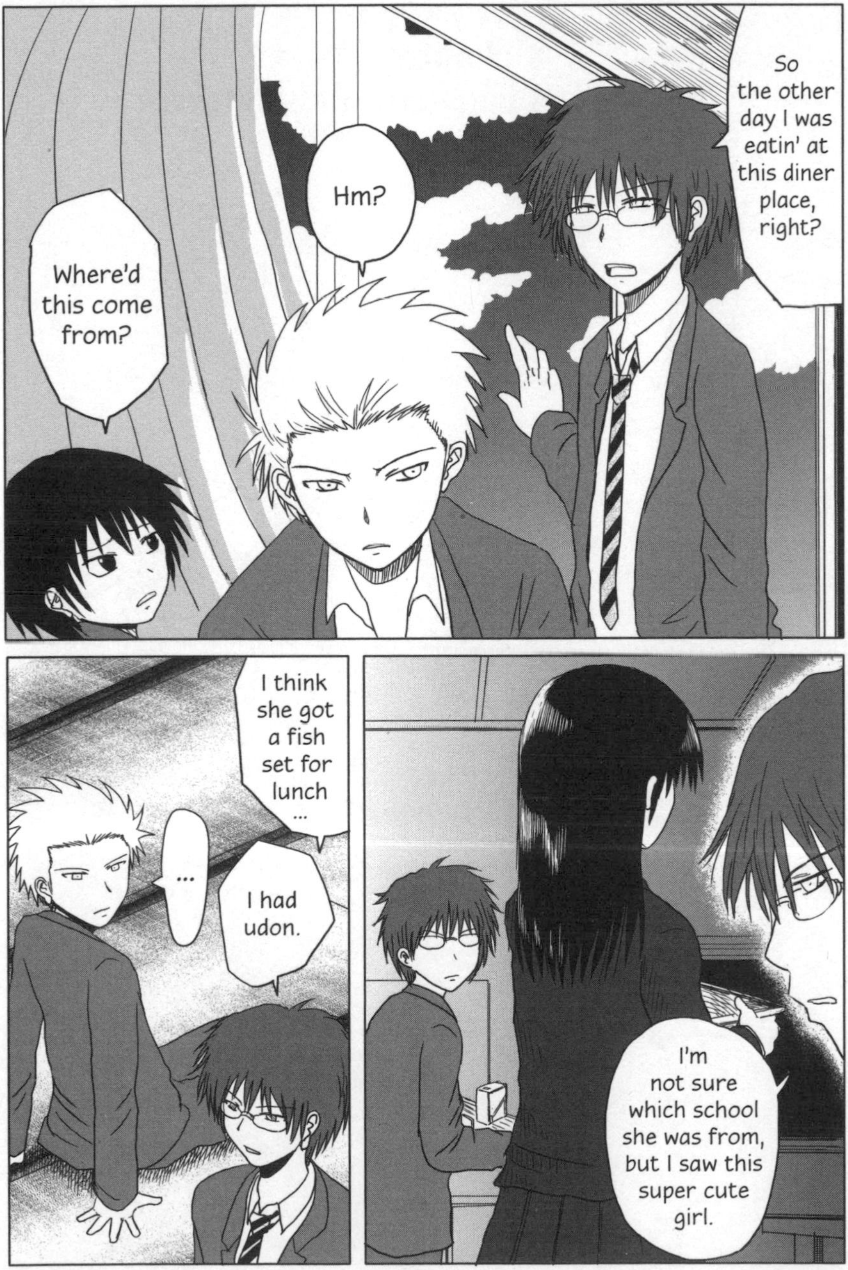
So the other day I was eatin' at this diner place, right?
Hm?
Where'd this come from?
I'm not sure which school she was from, but I saw this super cute girl.
I think she got a fish set for lunch ...
...
I had udon.

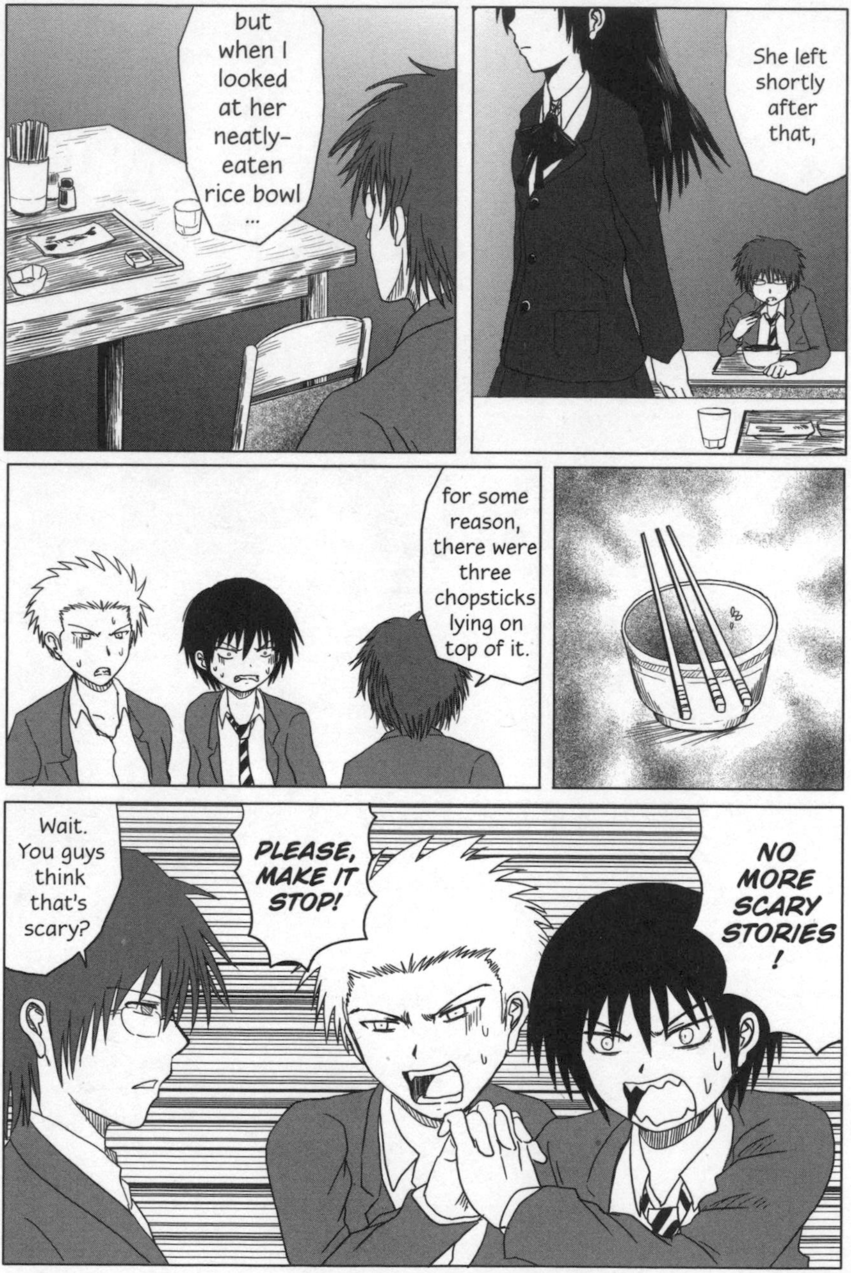
She left shortly after that,
but when I looked at her neatly-eaten rice bowl ...
for some reason, there were three chopsticks lying on top of it.
NO MORE SCARY STORIES!
PLEASE, MAKE IT STOP!
Wait. You guys think that's scary?

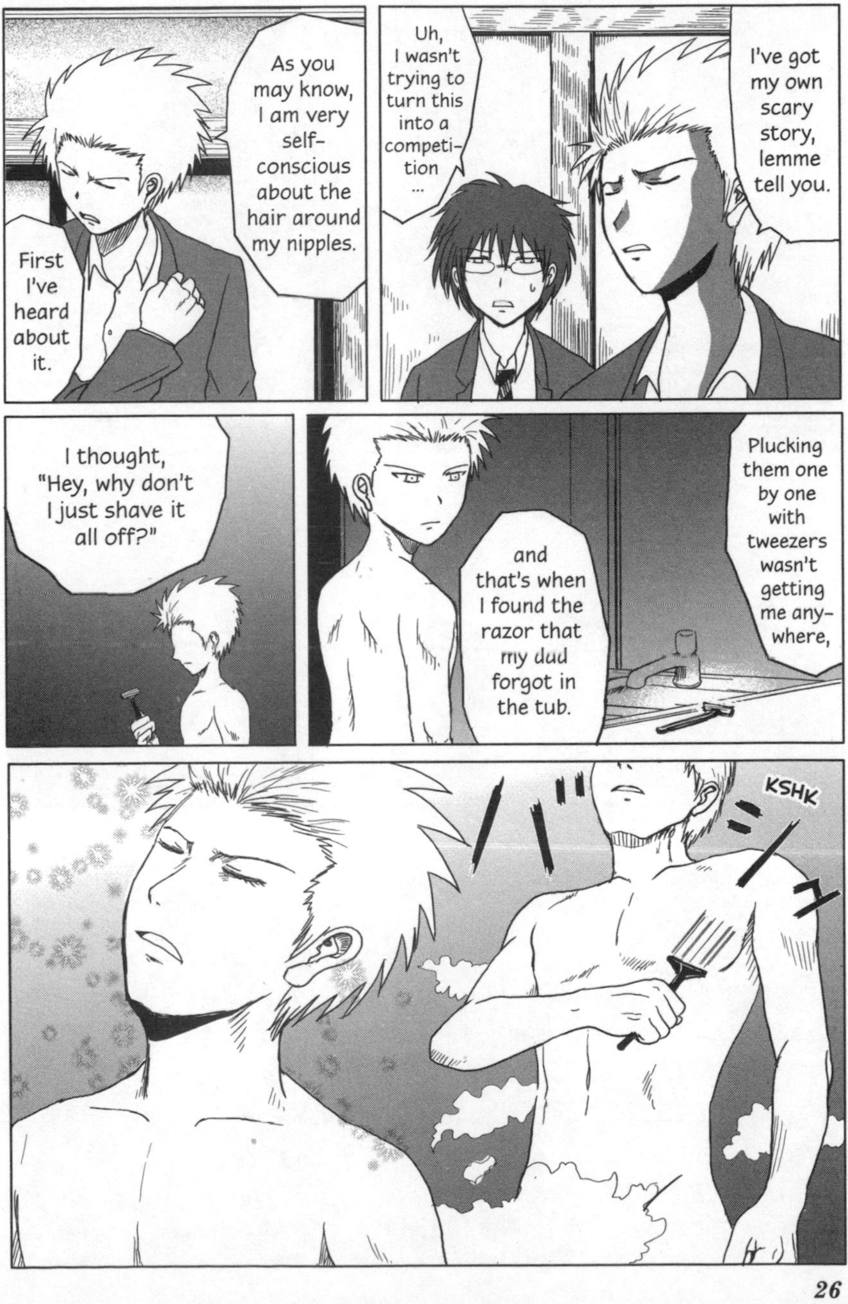
I've got my own scary story, lemme tell you.
Uh, I wasn't trying to turn this into a competition ...
As you may know, I am very self-conscious about the hair around my nipples.
First I've heard about it.
Plucking them one by one with tweezers wasn't getting me anywhere,
and that's when I found the razor that my dad forgot in the tub.
I thought, "Hey, why don't I just shave it all off?"
KSHK

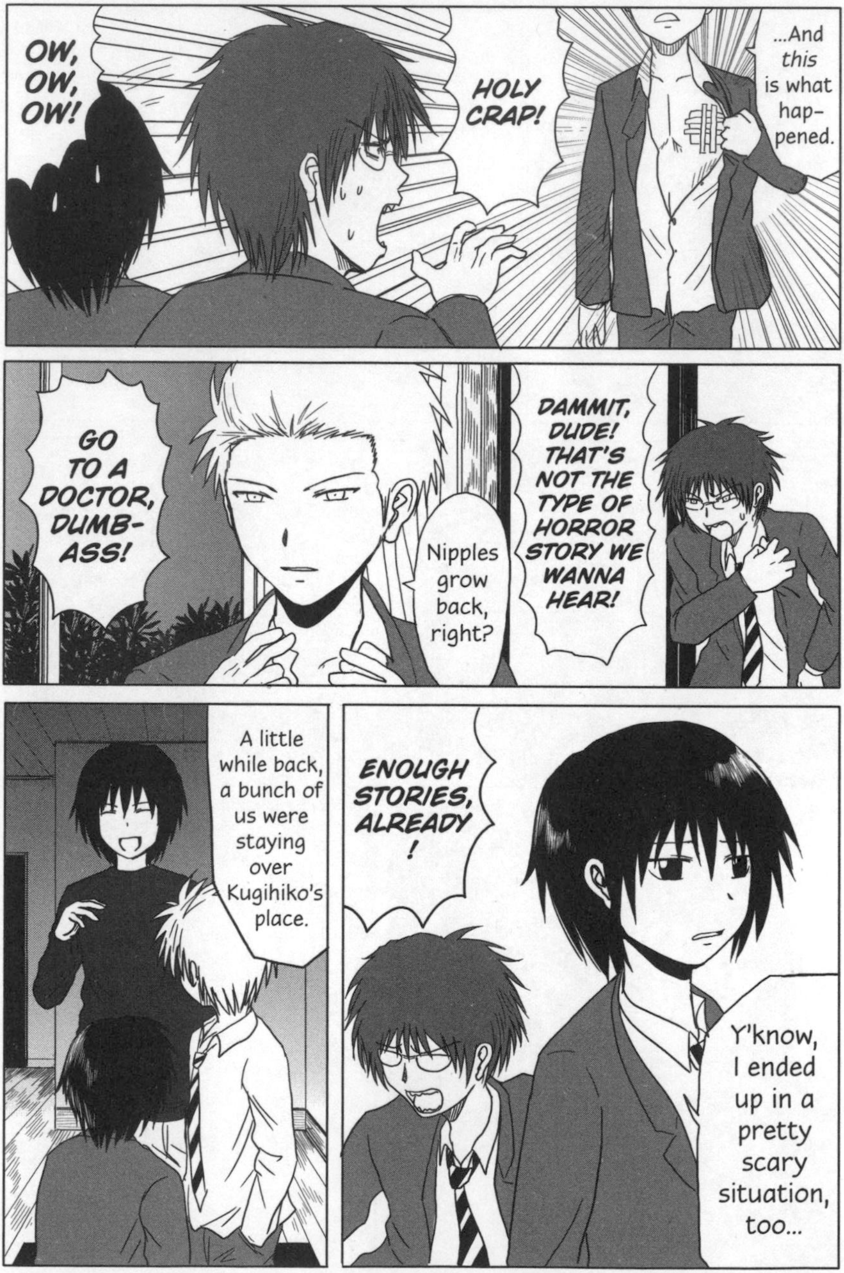
...And this is what hap-pened.
HOLY CRAP!
OW, OW, OW!
DAMMIT, DUDE! THAT'S NOT THE TYPE OF HORROR STORY WE WANNA HEAR!
Nipples grow back, right?
GO TO A DOCTOR, DUMB-ASS!
ENOUGH STORIES, ALREADY!
Y'know, I ended up in a pretty scary situation, too...
A little while back, a bunch of us were staying over Kugihiko's place.

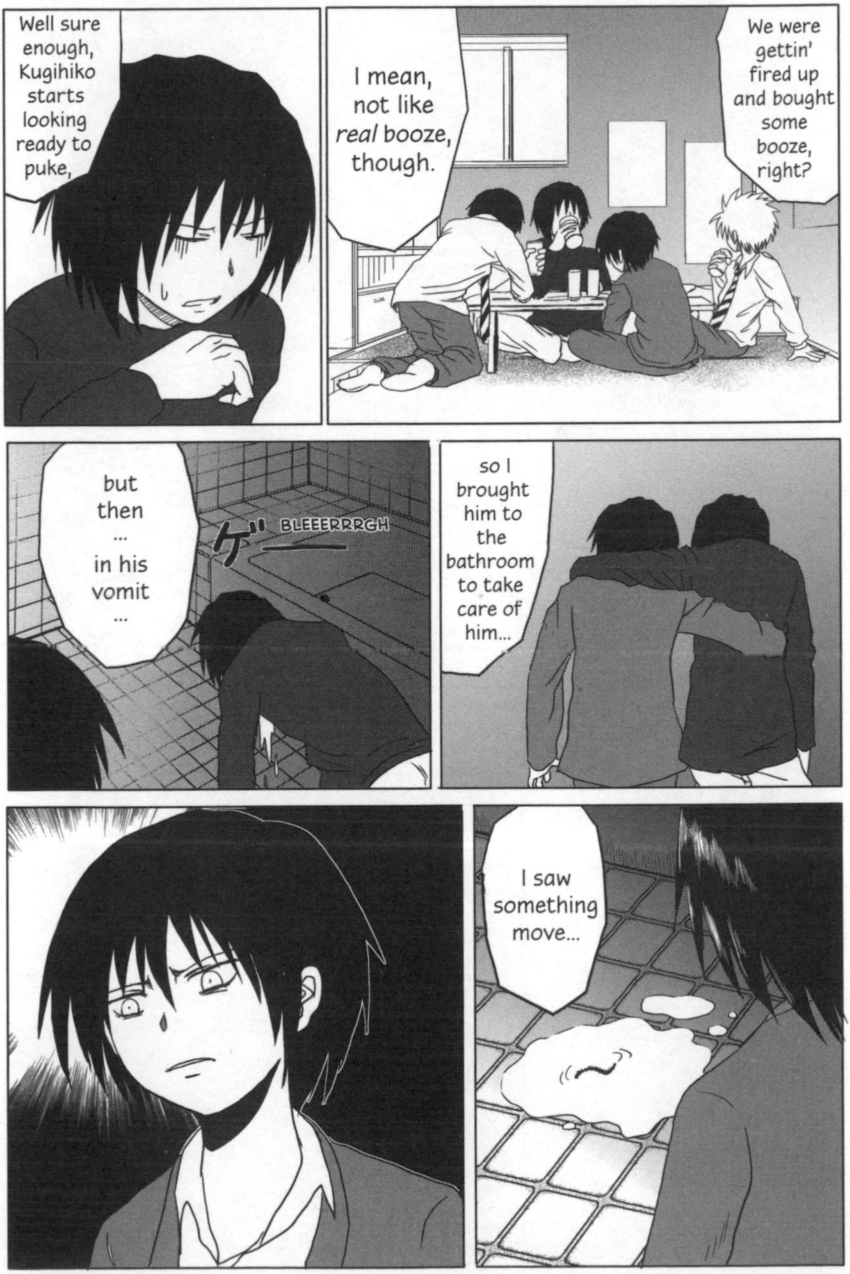

We were gettin' fired up and bought some booze, right?
I mean, not like *real* booze, though.
Well sure enough, Kugihiko starts looking ready to puke,
so I brought him to the bathroom to take care of him...
ゲー BLEEERRRGH
but then ... in his vomit ...
I saw something move...

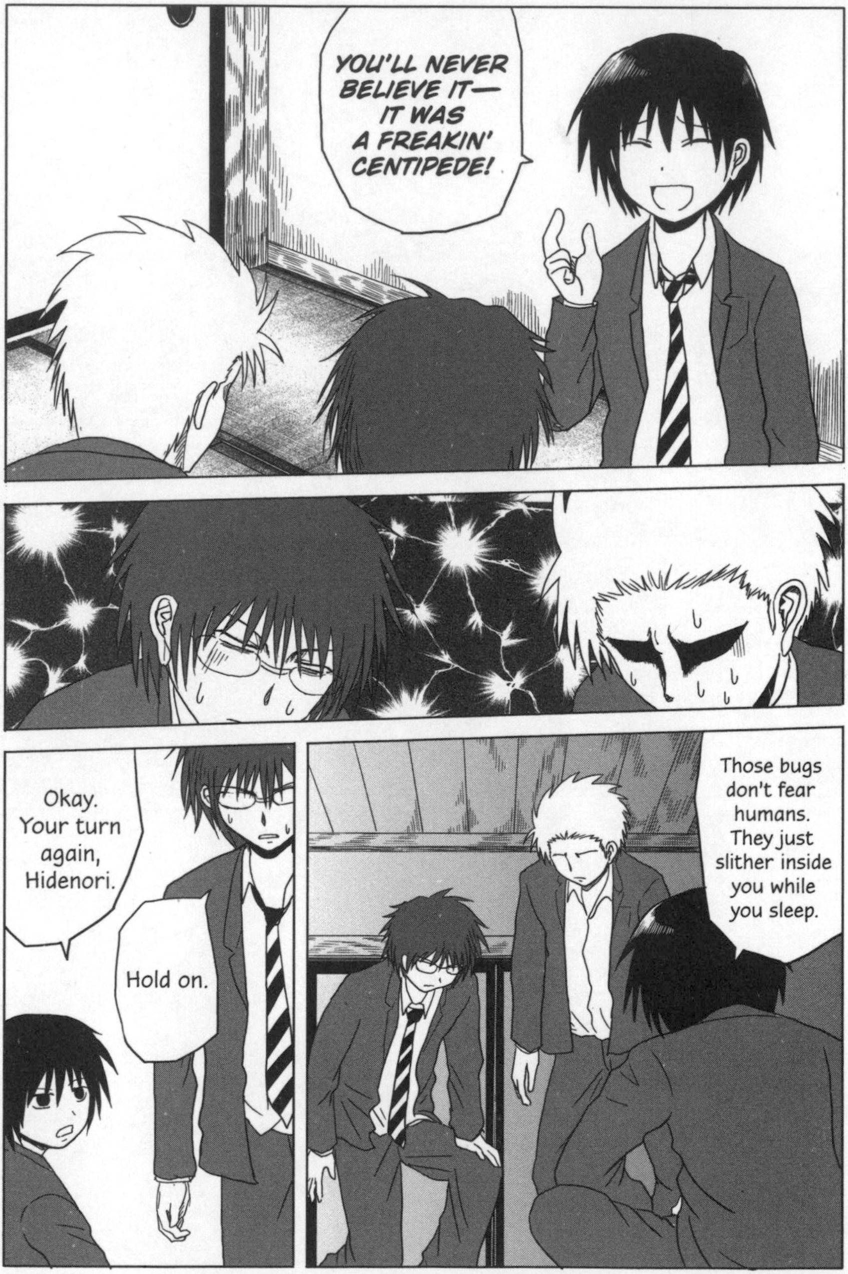
YOU'LL NEVER BELIEVE IT—IT WAS A FREAKIN' CENTIPEDE!
Those bugs don't fear humans. They just slither inside you while you sleep.
Okay. Your turn again, Hidenori.
Hold on.

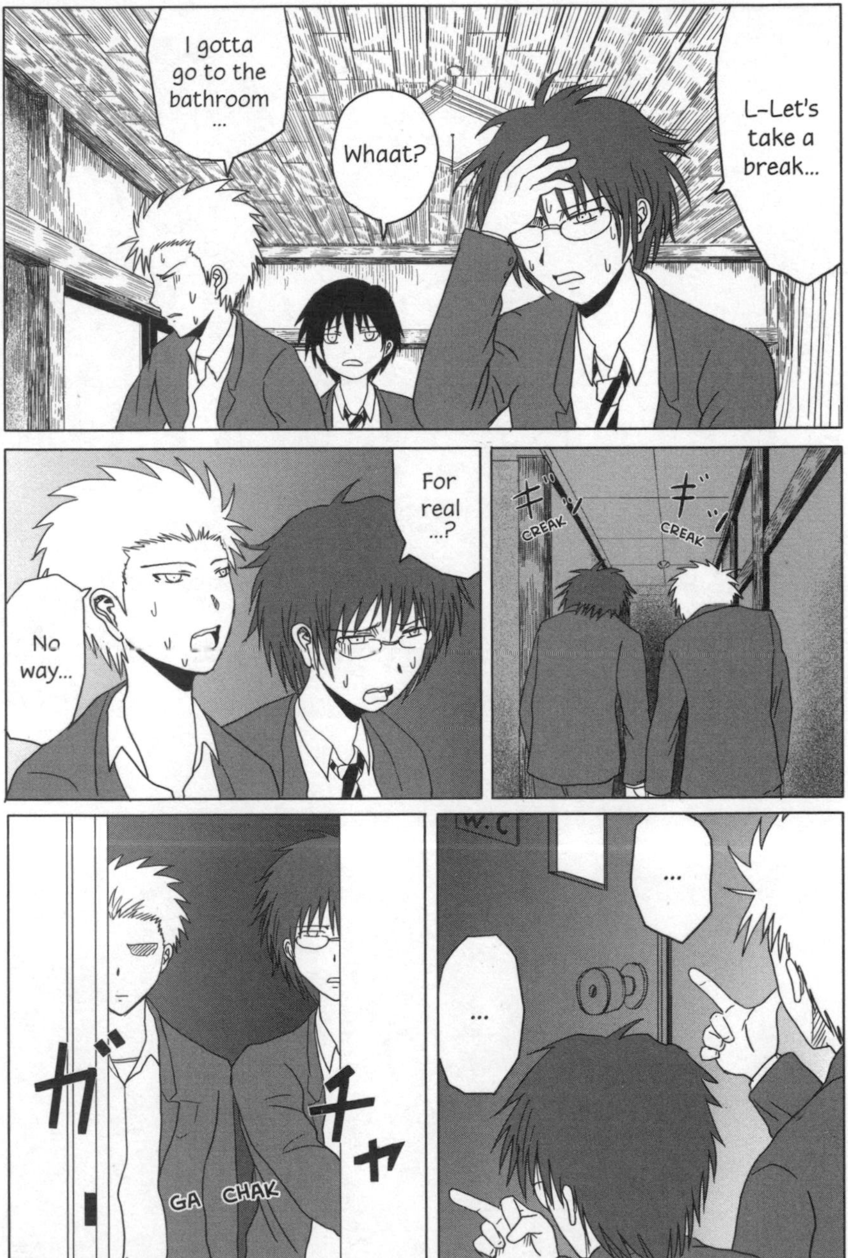
L-Let's take a break...
Whaat?
I gotta go to the bathroom ...
ギッ
CREAK
ギッ
CREAK
For real ...?
No way...
...
...
ガチャ
GA CHAK

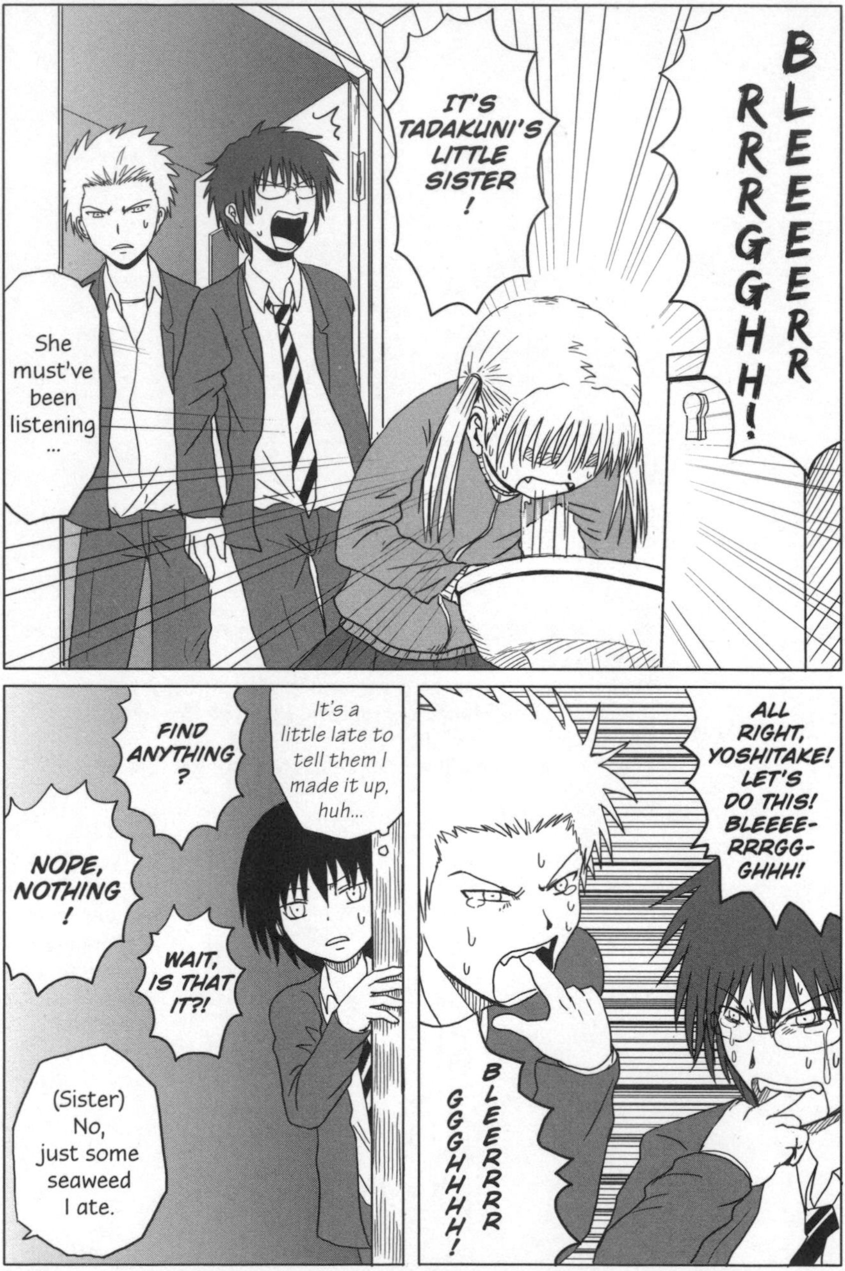
BLEEEERR
RRRGGHH!
IT'S TADAKUNI'S LITTLE SISTER!
She must've been listening...
ALL RIGHT, YOSHITAKE! LET'S DO THIS! BLEEEE-RRRGG-GHHH!
BLEERRRR
GGGHHHH!
It's a little late to tell them I made it up, huh...
FIND ANYTHING?
NOPE, NOTHING!
WAIT, IS THAT IT?!
(Sister) No, just some seaweed I ate.

The official title of this manga is "The Absolutely
Pointless Daily Lives of High School Boys."
That was the title of the manga when I submitted it to
the Square Enix Manga Contest and received the Judges'
Choice award.
I don't even know when it got shortened to what it is now.

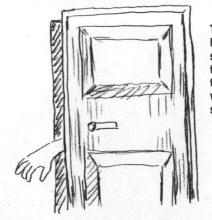

Tadakuni's
little sister
showed up in
that manga,
too, but this
was all you
saw of her.

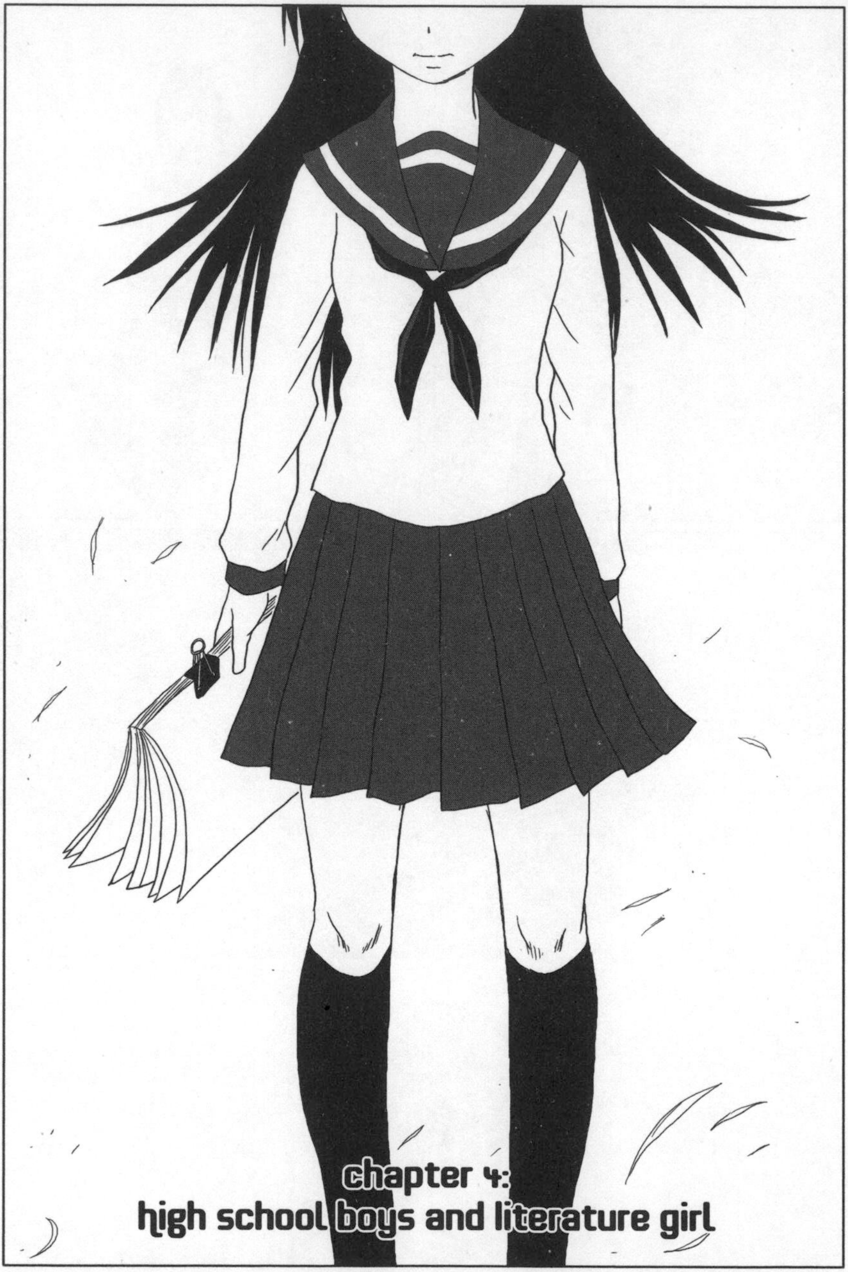
chapter 4:
high school boys and literature girl

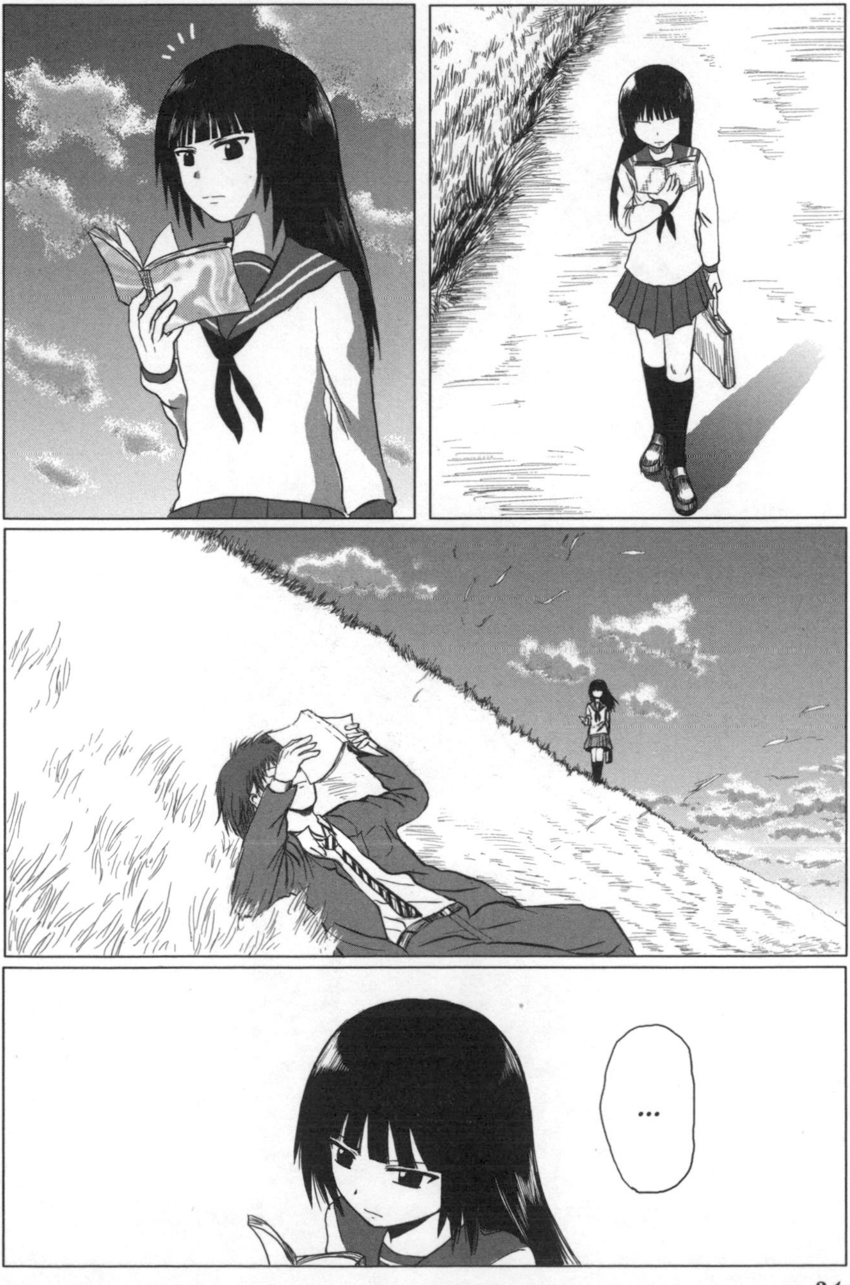
...

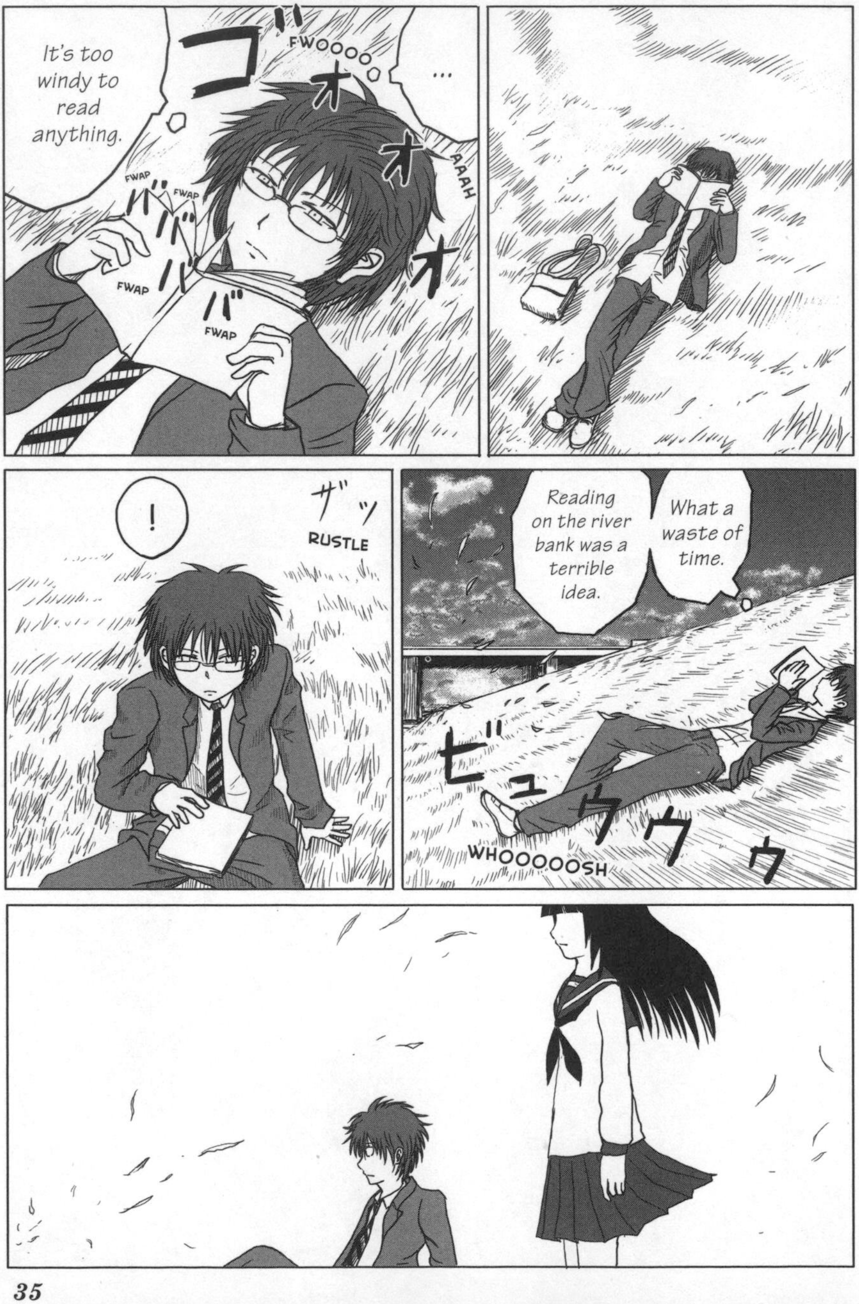
...
ゴオオオ
FWOOOO
AAAH
It's too windy to read anything.
バババ
FWAP
FWAP
FWAP
FWAP
What a waste of time.
Reading on the river bank was a terrible idea.
ビュウウウ
WHOOOOOSH
ザッ
RUSTLE
!

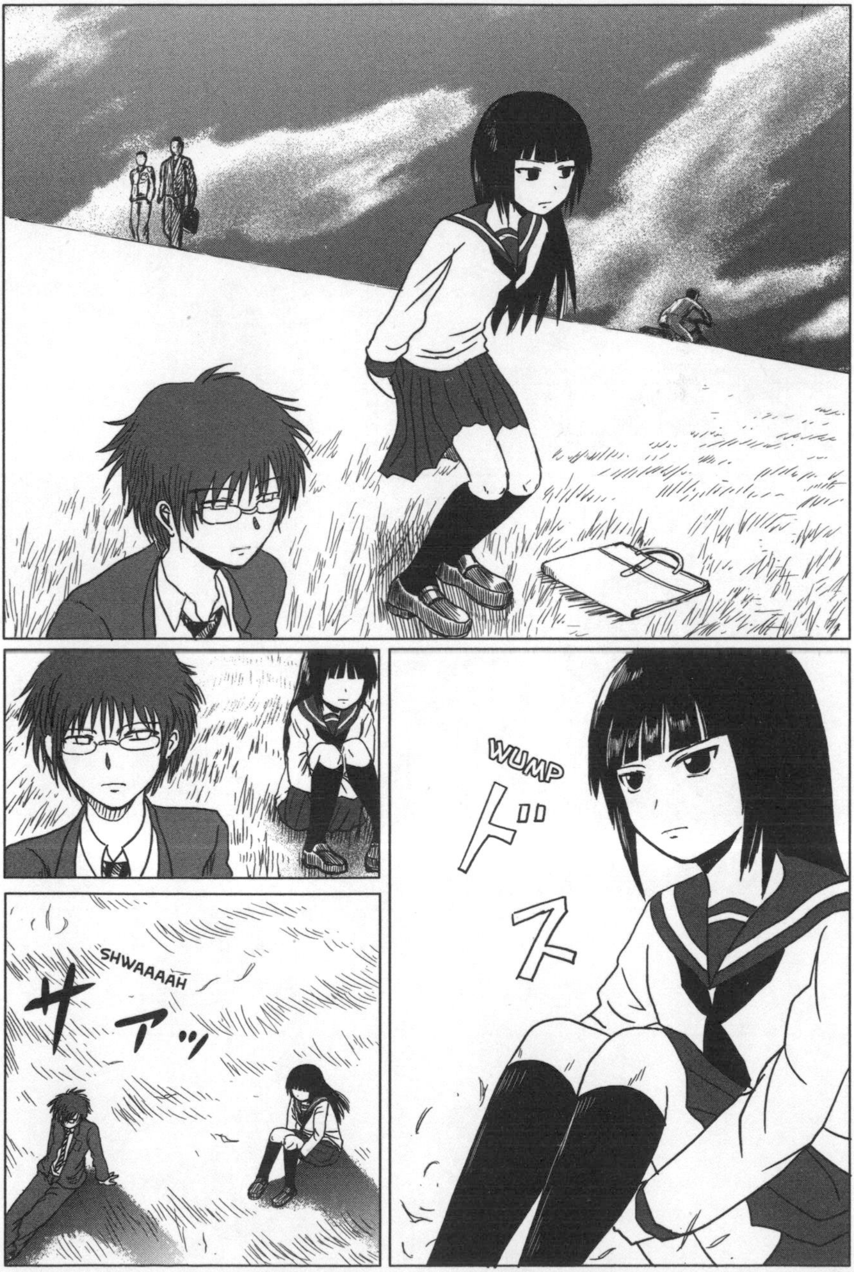
WUMP
ドス
SHWAAAAH
サアッ

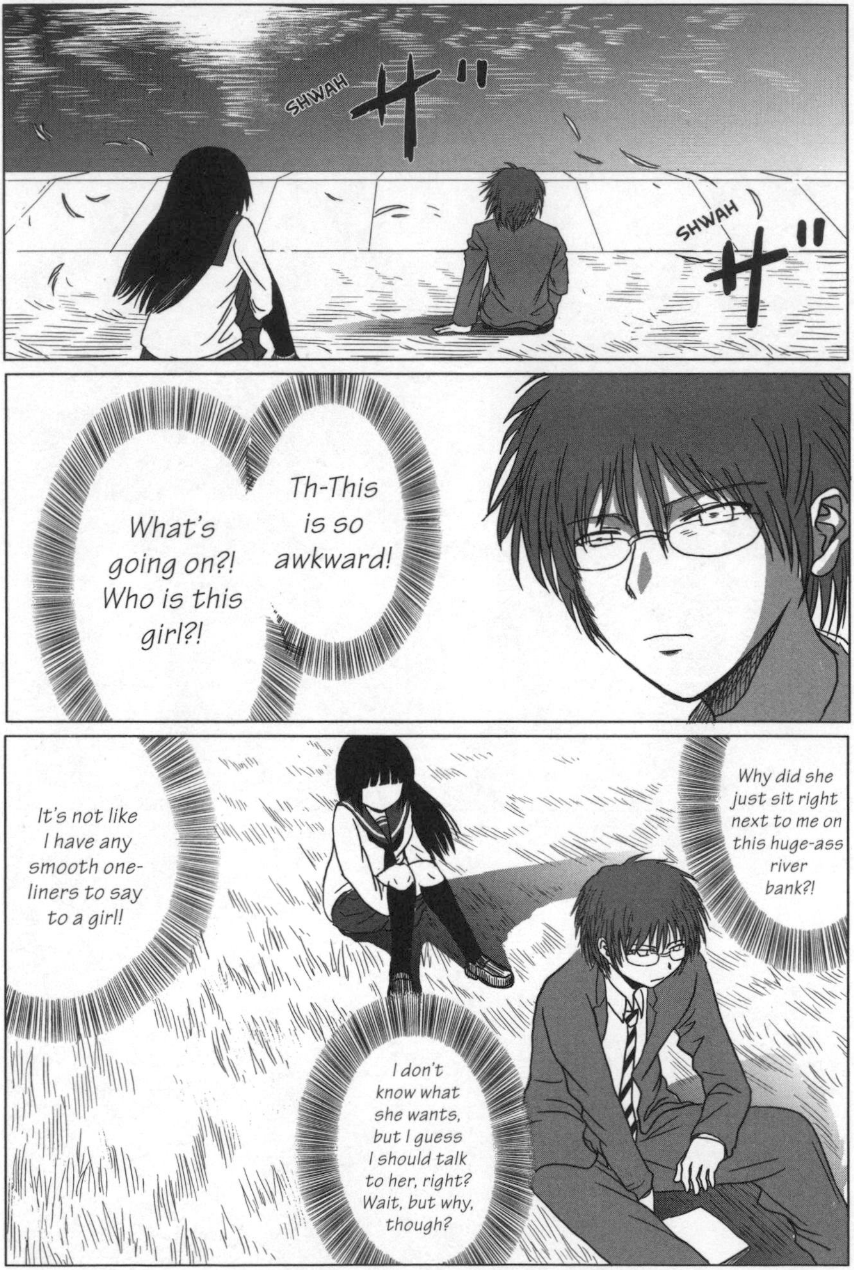
SHWAH
SHWAH
Th-This is so awkward!
What's going on?! Who is this girl?!
Why did she just sit right next to me on this huge-ass river bank?!
It's not like I have any smooth one-liners to say to a girl!
I don't know what she wants, but I guess I should talk to her, right? Wait, but why, though?

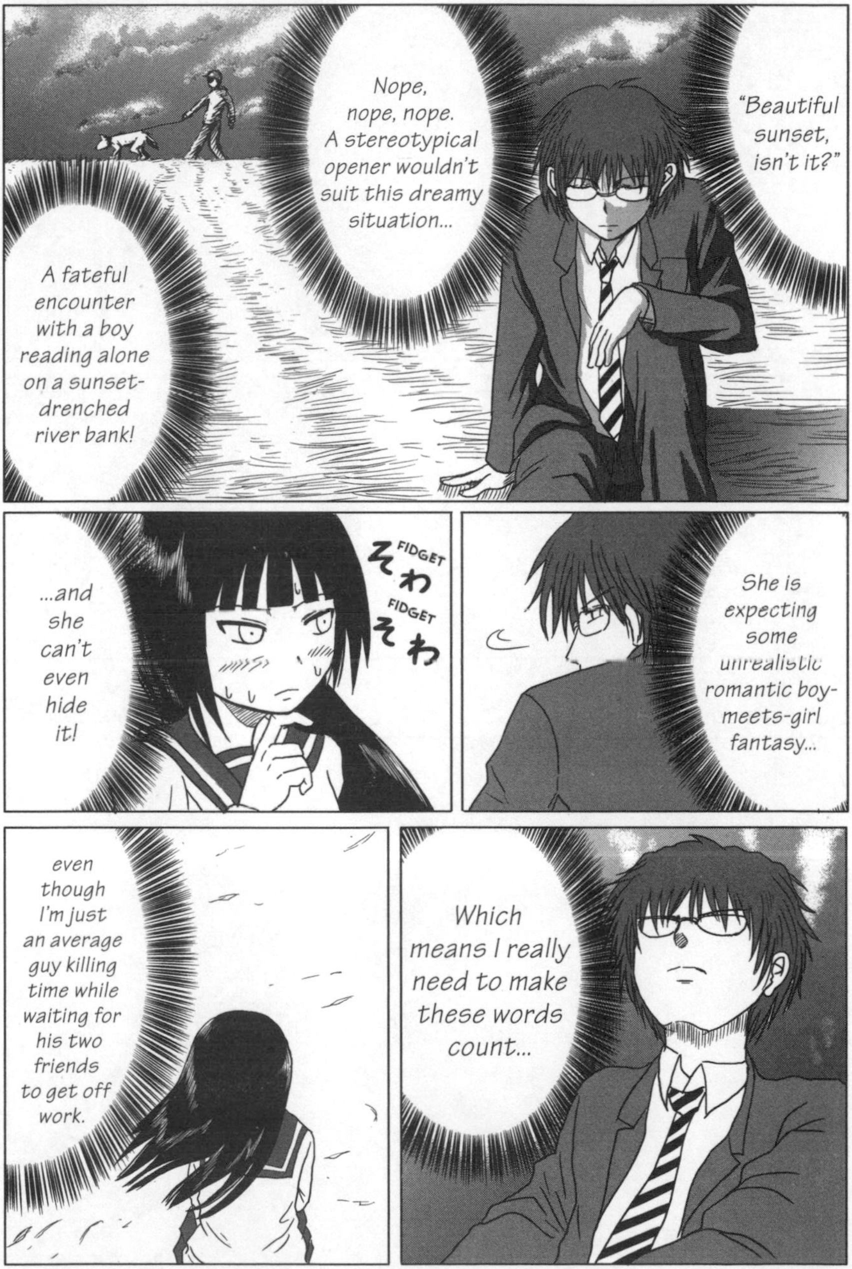
"Beautiful sunset, isn't it?"
Nope, nope, nope. A stereotypical opener wouldn't suit this dreamy situation...
A fateful encounter with a boy reading alone on a sunset-drenched river bank!
She is expecting some unrealistic romantic boy-meets-girl fantasy...
そわ FIDGET
そわ FIDGET
...and she can't even hide it!
Which means I really need to make these words count...
even though I'm just an average guy killing time while waiting for his two friends to get off work.

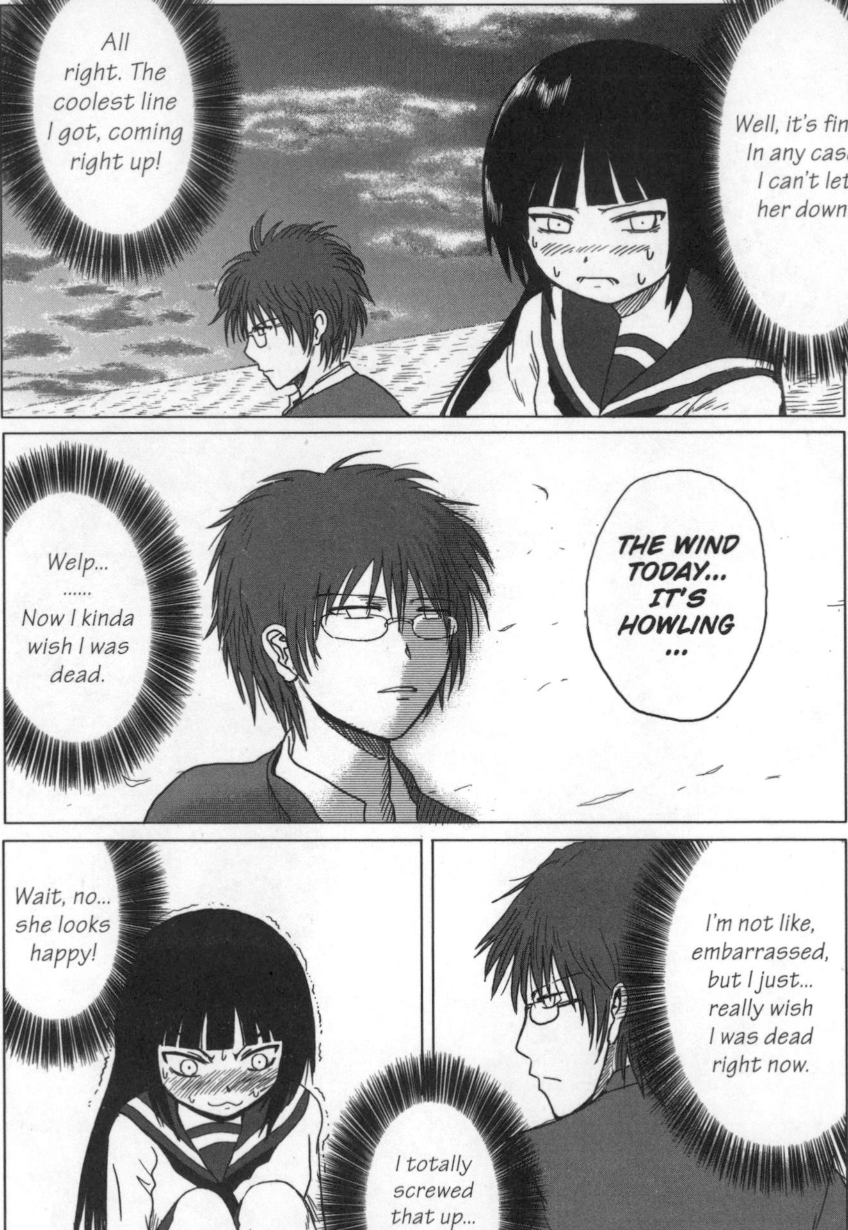
Well, it's fine... In any case, I can't let her down!
All right. The coolest line I got, coming right up!
THE WIND TODAY... IT'S HOWLING...
Welp... ...... Now I kinda wish I was dead.
I'm not like, embarrassed, but I just... really wish I was dead right now.
I totally screwed that up...
Wait, no... she looks happy!

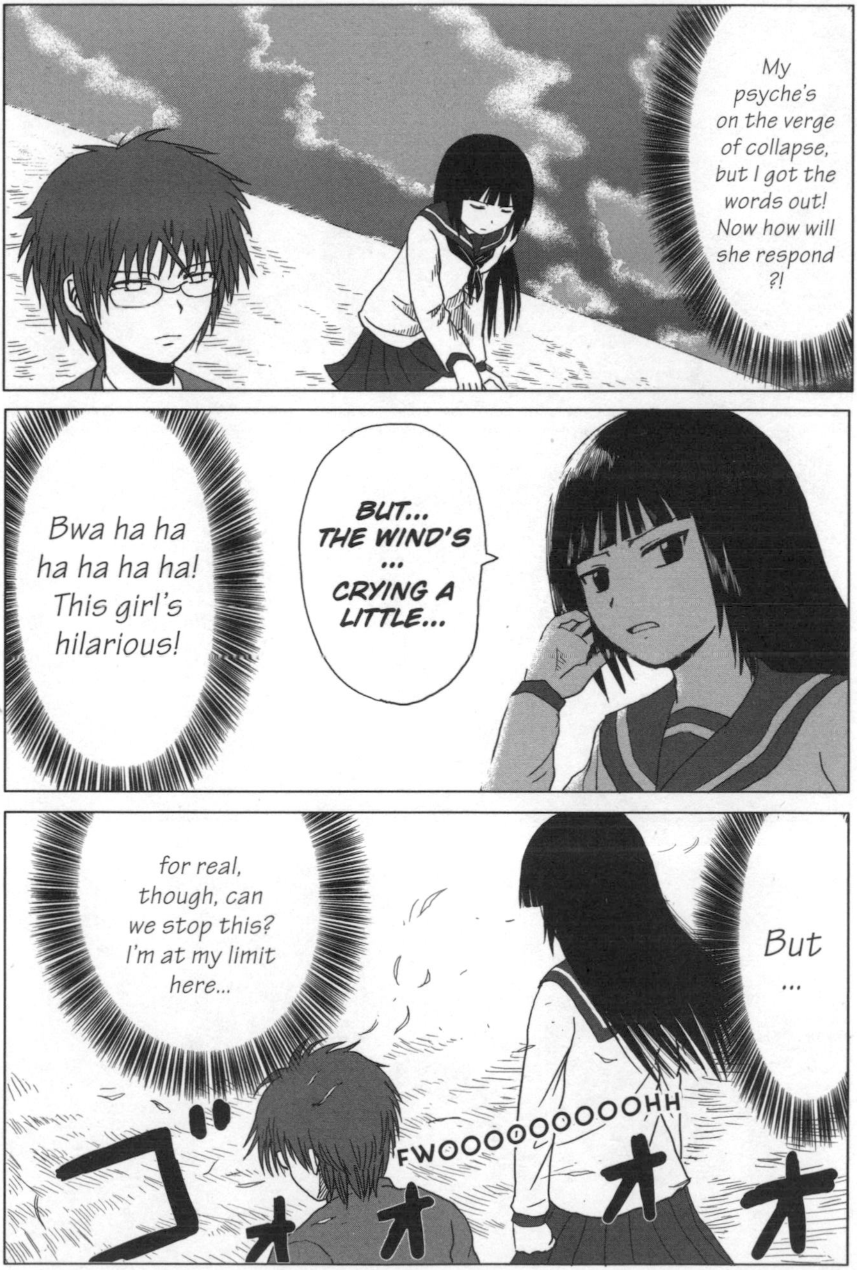
My psyche's on the verge of collapse, but I got the words out! Now how will she respond ?!
BUT... THE WIND'S ... CRYING A LITTLE...
Bwa ha ha ha ha ha ha! This girl's hilarious!
But ...
for real, though, can we stop this? I'm at my limit here...
ゴォオオ
FWOOOOOOOOOOHH

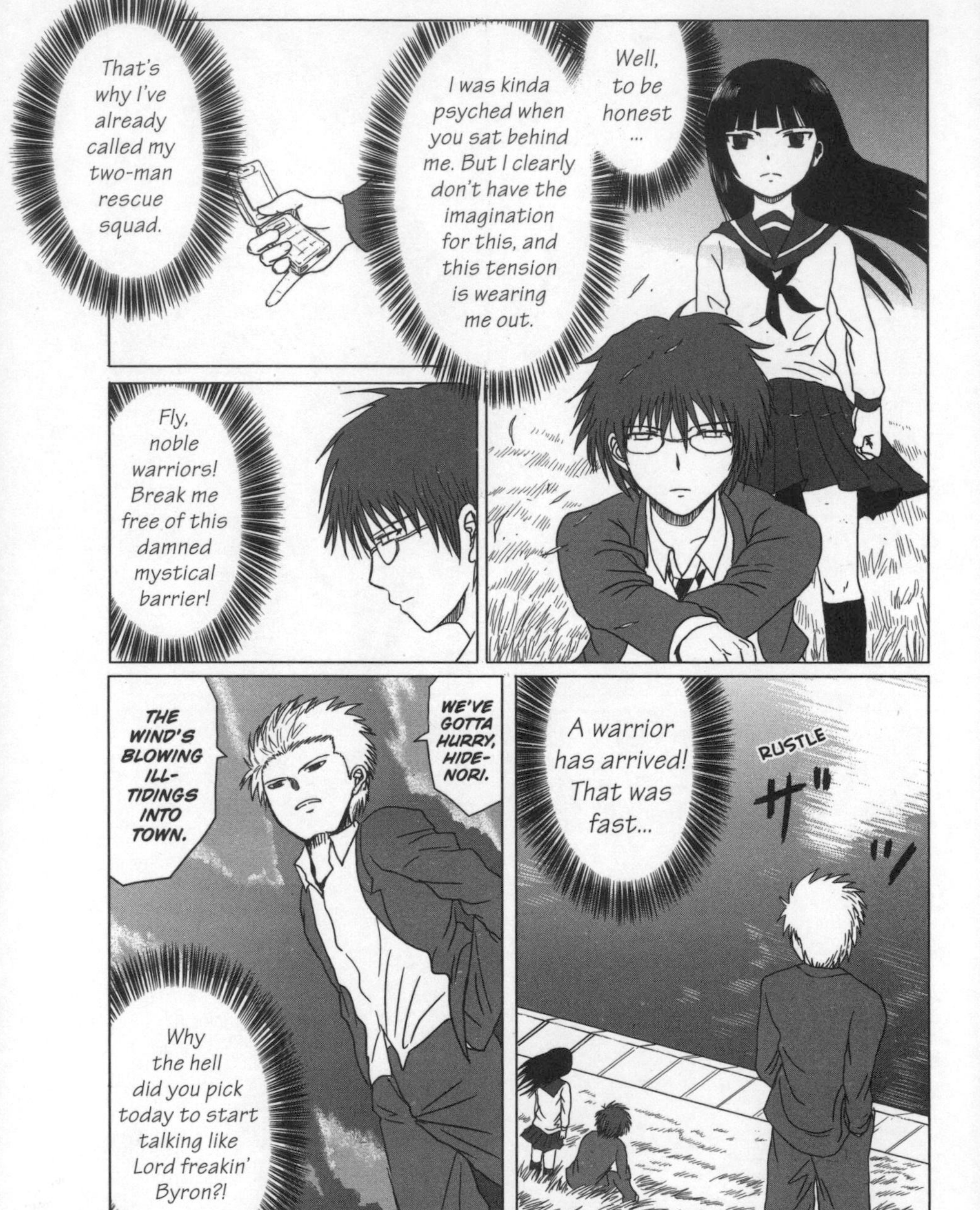
Well, to be honest ...
I was kinda psyched when you sat behind me. But I clearly don't have the imagination for this, and this tension is wearing me out.
That's why I've already called my two-man rescue squad.
Fly, noble warriors! Break me free of this damned mystical barrier!
A warrior has arrived! That was fast...
RUSTLE
WE'VE GOTTA HURRY, HIDE-NORI.
THE WIND'S BLOWING ILL-TIDINGS INTO TOWN.
Why the hell did you pick today to start talking like Lord freakin' Byron?!

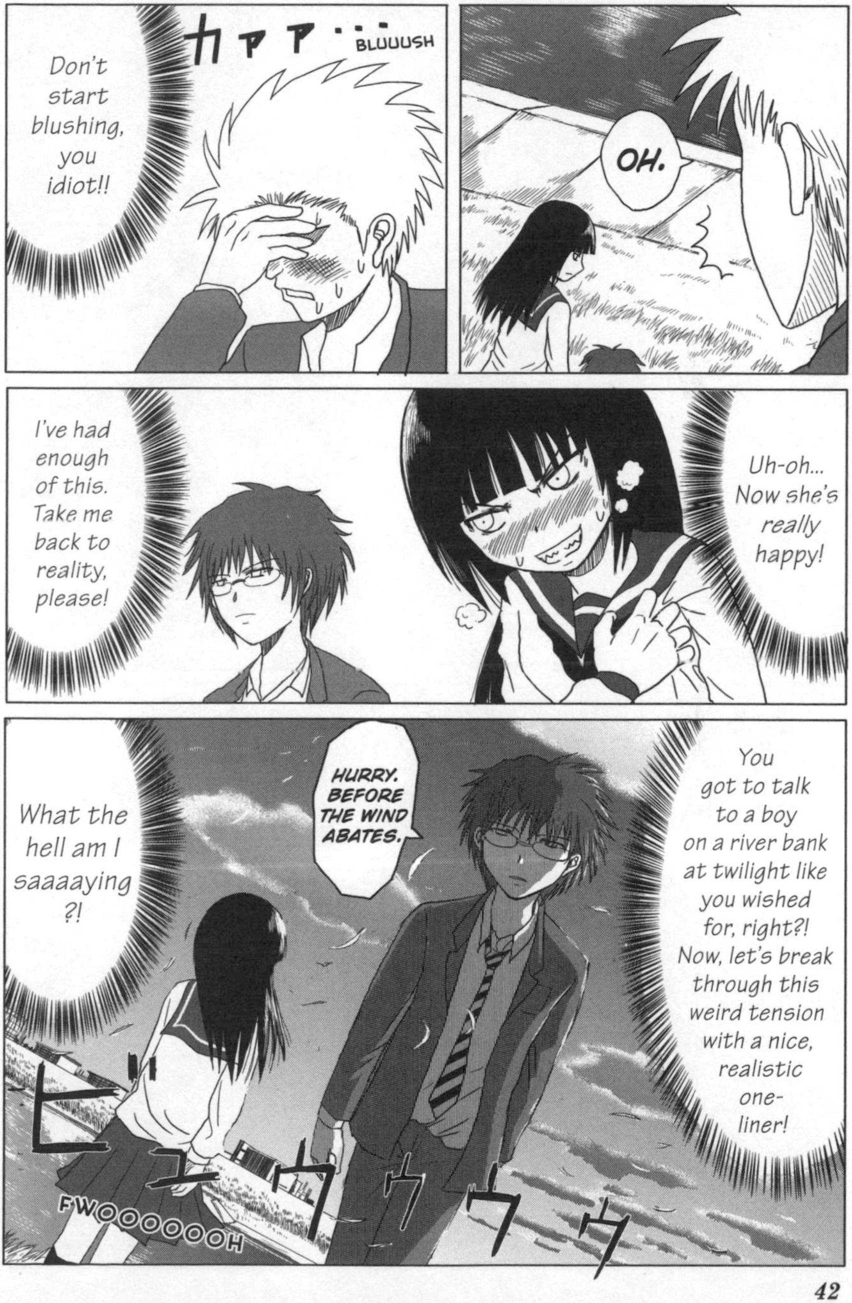
OH.
カァア...
BLUUUSH
Don't start blushing, you idiot!!
Uh-oh... Now she's really happy!
I've had enough of this. Take me back to reality, please!
You got to talk to a boy on a river bank at twilight like you wished for, right?! Now, let's break through this weird tension with a nice, realistic one-liner!
HURRY. BEFORE THE WIND ABATES.
What the hell am I saaaaying?!
ヒュウウウウウ
FWOOOOOOOH

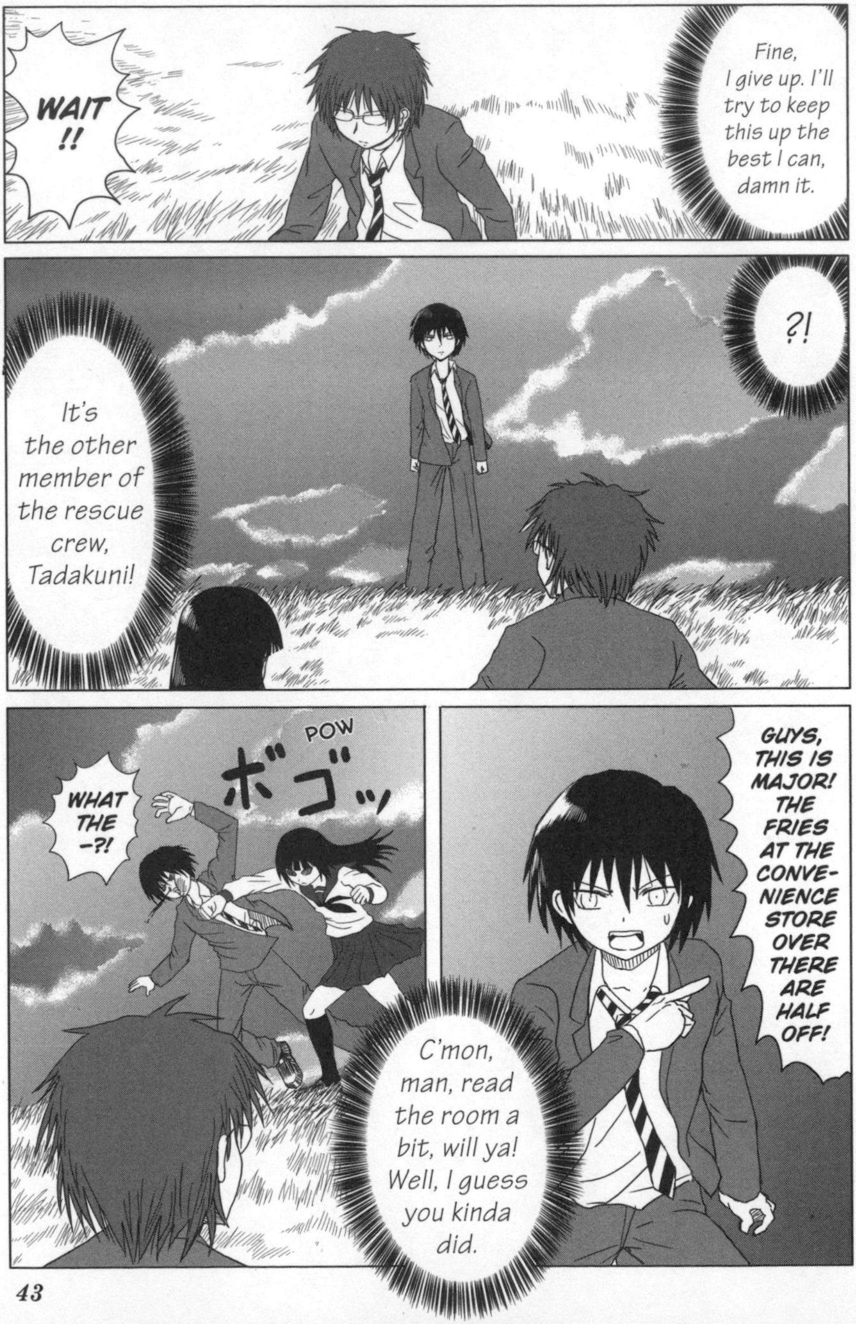
Fine, I give up. I'll try to keep this up the best I can, damn it.
WAIT !!
?!
It's the other member of the rescue crew, Tadakuni!
GUYS, THIS IS MAJOR! THE FRIES AT THE CONVE-NIENCE STORE OVER THERE ARE HALF OFF!
C'mon, man, read the room a bit, will ya! Well, I guess you kinda did.
POW
ボゴッ
WHAT THE -?!

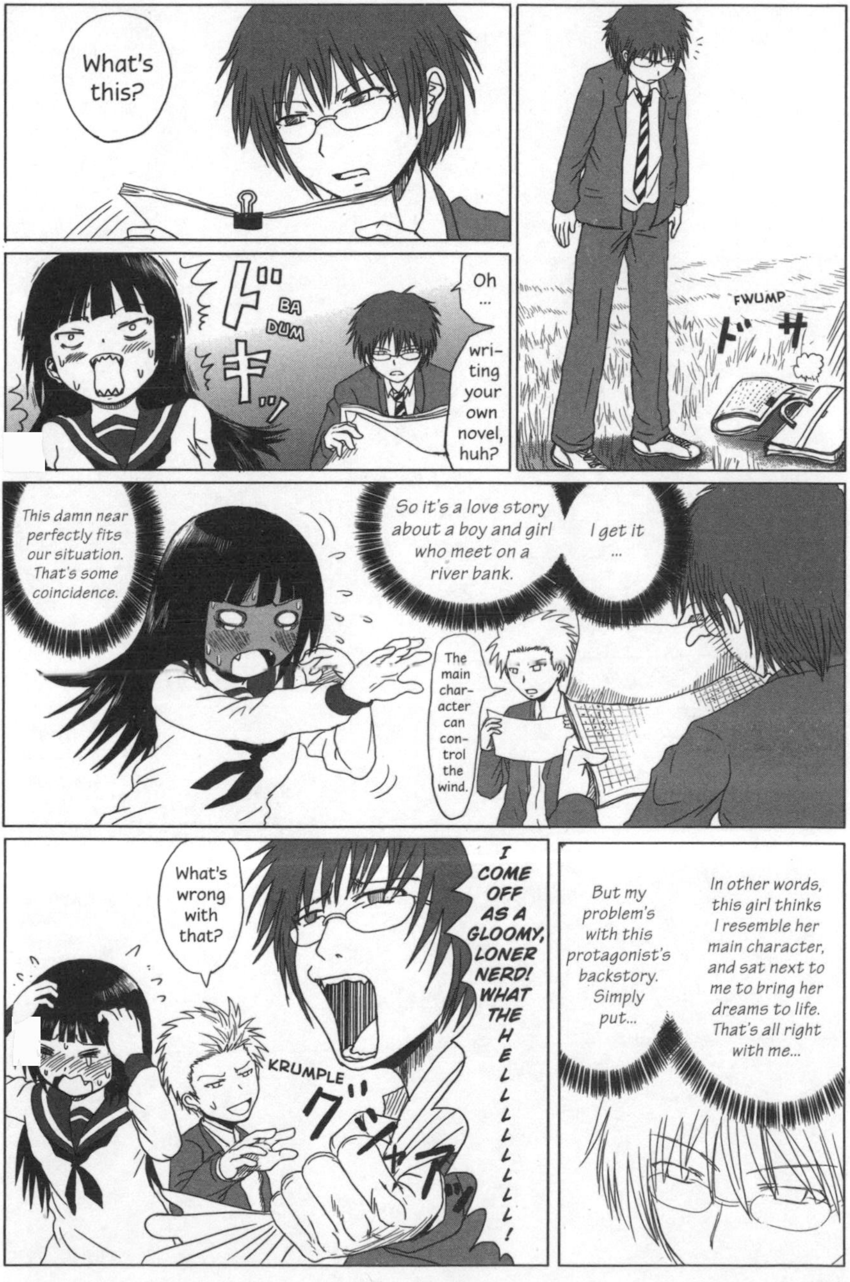
FWUMP
ドサ
What's this?
Oh ... writing your own novel, huh?
BA DUM
ドキッ
I get it ...
So it's a love story about a boy and girl who meet on a river bank.
This damn near perfectly fits our situation. That's some coincidence.
The main character can control the wind.
In other words, this girl thinks I resemble her main character, and sat next to me to bring her dreams to life. That's all right with me...
But my problem's with this protagonist's backstory. Simply put...
I COME OFF AS A GLOOMY, LONER NERD! WHAT THE HELLLLLLLLLLLL!
What's wrong with that?
KRUMPLE
グシャ

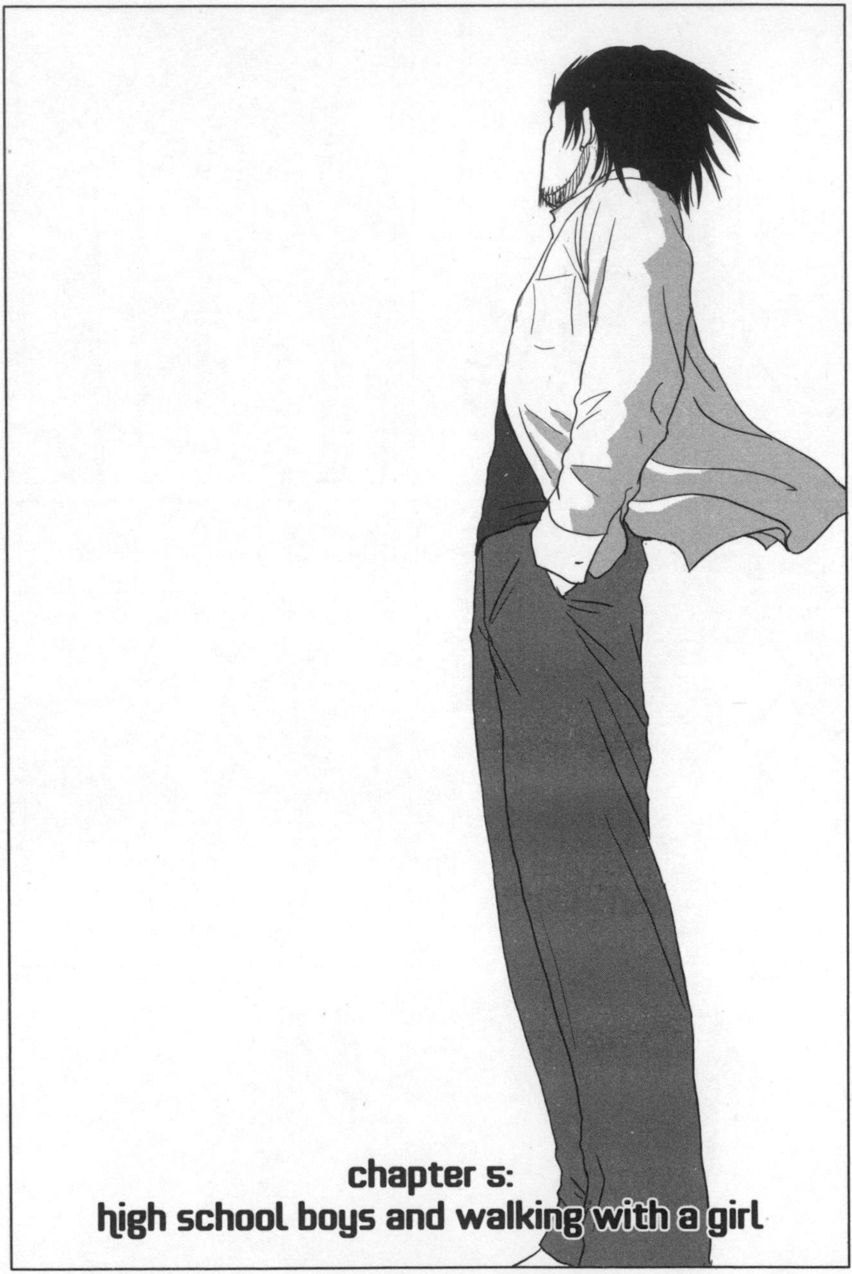

chapter 5:
high school boys and walking with a girl

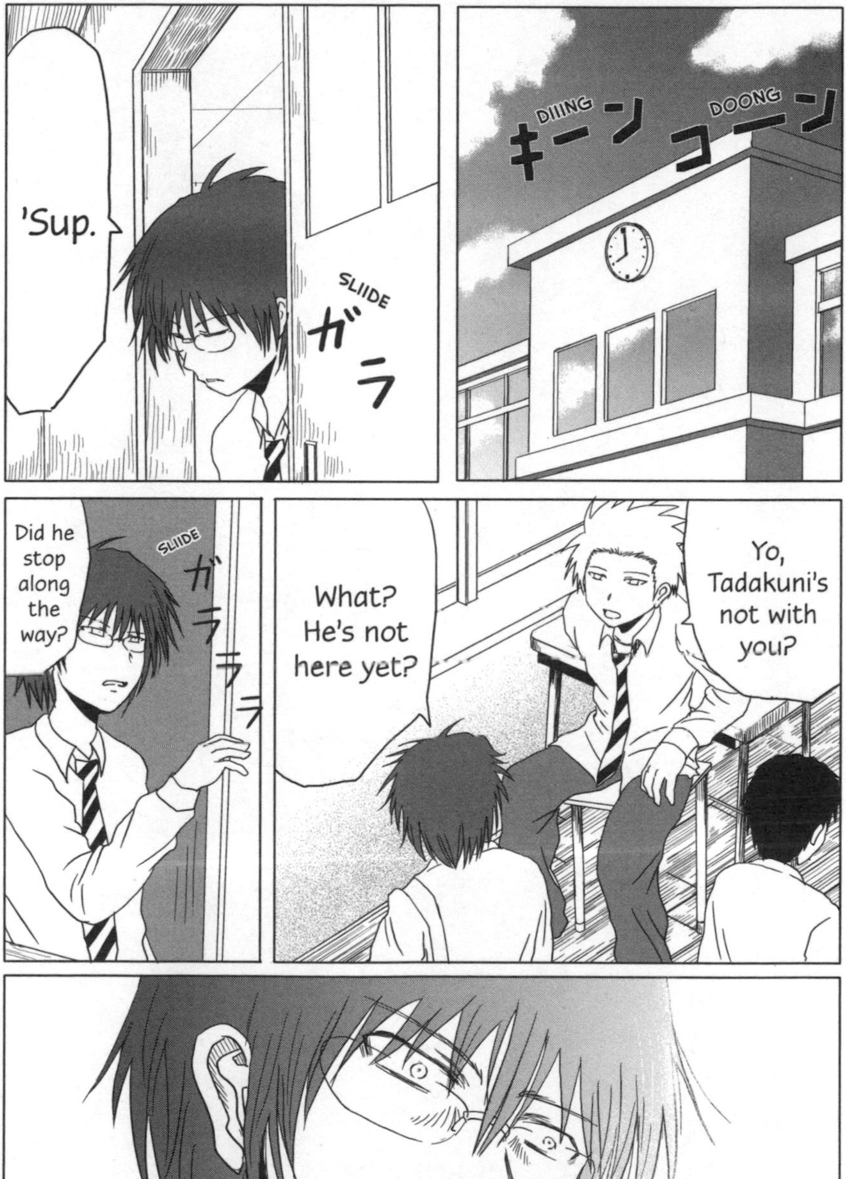
DIIING
キーン
DOONG
コーン
'Sup.
SLIIDE
ガラ
Yo, Tadakuni's not with you?
What? He's not here yet?
SLIIDE
ガラララ
Did he stop along the way?

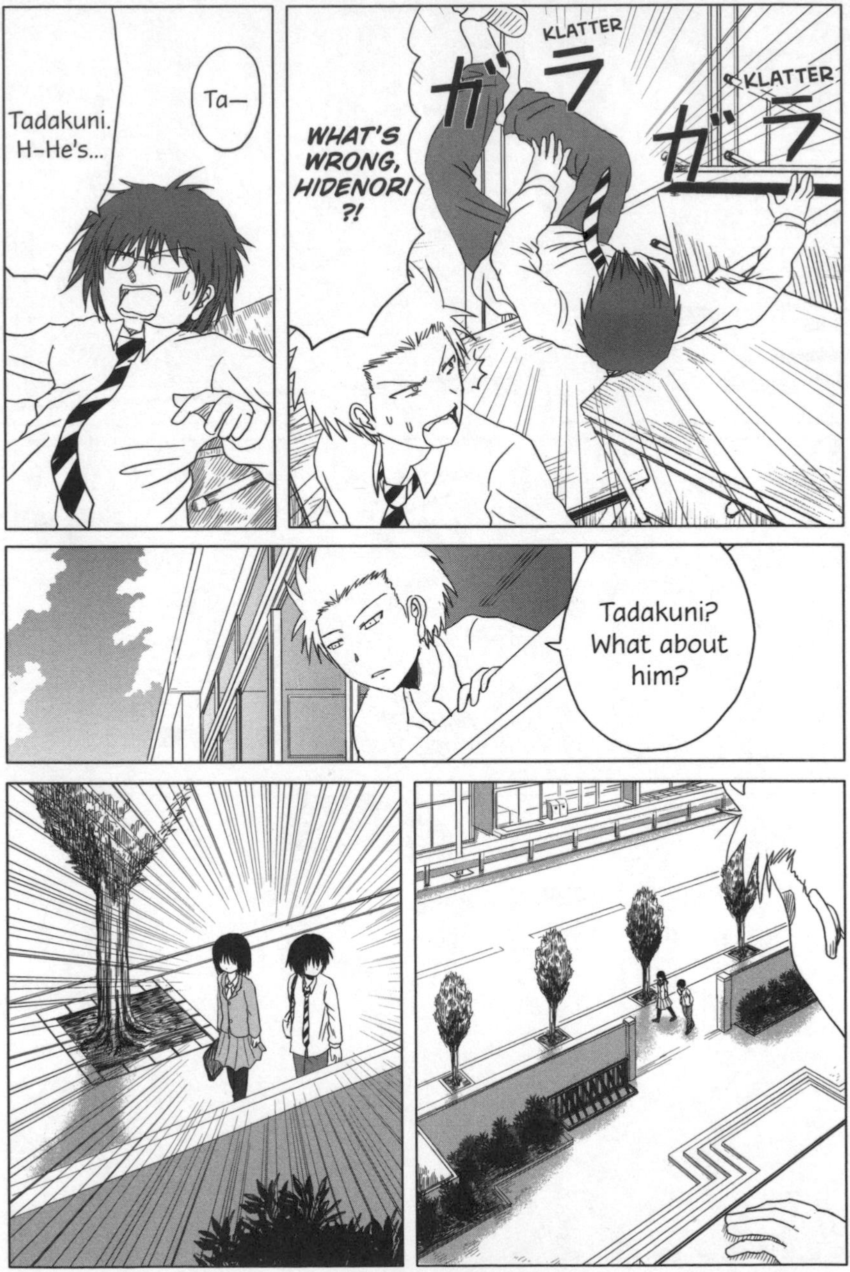
KLATTER
ガラ
KLATTER
ガラ
WHAT'S WRONG, HIDENORI?!
Ta—
Tadakuni. H-He's...
Tadakuni? What about him?

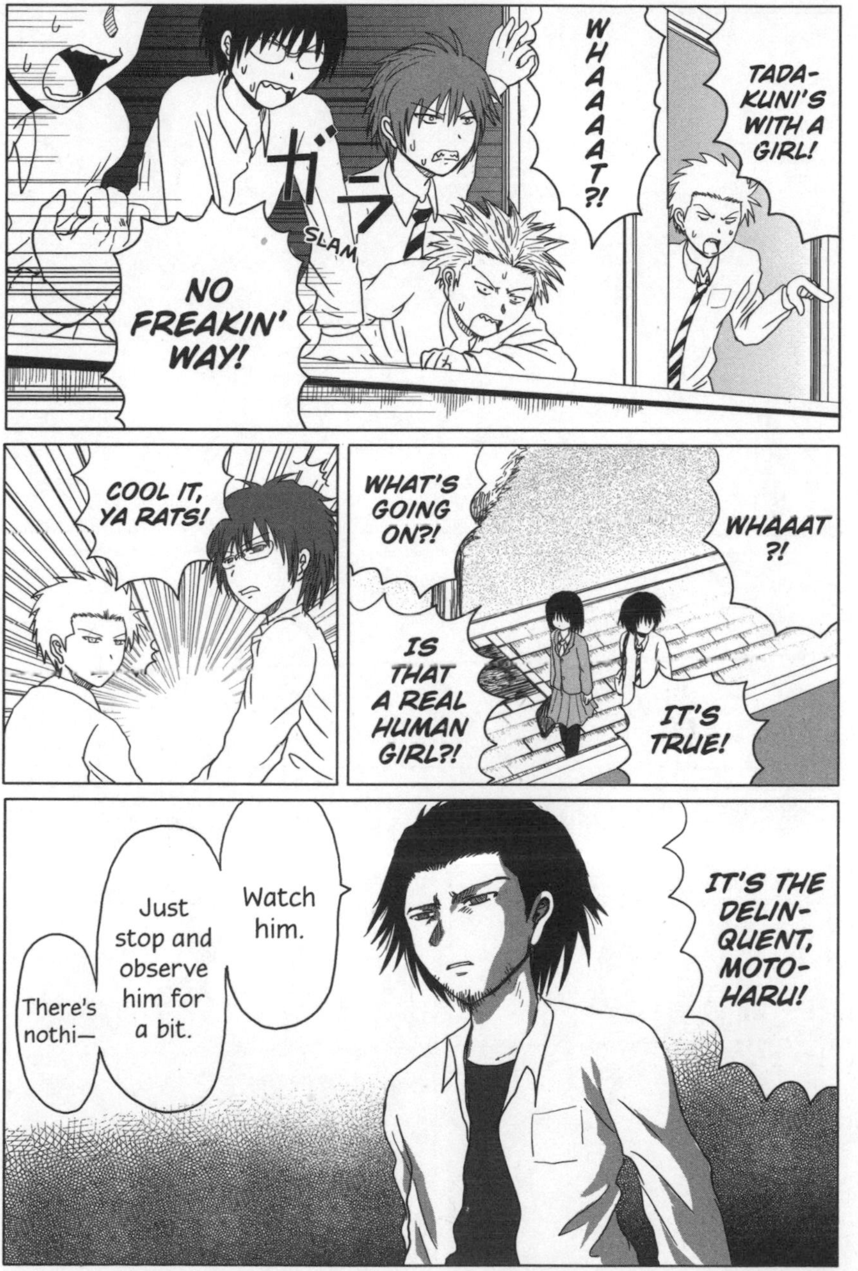
TADA-KUNI'S WITH A GIRL!
WHAAAAAT?!
ガラ
SLAM
NO FREAKIN' WAY!
WHAAAT?!
WHAT'S GOING ON?!
IT'S TRUE!
IS THAT A REAL HUMAN GIRL?!
COOL IT, YA RATS!
IT'S THE DELINQUENT, MOTO-HARU!
Watch him.
Just stop and observe him for a bit.
There's nothi—

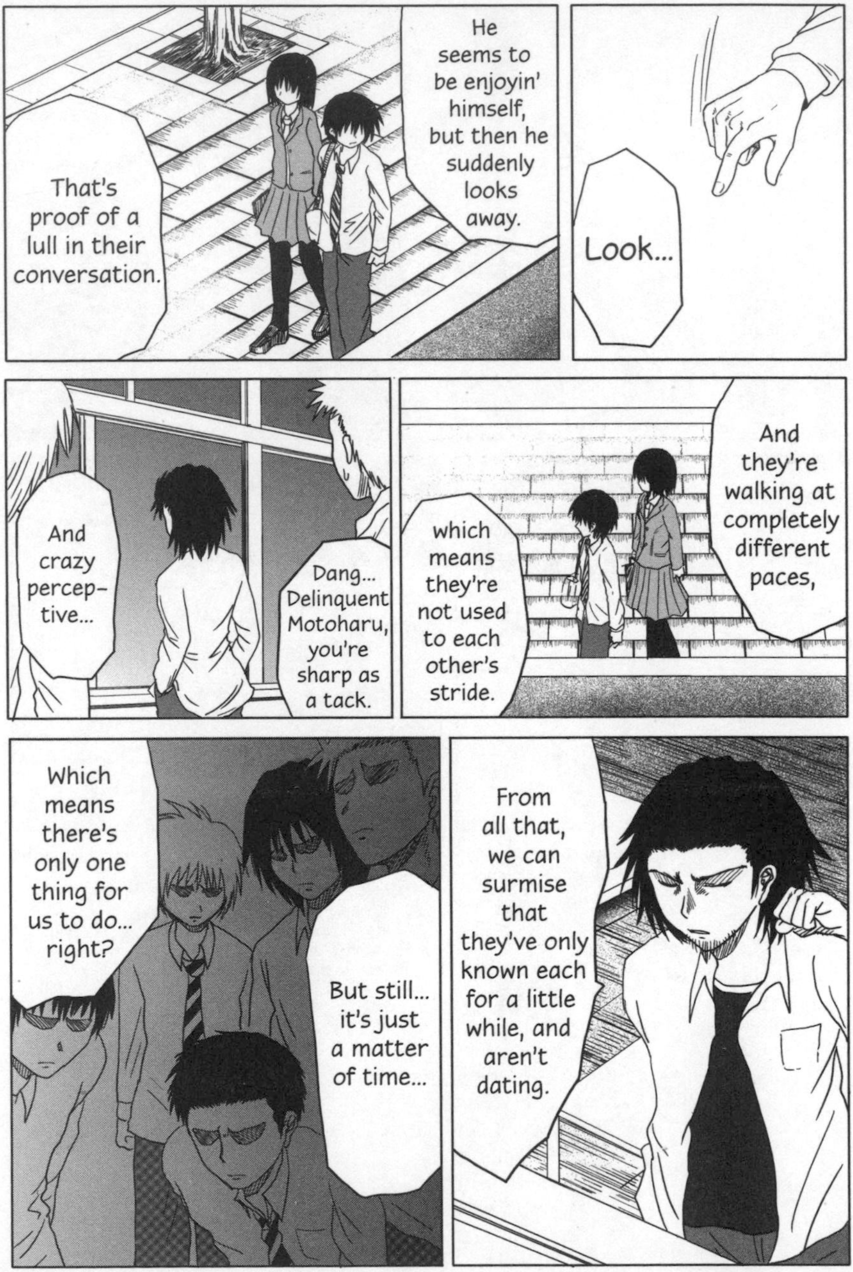
Look...
He seems to be enjoyin' himself, but then he suddenly looks away.
That's proof of a lull in their conversation.
And they're walking at completely different paces,
which means they're not used to each other's stride.
Dang... Delinquent Motoharu, you're sharp as a tack.
And crazy percep-tive...
From all that, we can surmise that they've only known each for a little while, and aren't dating.
Which means there's only one thing for us to do... right?
But still... it's just a matter of time...

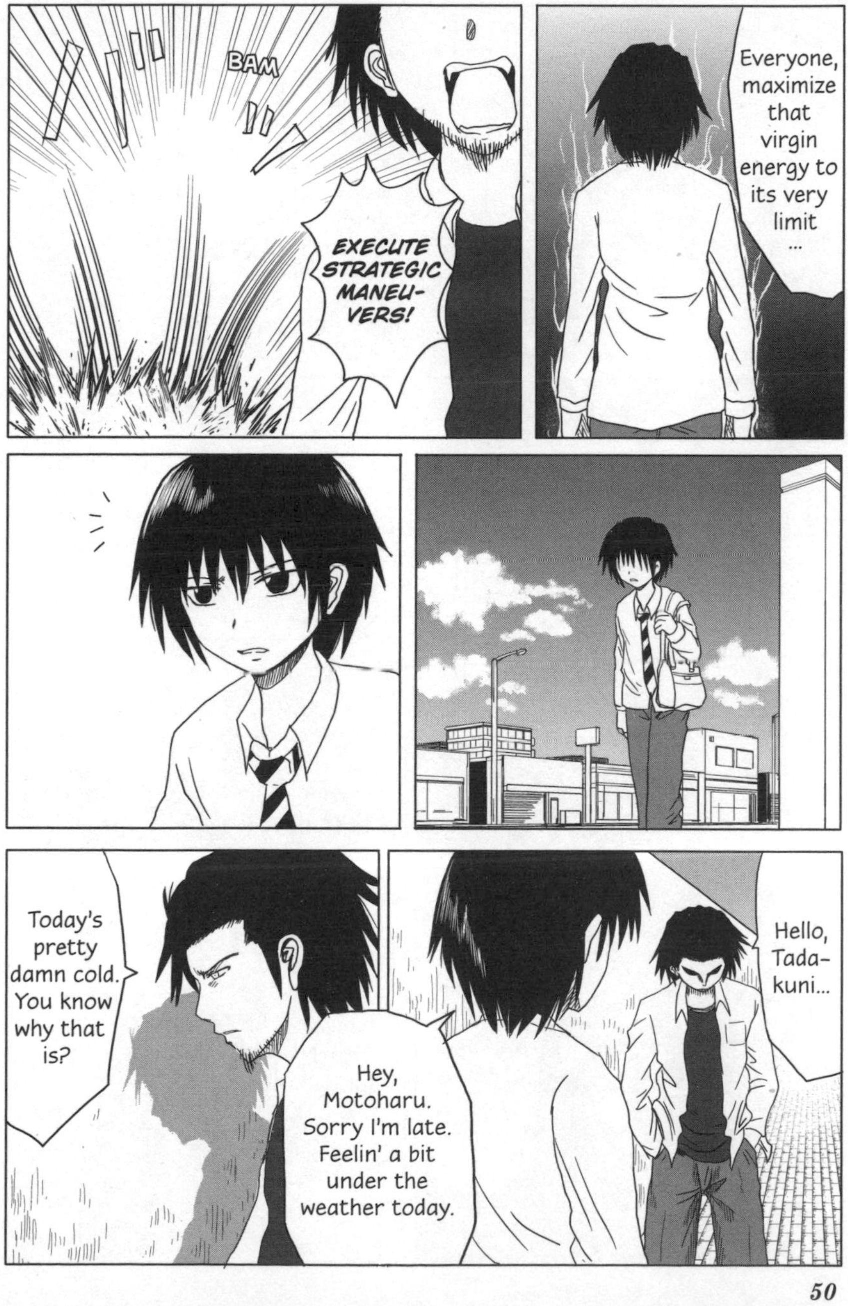
Everyone, maximize that virgin energy to its very limit ...
BAM
EXECUTE STRATEGIC MANEU-VERS!
Hello, Tada-kuni...
Hey, Motoharu. Sorry I'm late. Feelin' a bit under the weather today.
Today's pretty damn cold. You know why that is?

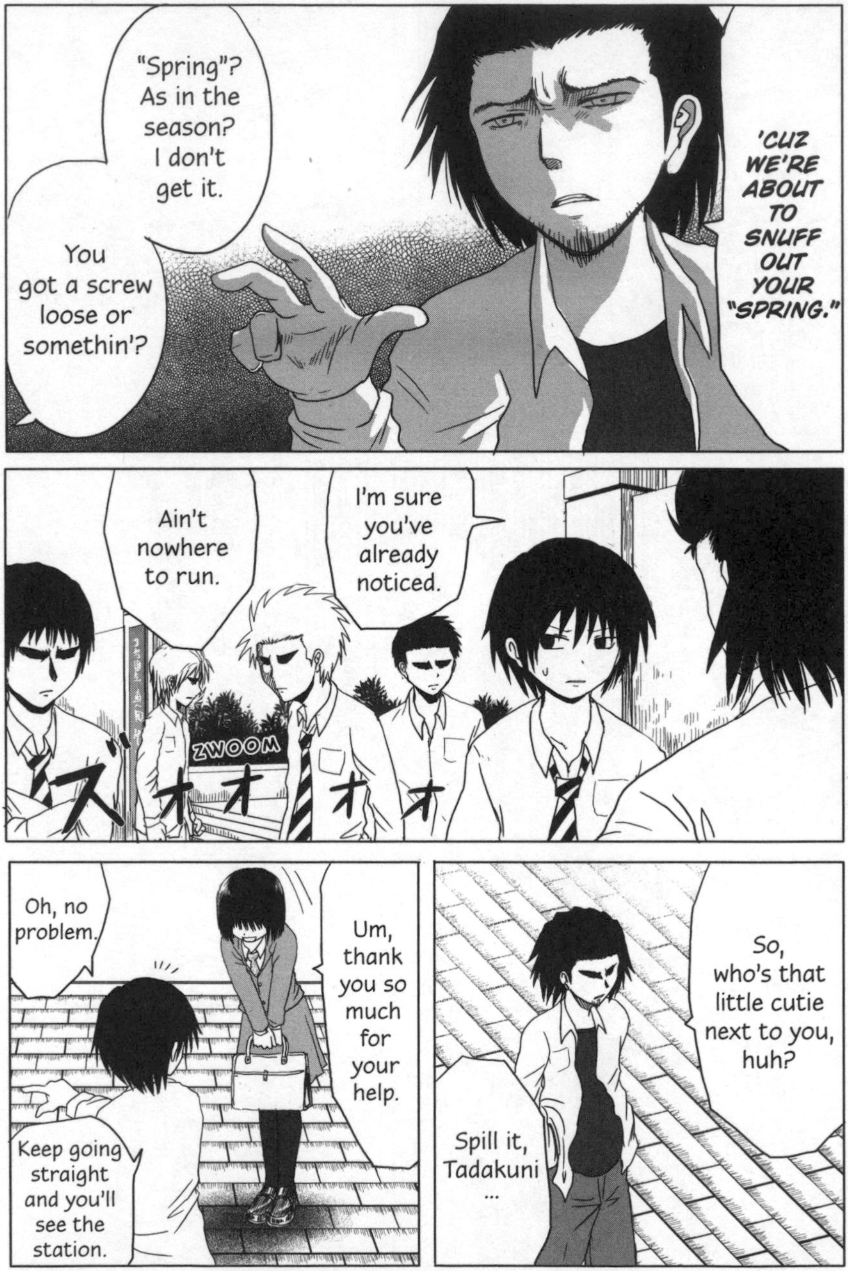

'CUZ WE'RE ABOUT TO SNUFF OUT YOUR "SPRING."
"Spring"? As in the season? I don't get it.
You got a screw loose or somethin'?
I'm sure you've already noticed.
Ain't nowhere to run.
ZWOOM
So, who's that little cutie next to you, huh?
Spill it, Tadakuni ...
Um, thank you so much for your help.
Oh, no problem.
Keep going straight and you'll see the station.

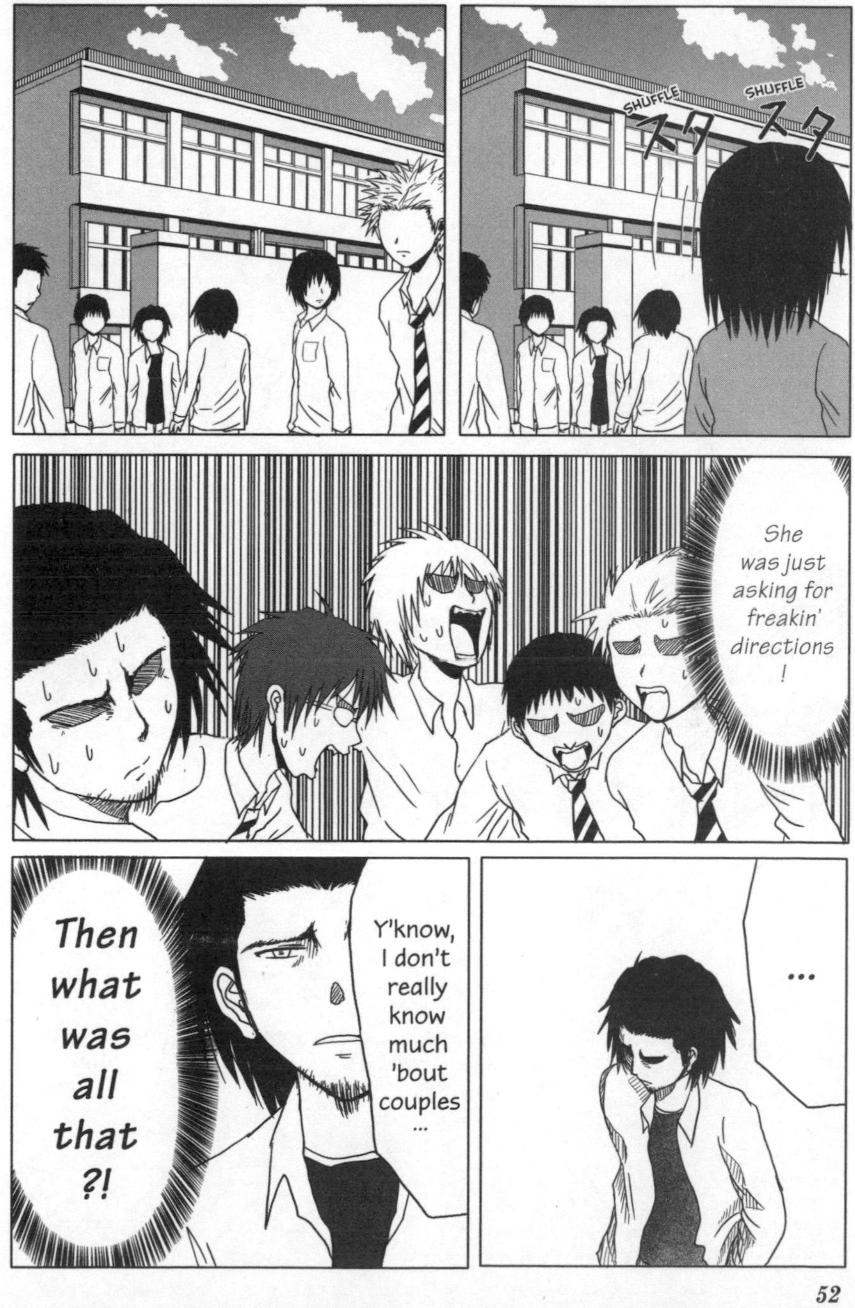
SHUFFLE スタ
SHUFFLE スタ
She was just asking for freakin' directions!
...
Y'know, I don't really know much 'bout couples...
Then what was all that?!

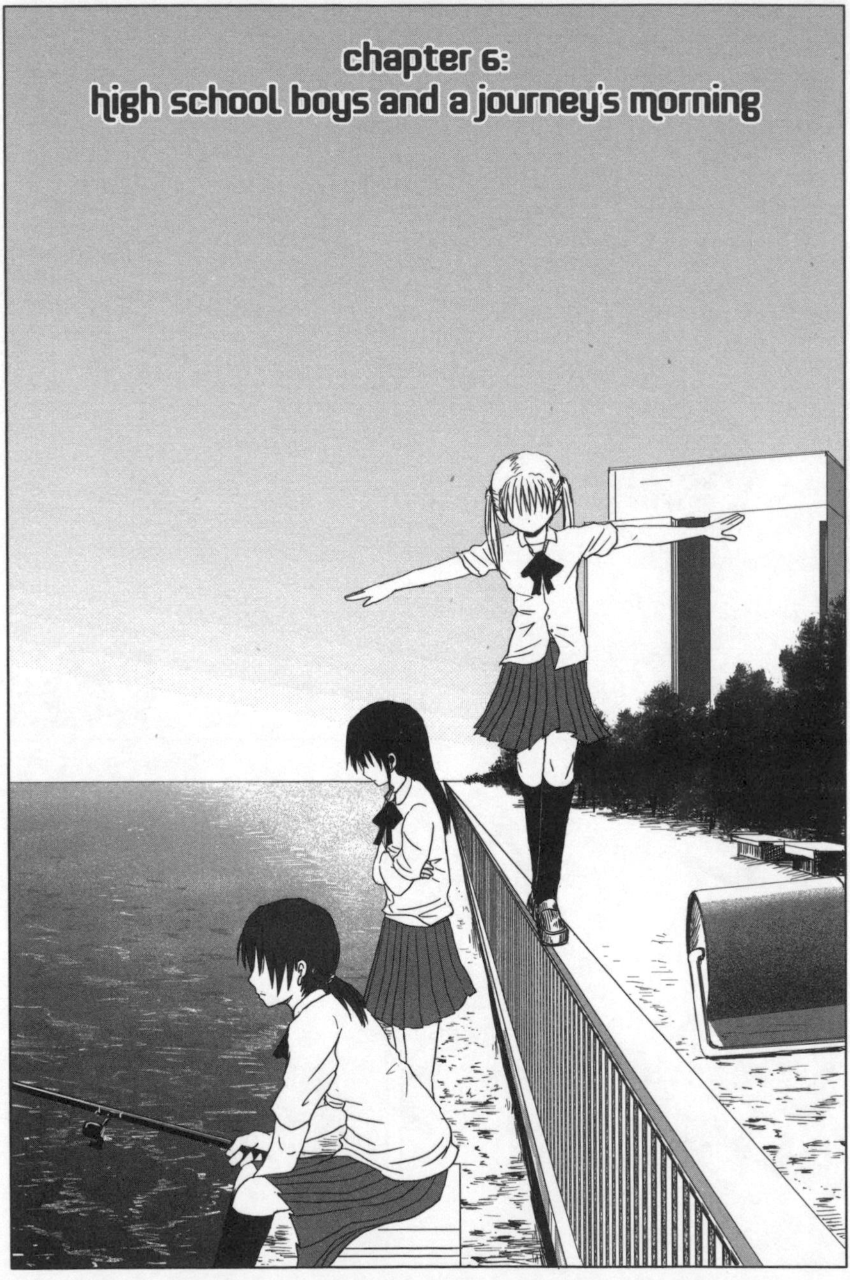
chapter 6:
high school boys and a journey's morning

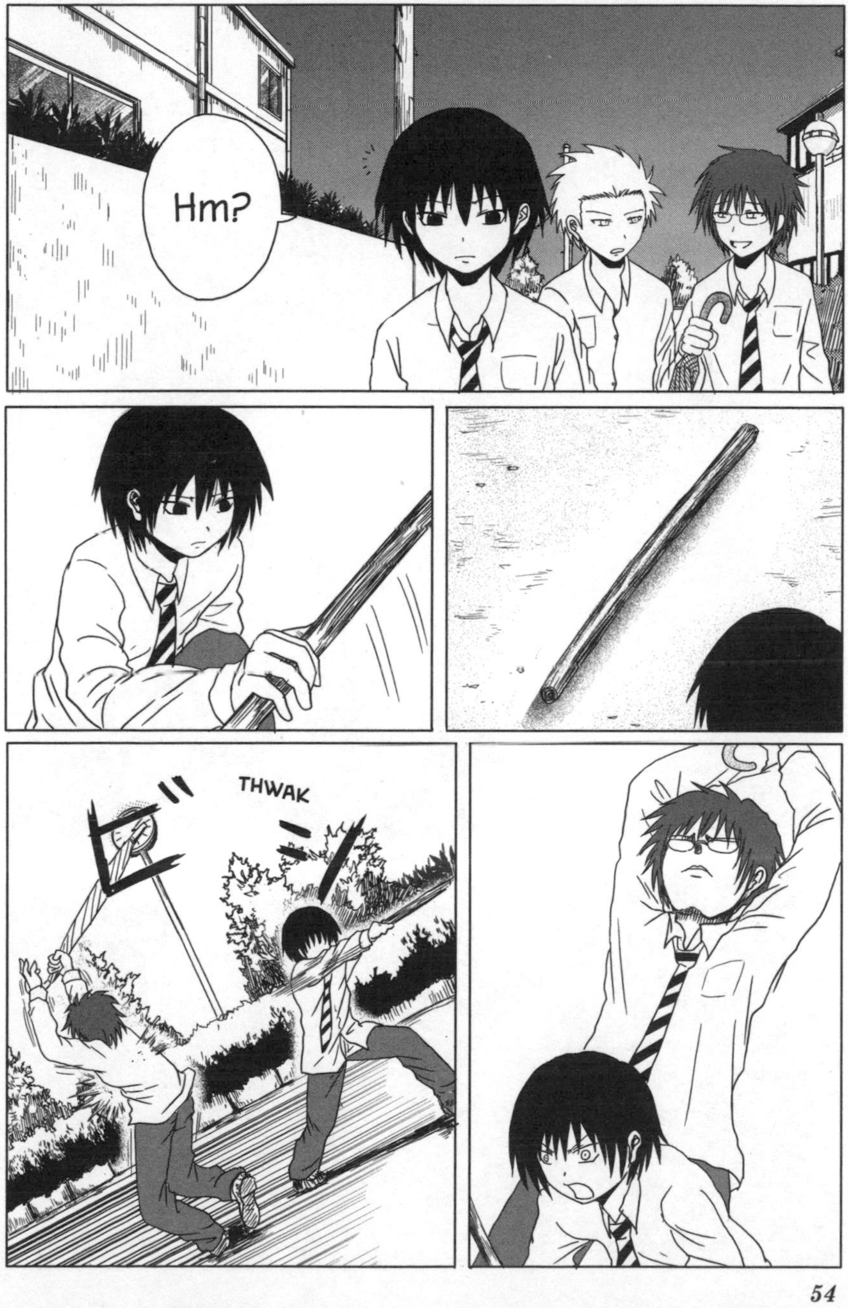
Hm?
THWAK

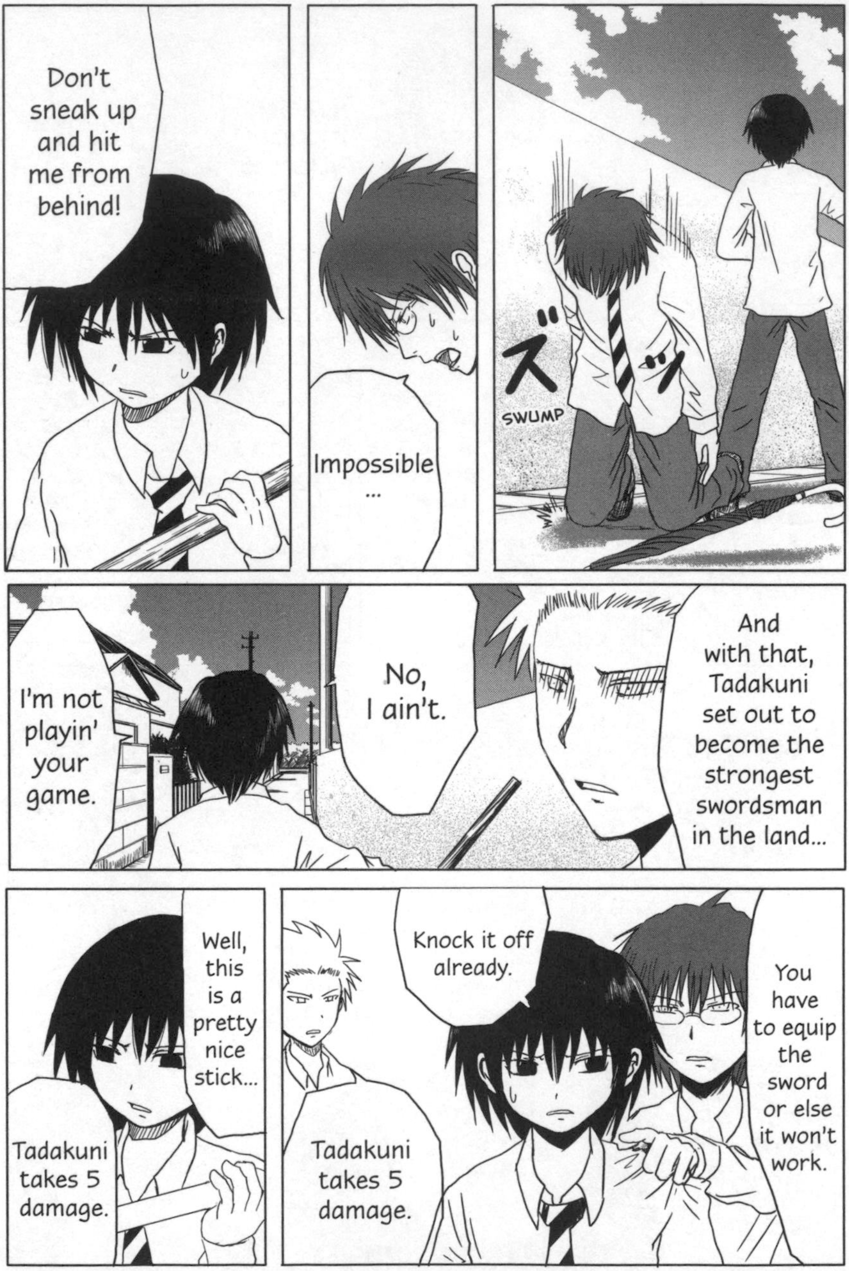
ズ
SWUMP
Impossible ...
Don't sneak up and hit me from behind!
And with that, Tadakuni set out to become the strongest swordsman in the land...
No, I ain't.
I'm not playin' your game.
Knock it off already.
You have to equip the sword or else it won't work.
Tadakuni takes 5 damage.
Well, this is a pretty nice stick...
Tadakuni takes 5 damage.

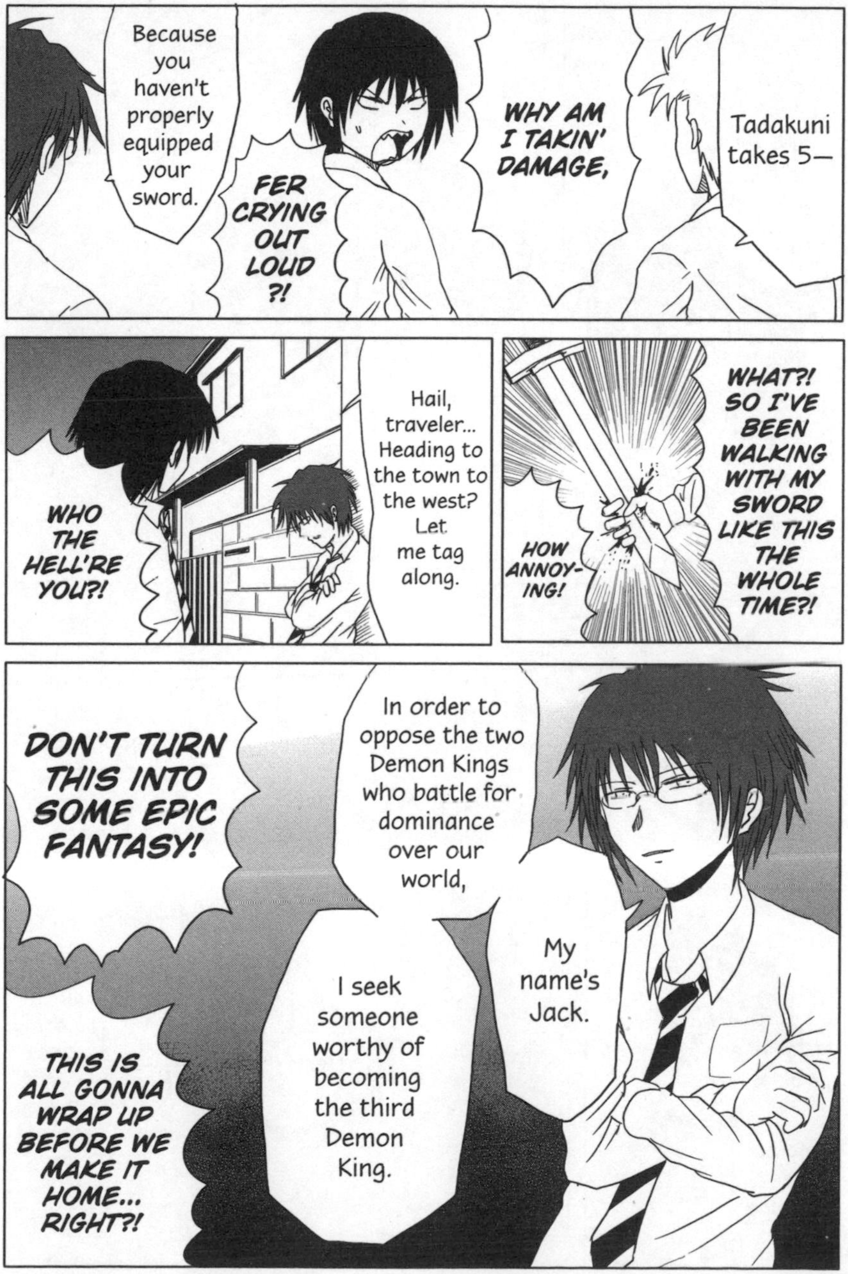
Tadakuni takes 5—
WHY AM I TAKIN' DAMAGE,
FER CRYING OUT LOUD ?!
Because you haven't properly equipped your sword.
WHAT?! SO I'VE BEEN WALKING WITH MY SWORD LIKE THIS THE WHOLE TIME?!
HOW ANNOY-ING!
Hail, traveler... Heading to the town to the west? Let me tag along.
WHO THE HELL'RE YOU?!
My name's Jack.
In order to oppose the two Demon Kings who battle for dominance over our world,
I seek someone worthy of becoming the third Demon King.
DON'T TURN THIS INTO SOME EPIC FANTASY!
THIS IS ALL GONNA WRAP UP BEFORE WE MAKE IT HOME... RIGHT?!

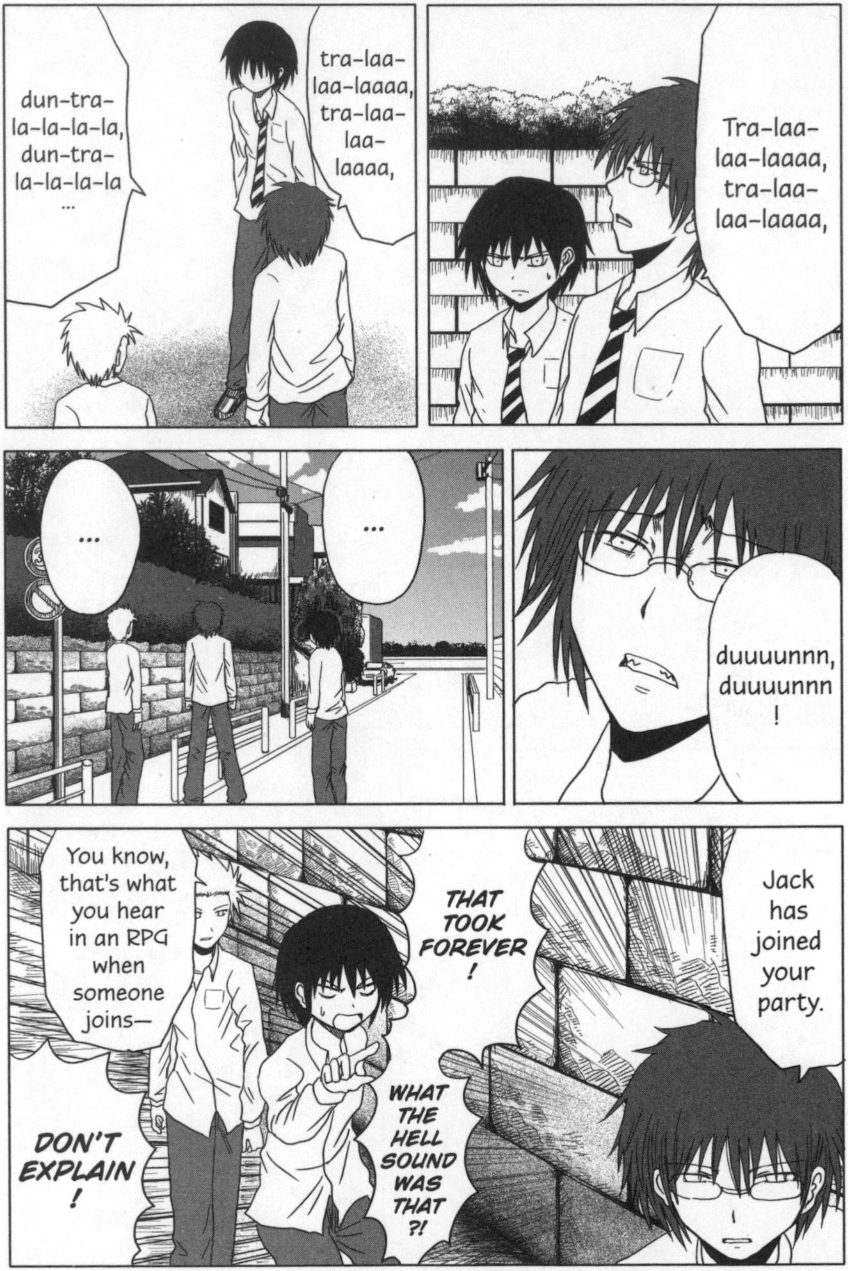
Tra-laa-laa-laaaa, tra-laa-laa-laaaa,
tra-laa-laa-laaaa, tra-laa-laa-laaaa,
dun-tra-la-la-la-la, dun-tra-la-la-la-la ...
duuuunnn, duuuunnn!
...
...
Jack has joined your party.
THAT TOOK FOREVER!
WHAT THE HELL SOUND WAS THAT?!
You know, that's what you hear in an RPG when someone joins—
DON'T EXPLAIN!

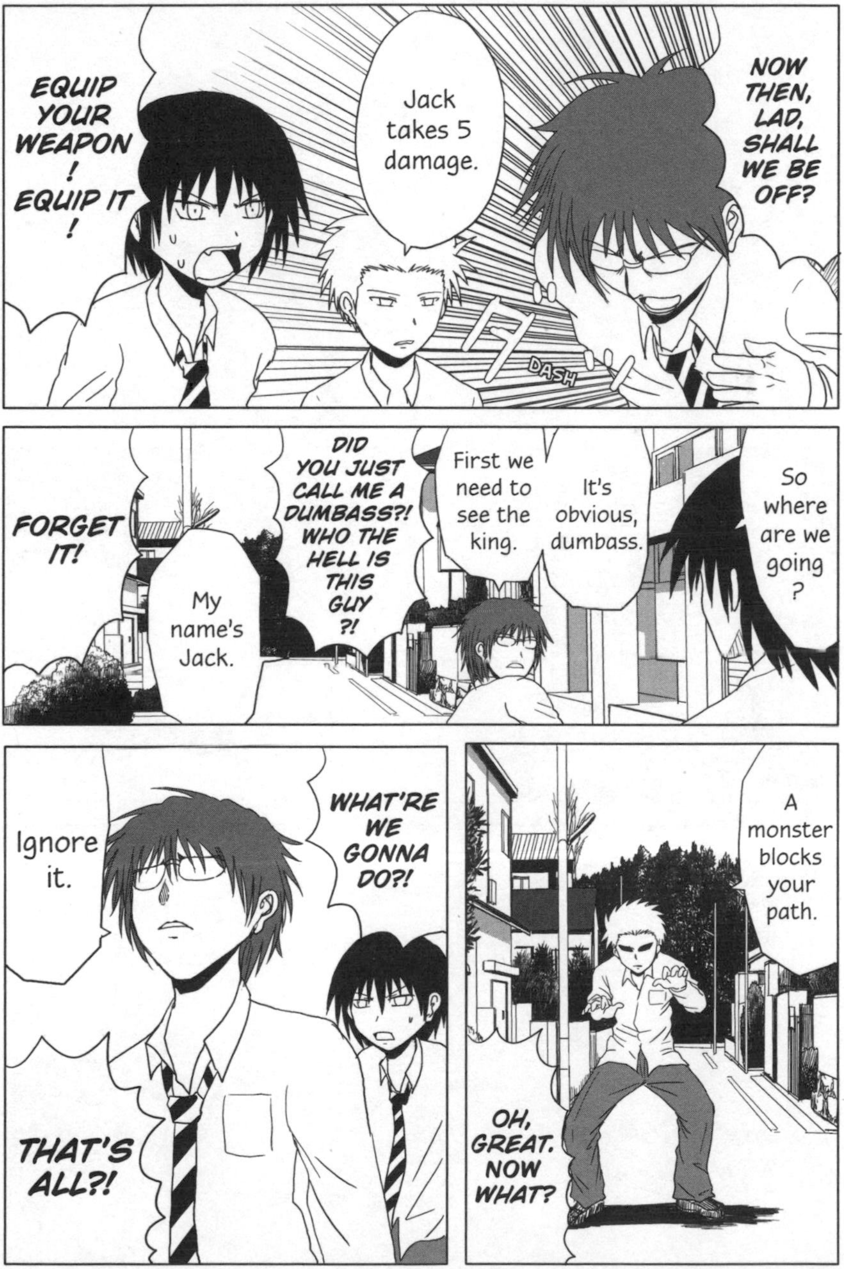
NOW THEN, LAD, SHALL WE BE OFF?
Jack takes 5 damage.
EQUIP YOUR WEAPON! EQUIP IT!
DASH
So where are we going?
It's obvious, dumbass.
First we need to see the king.
DID YOU JUST CALL ME A DUMBASS?! WHO THE HELL IS THIS GUY?!
FORGET IT!
My name's Jack.
A monster blocks your path.
OH, GREAT. NOW WHAT?
WHAT'RE WE GONNA DO?!
Ignore it.
THAT'S ALL?!

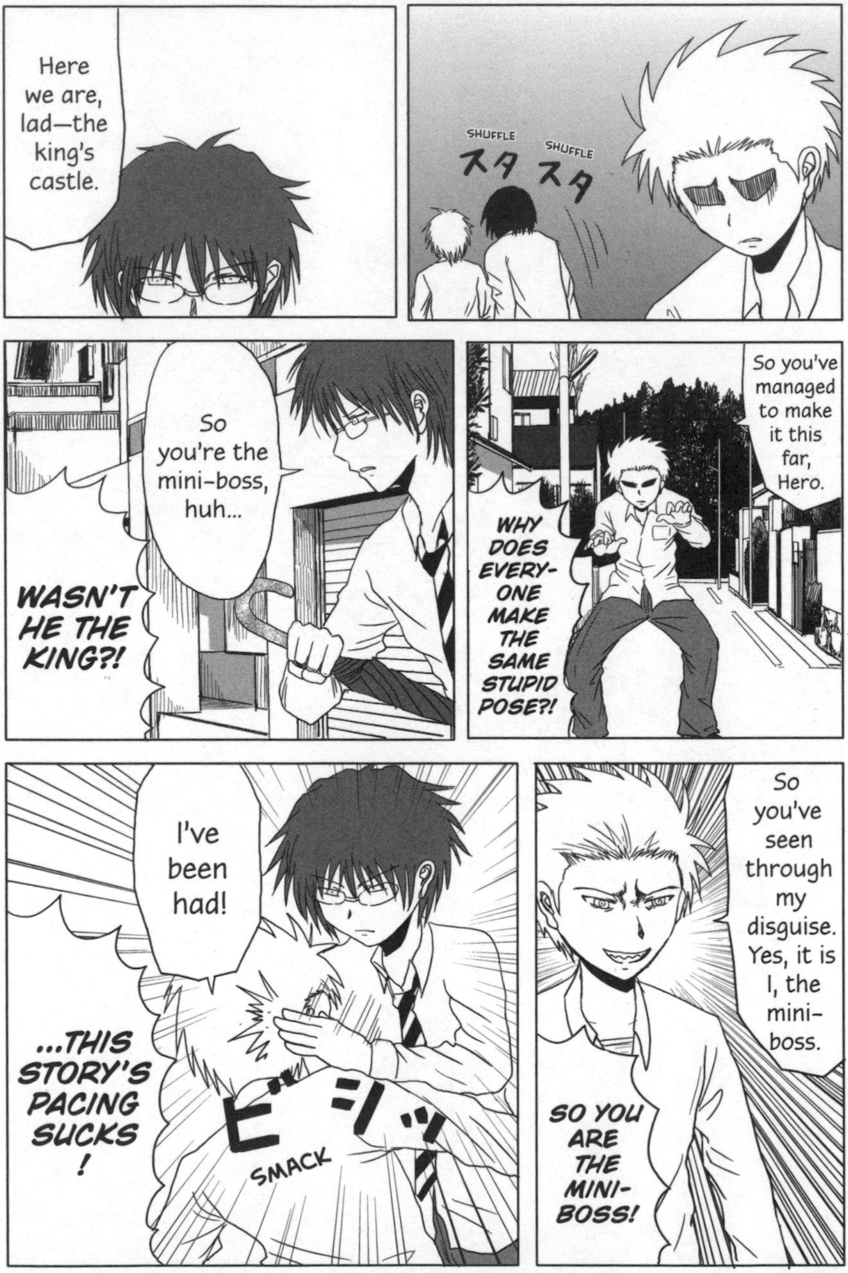

SHUFFLE
スタ
SHUFFLE
スタ
Here we are, lad—the king's castle.
So you've managed to make it this far, Hero.
WHY DOES EVERYONE MAKE THE SAME STUPID POSE?!
So you're the mini-boss, huh...
WASN'T HE THE KING?!
So you've seen through my disguise. Yes, it is I, the mini-boss.
SO YOU ARE THE MINI-BOSS!
I've been had!
ビシッ
SMACK
...THIS STORY'S PACING SUCKS!

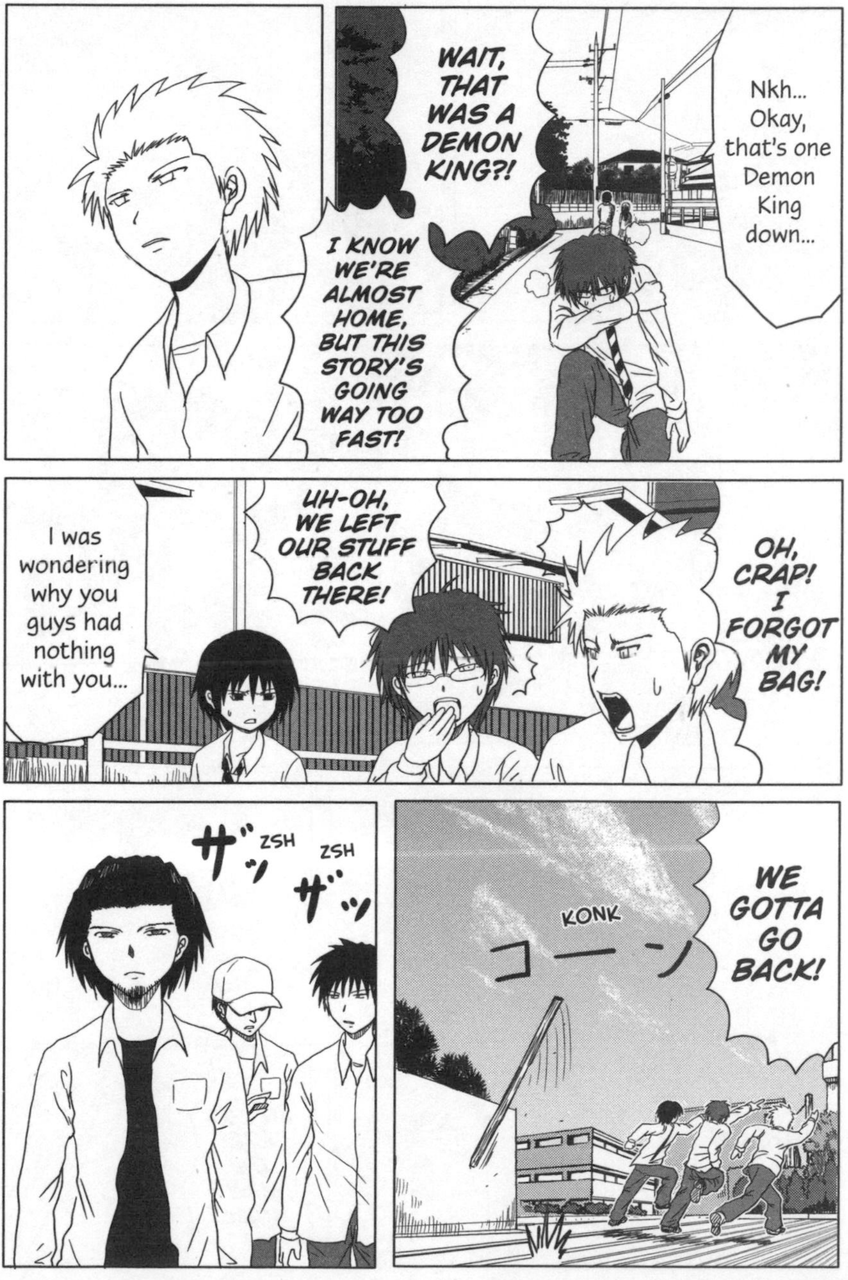
Nkh... Okay, that's one Demon King down...
WAIT, THAT WAS A DEMON KING?!
I KNOW WE'RE ALMOST HOME, BUT THIS STORY'S GOING WAY TOO FAST!
OH, CRAP! I FORGOT MY BAG!
UH-OH, WE LEFT OUR STUFF BACK THERE!
I was wondering why you guys had nothing with you...
WE GOTTA GO BACK!
コーーン
KONK
ザッ
ZSH
ザッ
ZSH

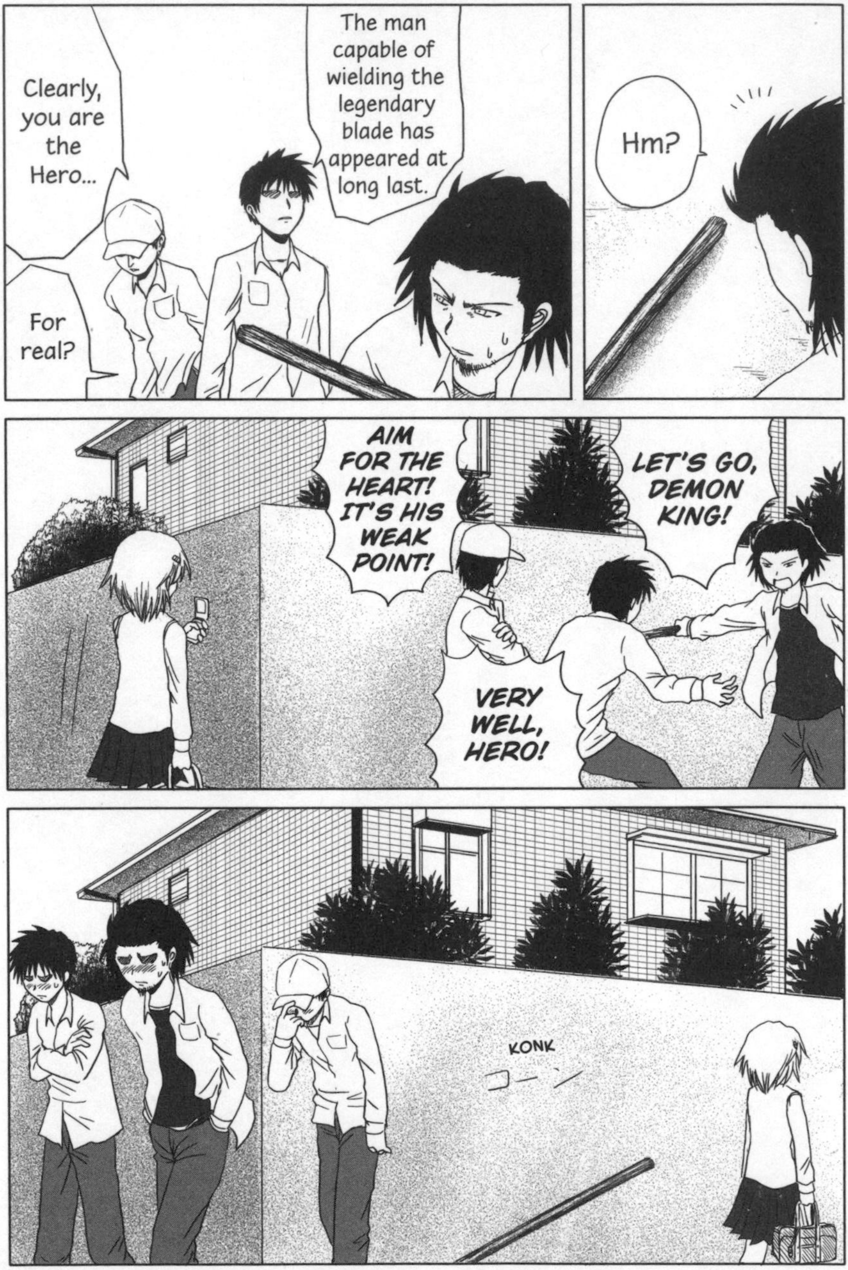
Hm?
The man capable of wielding the legendary blade has appeared at long last.
Clearly, you are the Hero...
For real?
LET'S GO, DEMON KING!
AIM FOR THE HEART! IT'S HIS WEAK POINT!
VERY WELL, HERO!
KONK

As small as she looks, she's 5'7"

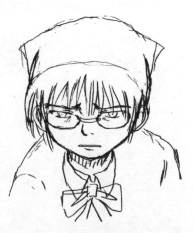

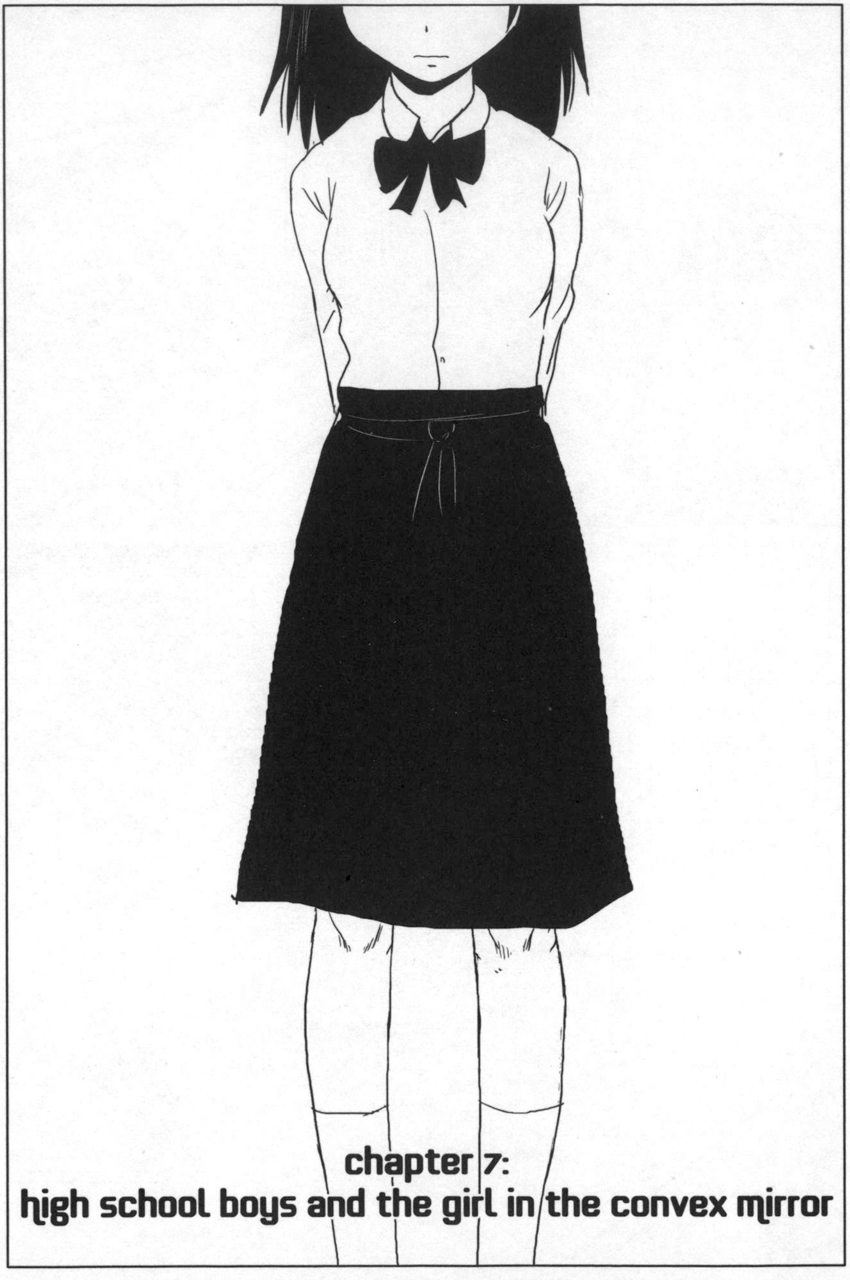

chapter 7:
high school boys and the girl in the convex mirror

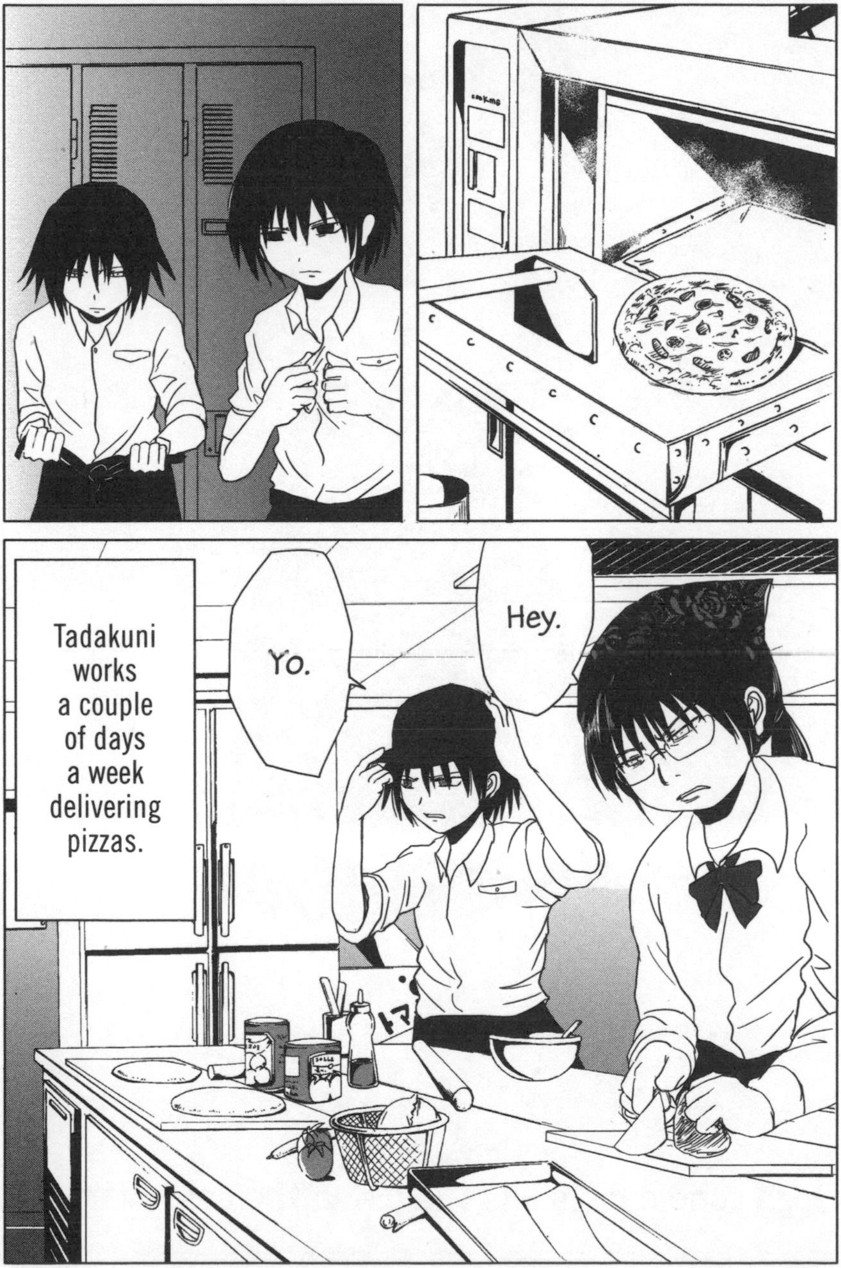
Hey.
Yo.
Tadakuni works a couple of days a week delivering pizzas.

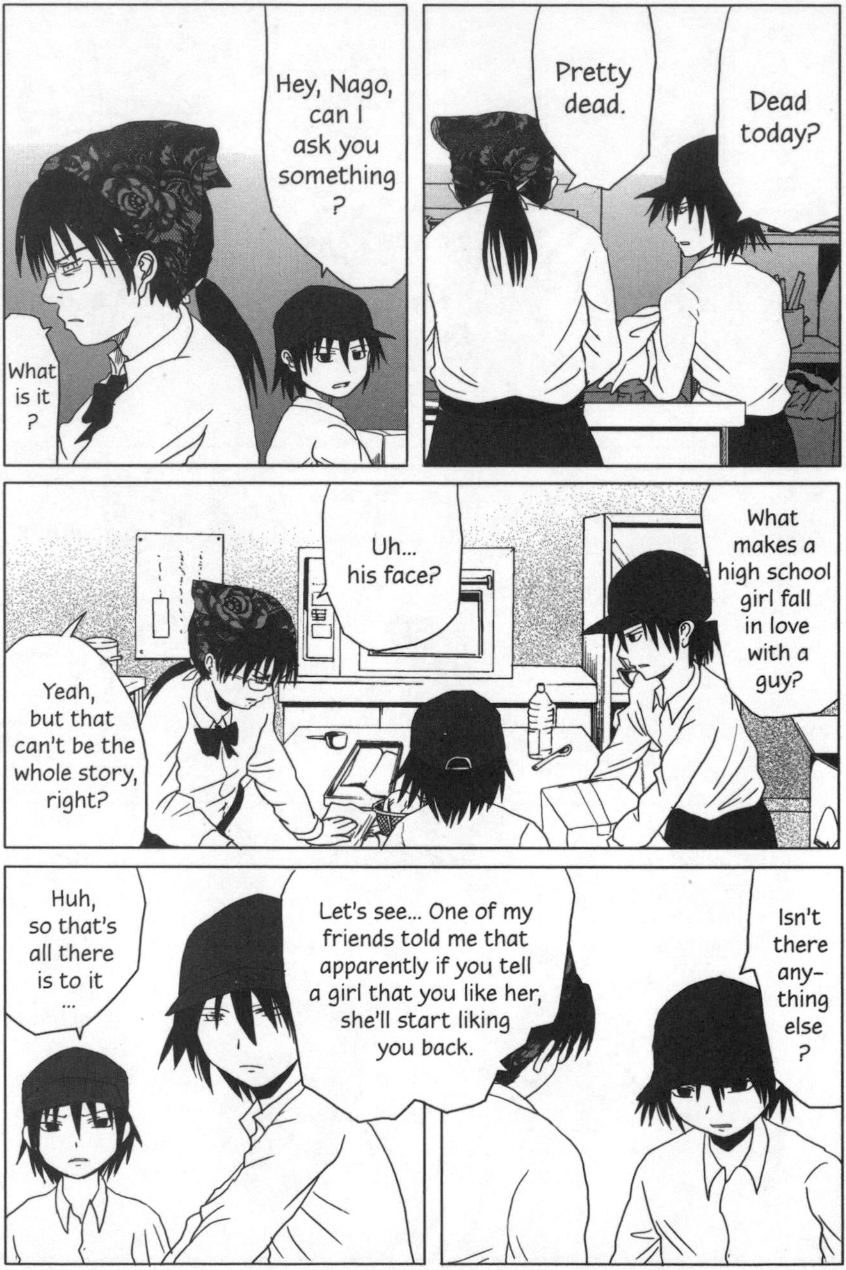
Dead today?
Pretty dead.
Hey, Nago, can I ask you something?
What is it?
What makes a high school girl fall in love with a guy?
Uh... his face?
Yeah, but that can't be the whole story, right?
Isn't there any-thing else?
Let's see... One of my friends told me that apparently if you tell a girl that you like her, she'll start liking you back.
Huh, so that's all there is to it...

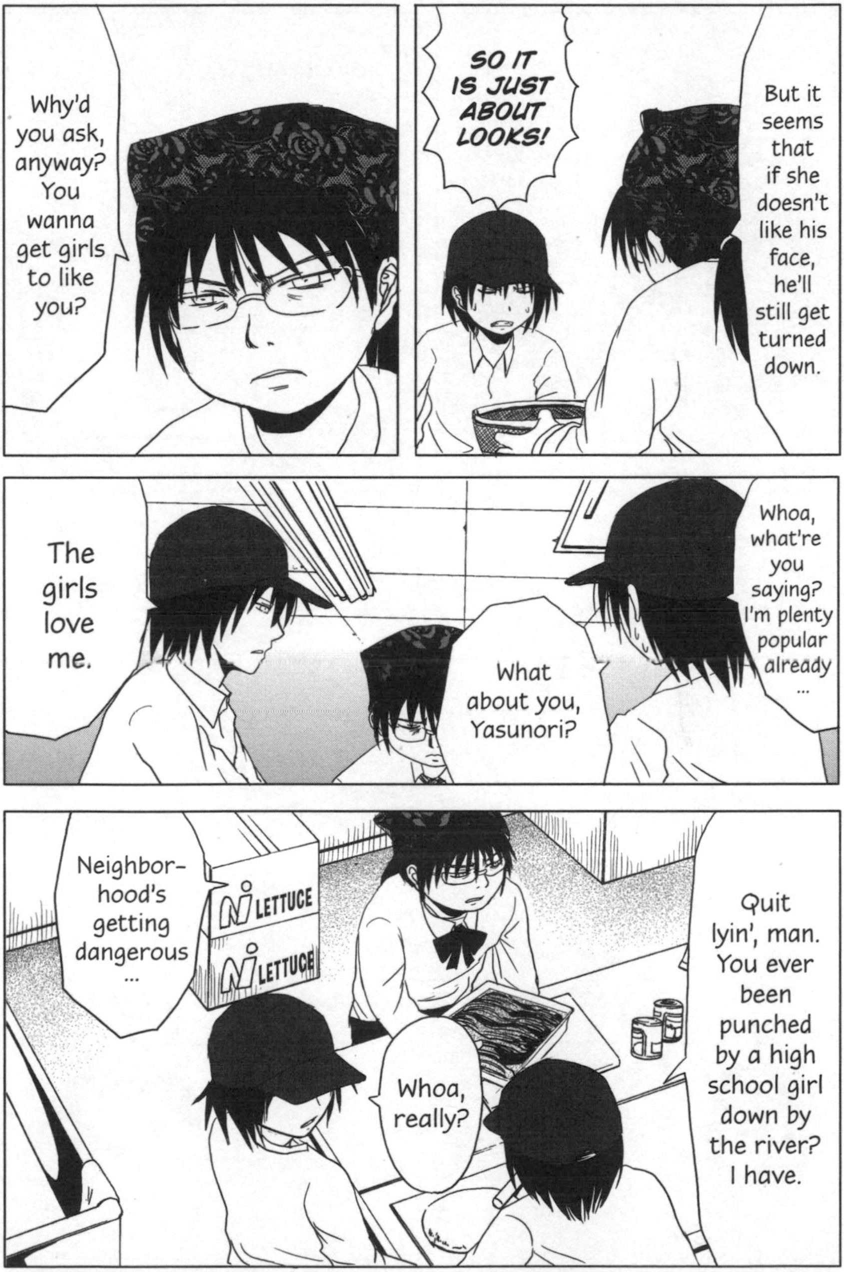
But it seems that if she doesn't like his face, he'll still get turned down.
SO IT IS JUST ABOUT LOOKS!
Why'd you ask, anyway? You wanna get girls to like you?
Whoa, what're you saying? I'm plenty popular already ...
What about you, Yasunori?
The girls love me.
Quit lyin', man. You ever been punched by a high school girl down by the river? I have.
Whoa, really?
Neighbor-hood's getting dangerous ...
LETTUCE
LETTUCE

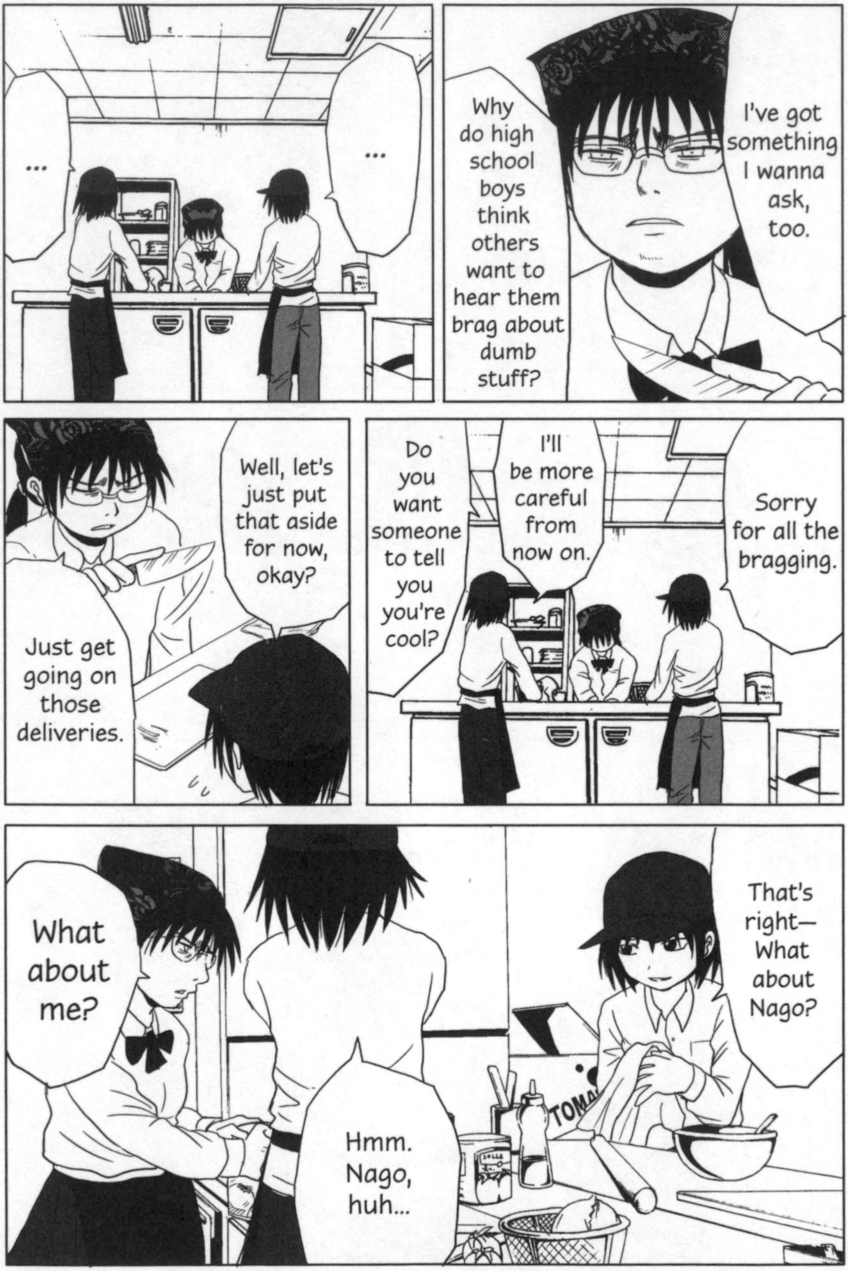
I've got something I wanna ask, too.
Why do high school boys think others want to hear them brag about dumb stuff?
...
...
Sorry for all the bragging.
I'll be more careful from now on.
Do you want someone to tell you you're cool?
Well, let's just put that aside for now, okay?
Just get going on those deliveries.
That's right— What about Nago?
Hmm. Nago, huh...
What about me?

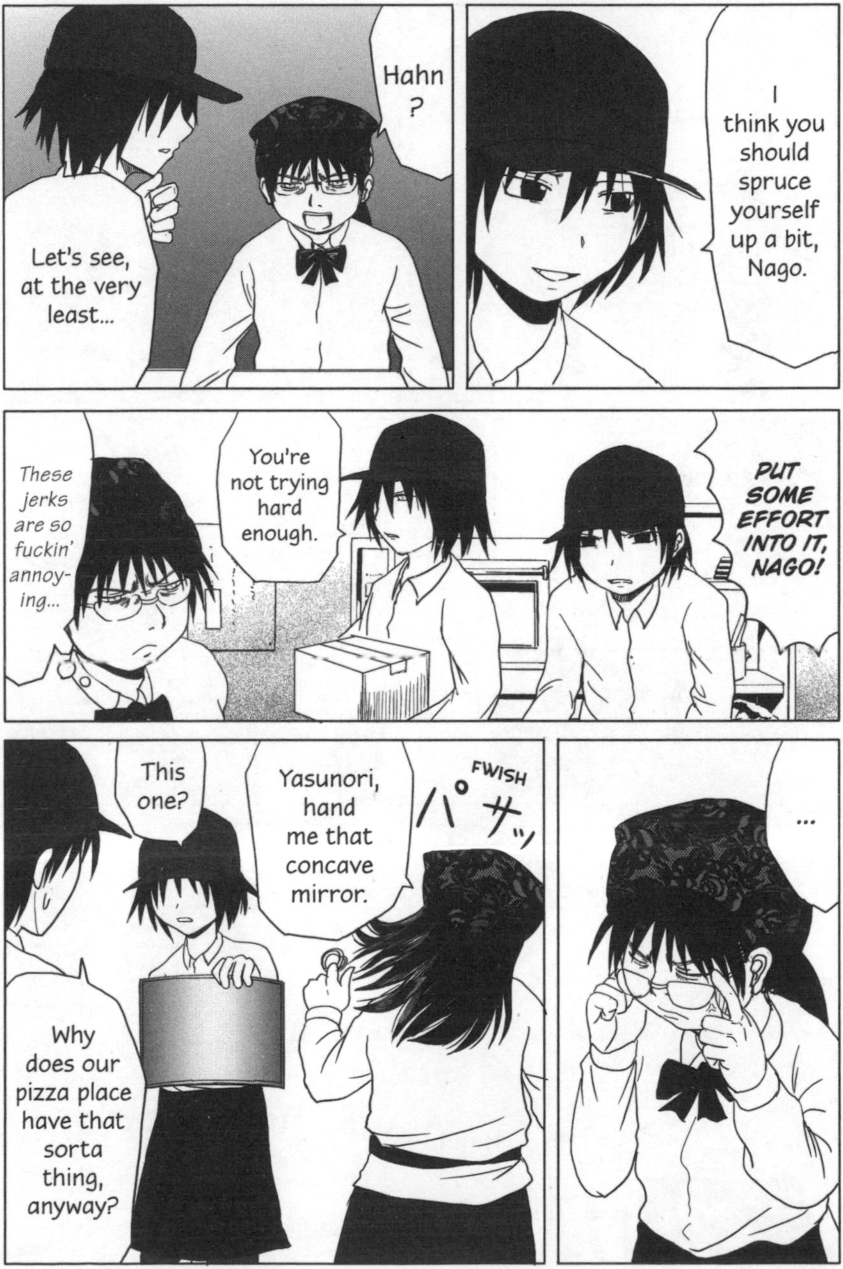
I think you should spruce yourself up a bit, Nago.
Hahn?
Let's see, at the very least...
PUT SOME EFFORT INTO IT, NAGO!
You're not trying hard enough.
These jerks are so fuckin' annoying...
...
FWISH
パサッ
Yasunori, hand me that concave mirror.
This one?
Why does our pizza place have that sorta thing, anyway?

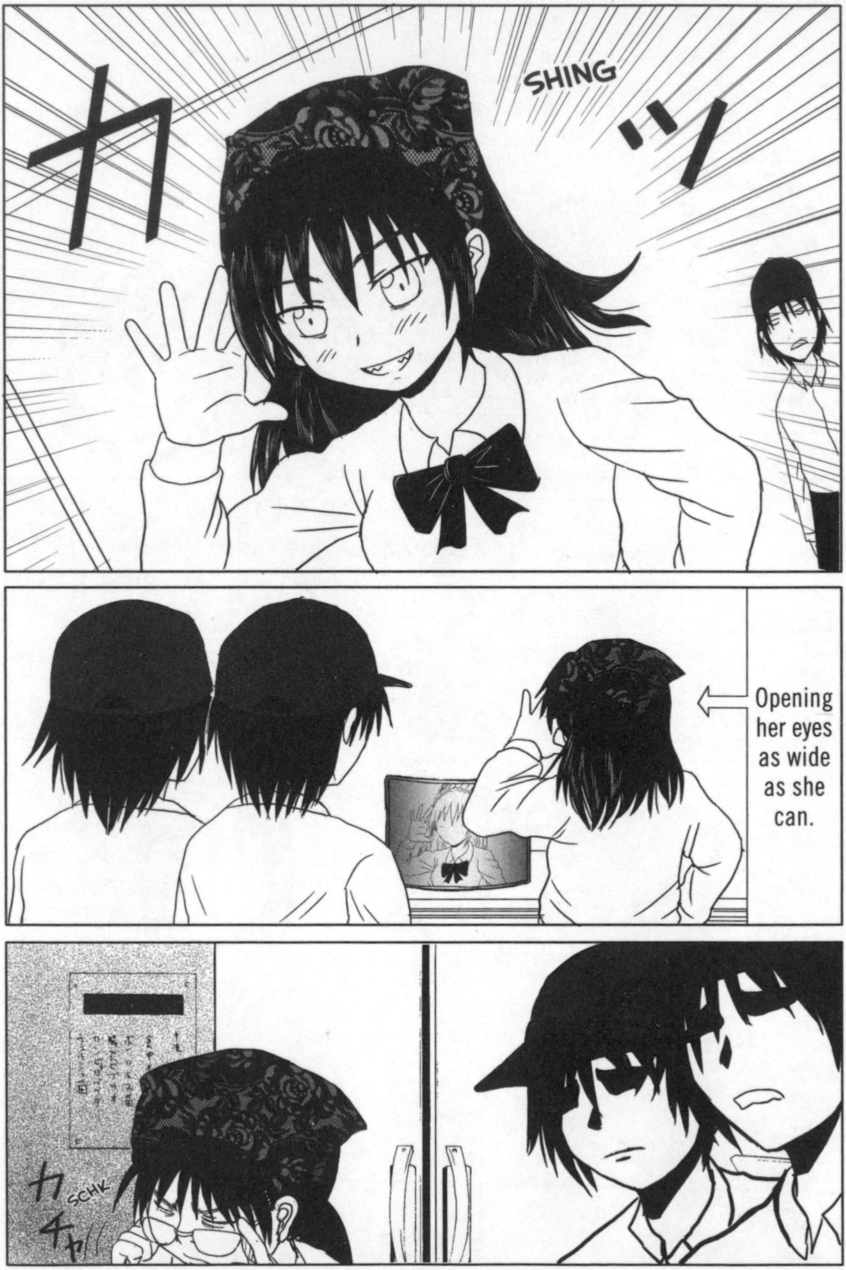
カッ
SHING
Opening her eyes as wide as she can.
カチャ
SCHK

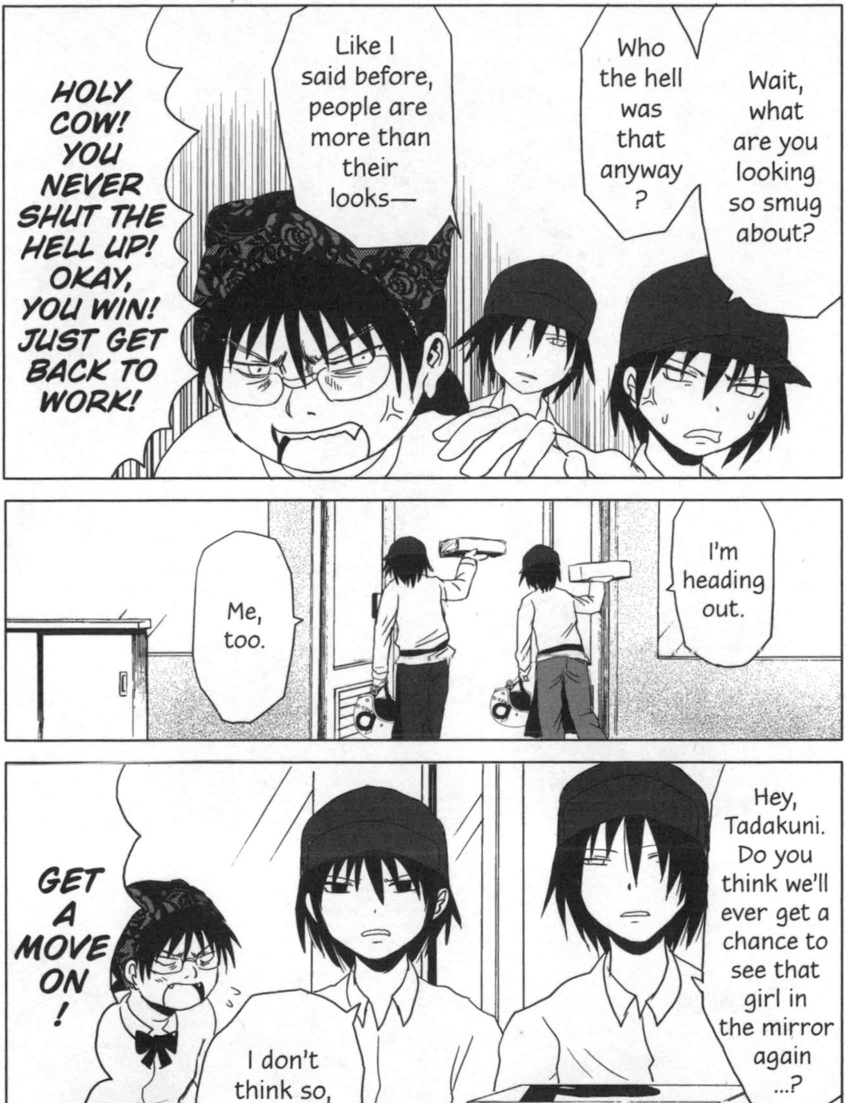
Wait, what are you looking so smug about?
Who the hell was that anyway?
Like I said before, people are more than their looks—
HOLY COW! YOU NEVER SHUT THE HELL UP! OKAY, YOU WIN! JUST GET BACK TO WORK!
I'm heading out.
Me, too.
Hey, Tadakuni. Do you think we'll ever get a chance to see that girl in the mirror again ...?
I don't think so, man... but I'll never give up.
GET A MOVE ON!
PIZZA-LE
ZA-LE

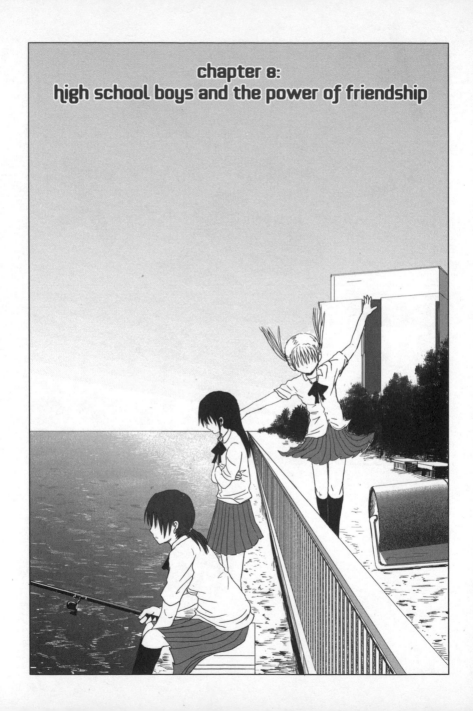

chapter 8:
high school boys and the power of friendship

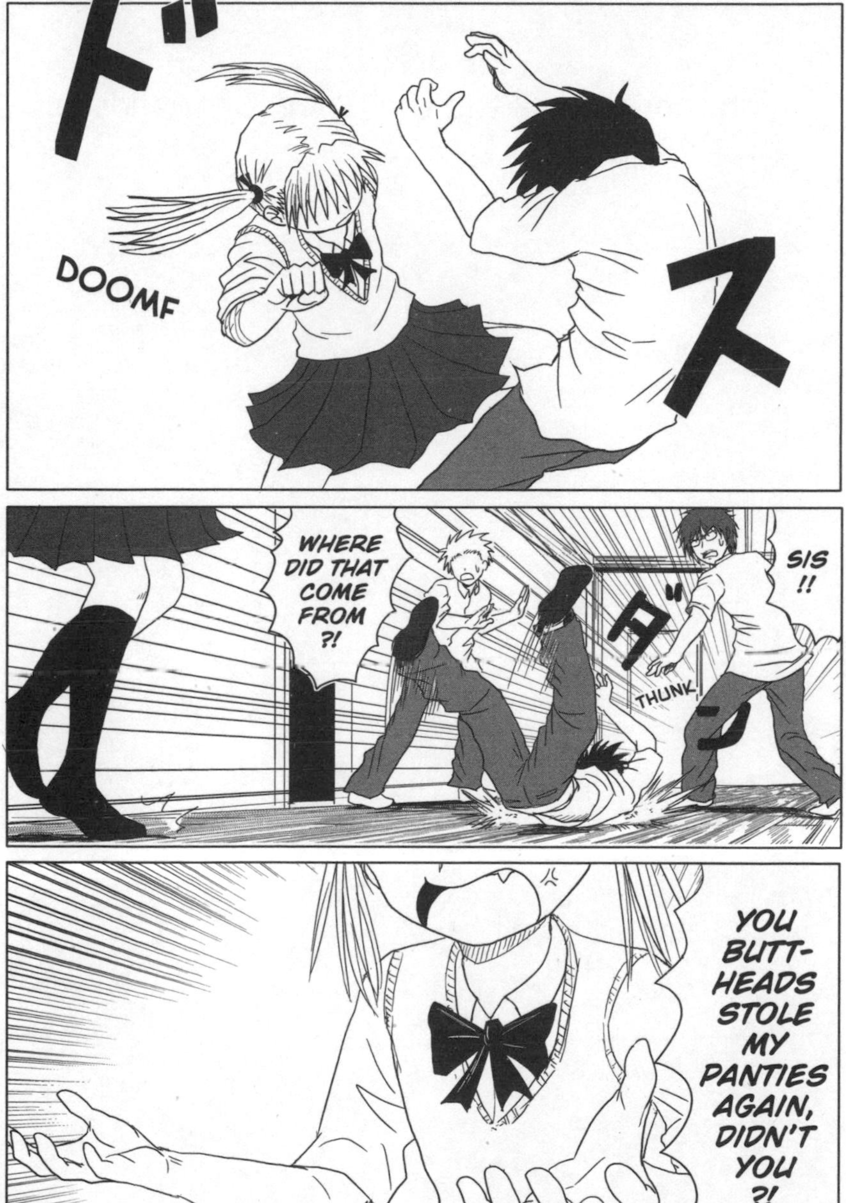
ドス
DOOMF
SIS!!
ダン
THUNK
WHERE DID THAT COME FROM?!
YOU BUTT-HEADS STOLE MY PANTIES AGAIN, DIDN'T YOU?!

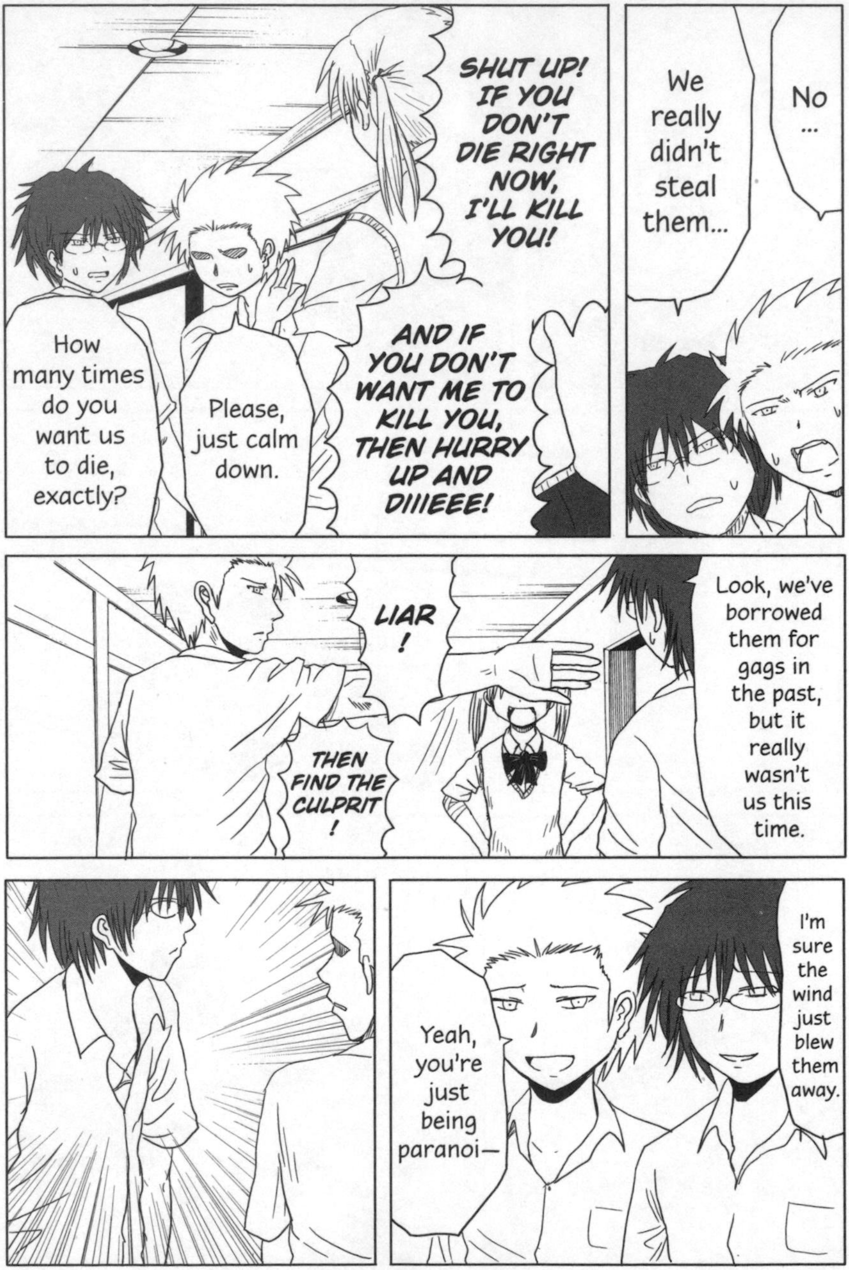
No ...
We really didn't steal them...
SHUT UP! IF YOU DON'T DIE RIGHT NOW, I'LL KILL YOU!
AND IF YOU DON'T WANT ME TO KILL YOU, THEN HURRY UP AND DIIIEEE!
Please, just calm down.
How many times do you want us to die, exactly?
Look, we've borrowed them for gags in the past, but it really wasn't us this time.
LIAR!
THEN FIND THE CULPRIT!
I'm sure the wind just blew them away.
Yeah, you're just being paranoi—

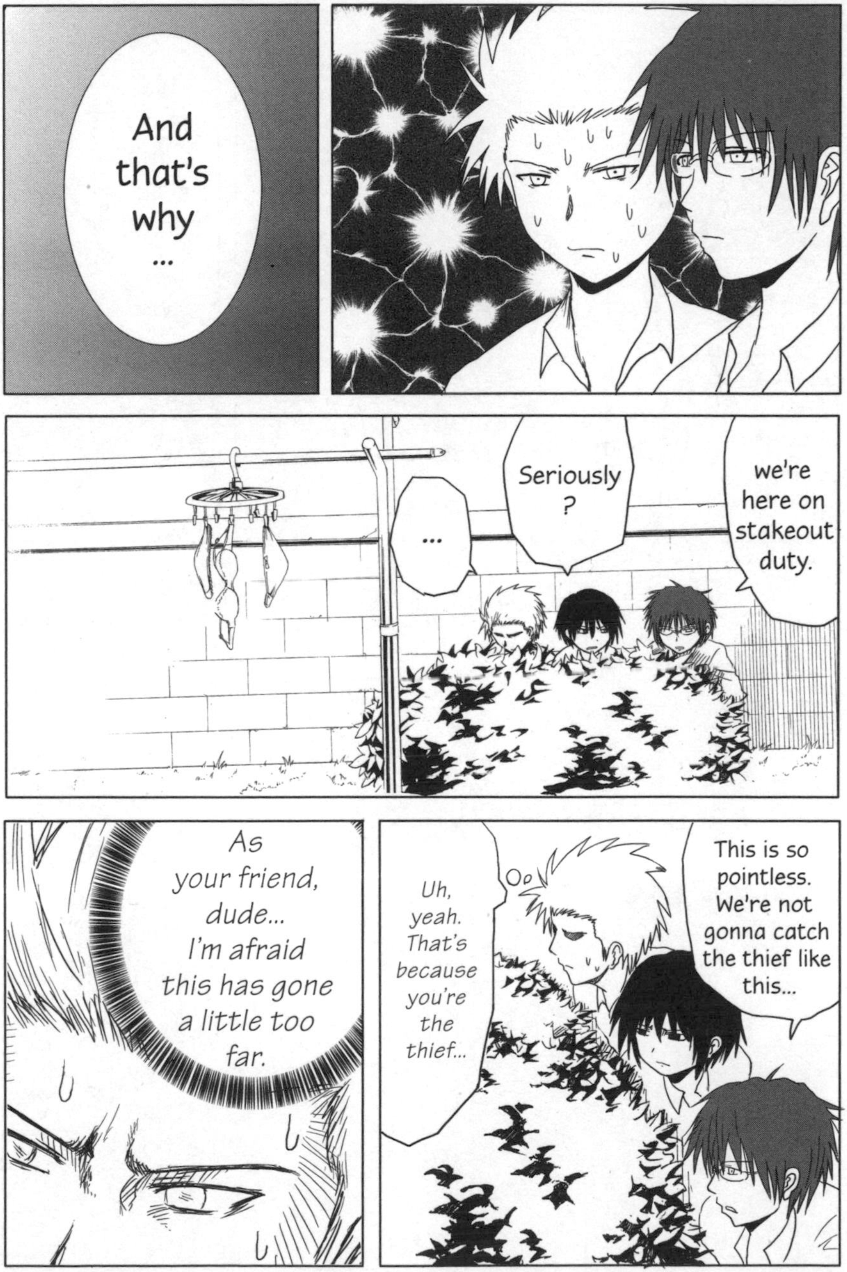
And that's why ...
we're here on stakeout duty.
Seriously ?
...
This is so pointless. We're not gonna catch the thief like this...
Uh, yeah. That's because you're the thief...
As your friend, dude... I'm afraid this has gone a little too far.

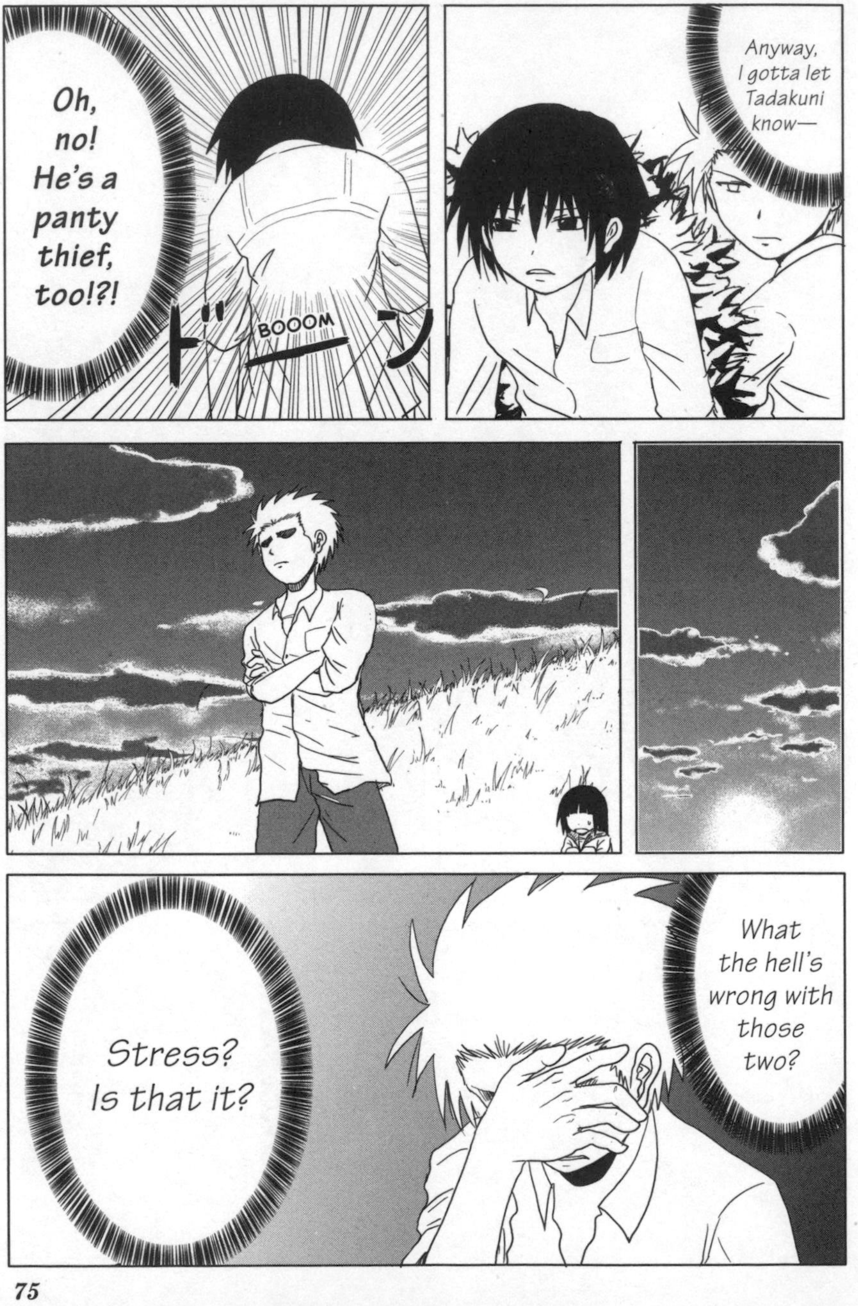
Anyway, I gotta let Tadakuni know—
Oh, no! He's a panty thief, too!?!
ドーン
BOOOM
What the hell's wrong with those two?
Stress? Is that it?

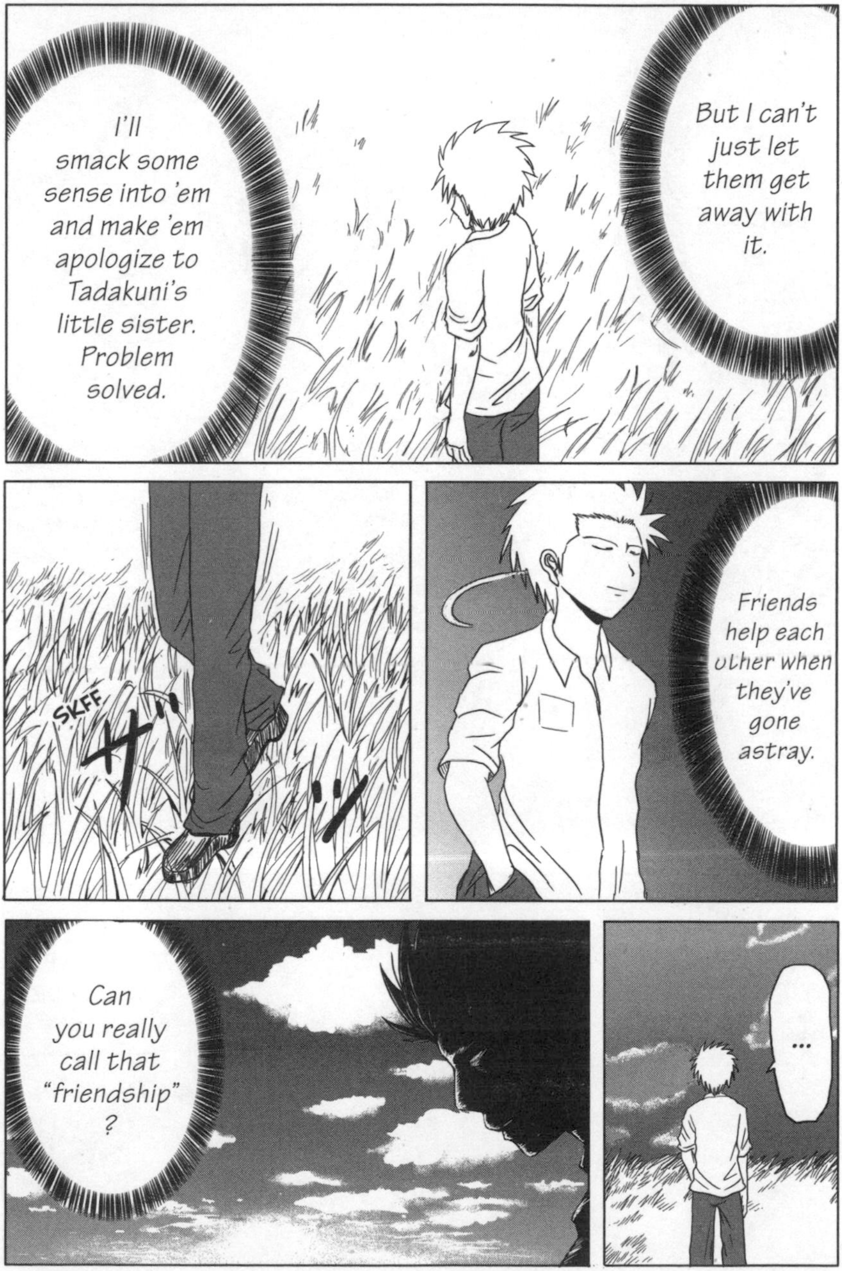
But I can't just let them get away with it.
I'll smack some sense into 'em and make 'em apologize to Tadakuni's little sister. Problem solved.
Friends help each other when they've gone astray.
SKFF
...
Can you really call that "friendship"?

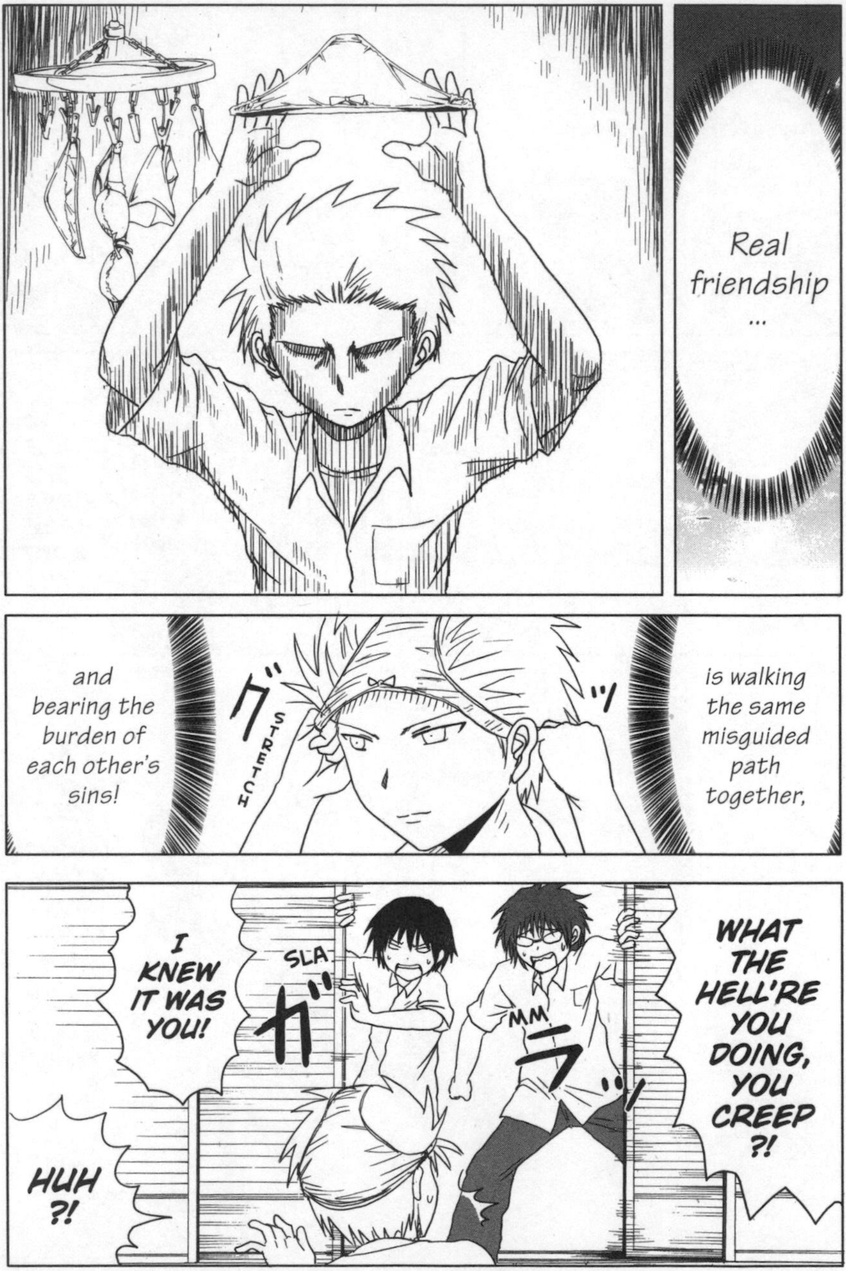
Real friendship ...
is walking the same misguided path together,
ツ
グ
STRETCH
and bearing the burden of each other's sins!
WHAT THE HELL'RE YOU DOING, YOU CREEP?!
MM
ラッ
SLA
ガ
I KNEW IT WAS YOU!
HUH?!

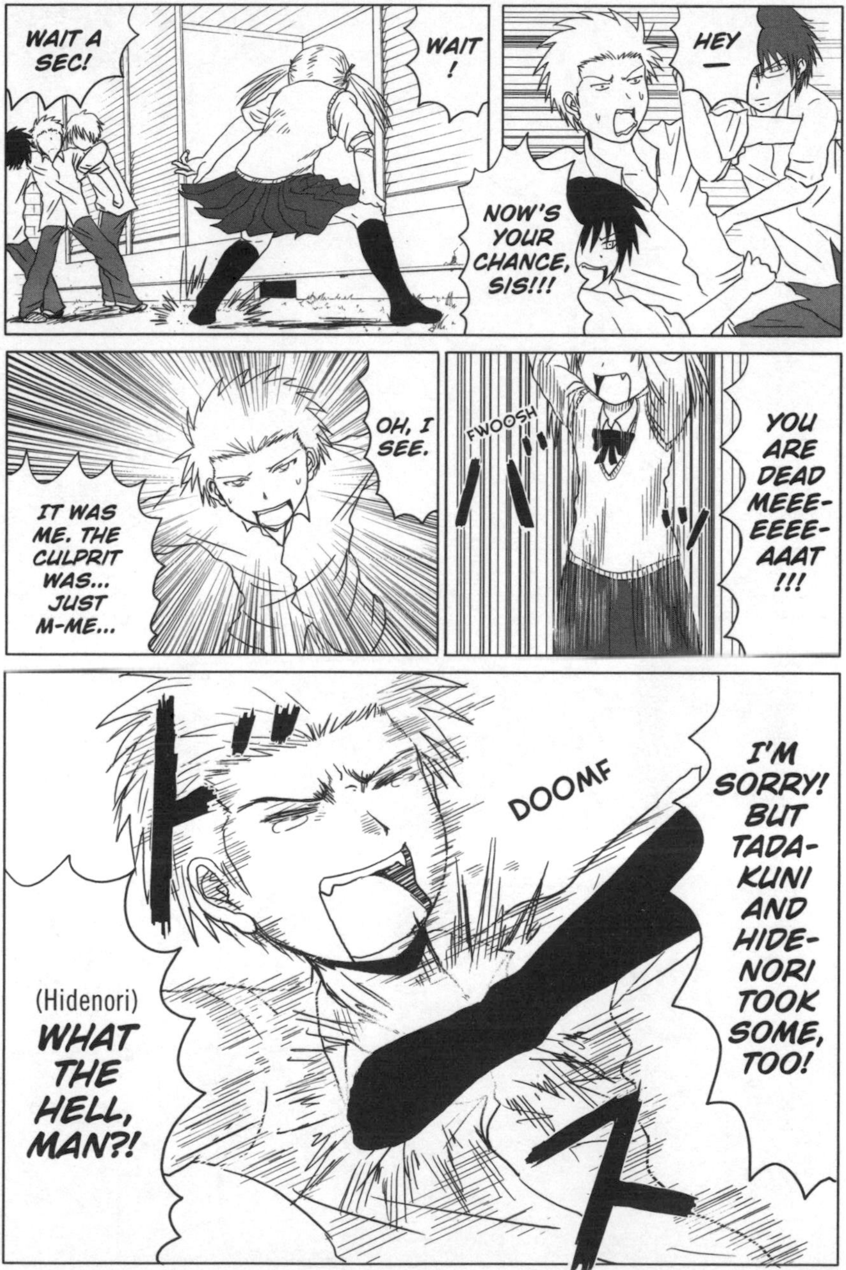

HEY —
NOW'S YOUR CHANCE, SIS!!!
WAIT !
WAIT A SEC!
YOU ARE DEAD MEEE-EEEE-AAAT !!!
FWOOSH
OH, I SEE.
IT WAS ME. THE CULPRIT WAS... JUST M-ME...
I'M SORRY! BUT TADA-KUNI AND HIDE-NORI TOOK SOME, TOO!
DOOMF
(Hidenori) WHAT THE HELL, MAN?!

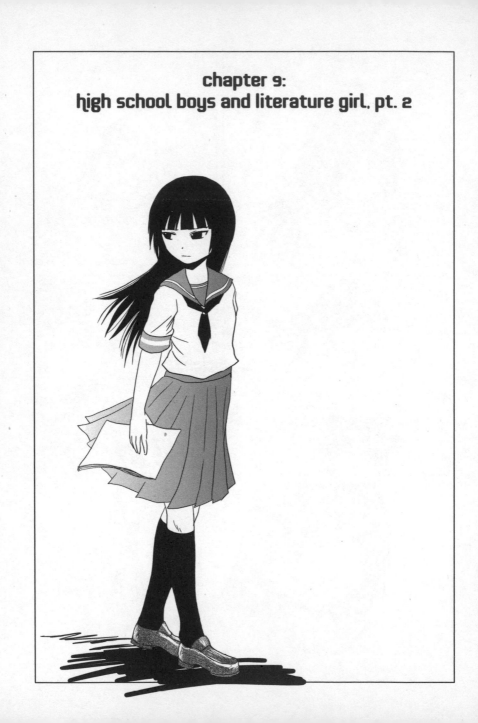

chapter 9:
high school boys and literature girl, pt. 2

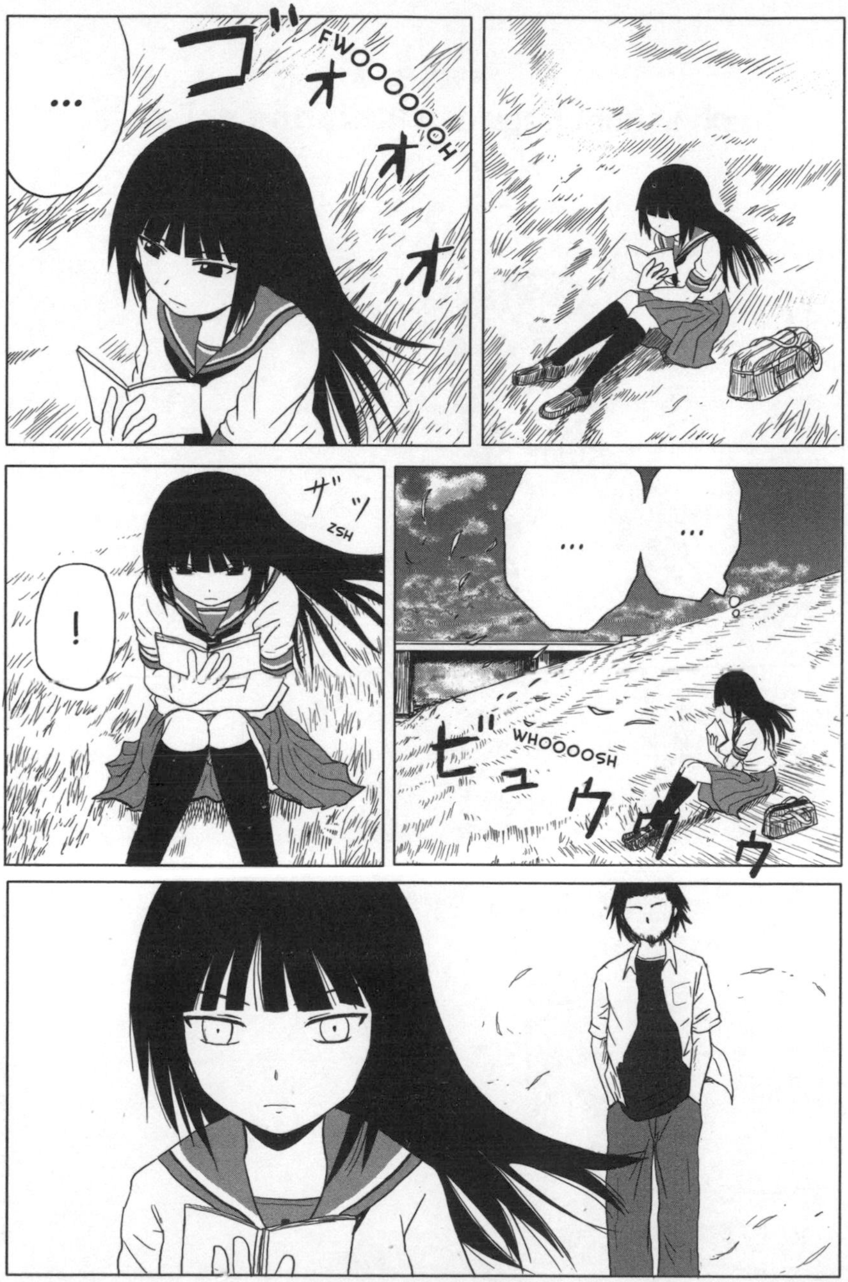
...
ゴオオオ
FWOOOOOOOH
...
...
ビュウウウウ
WHOOOOSH
ザッ
ZSH
!

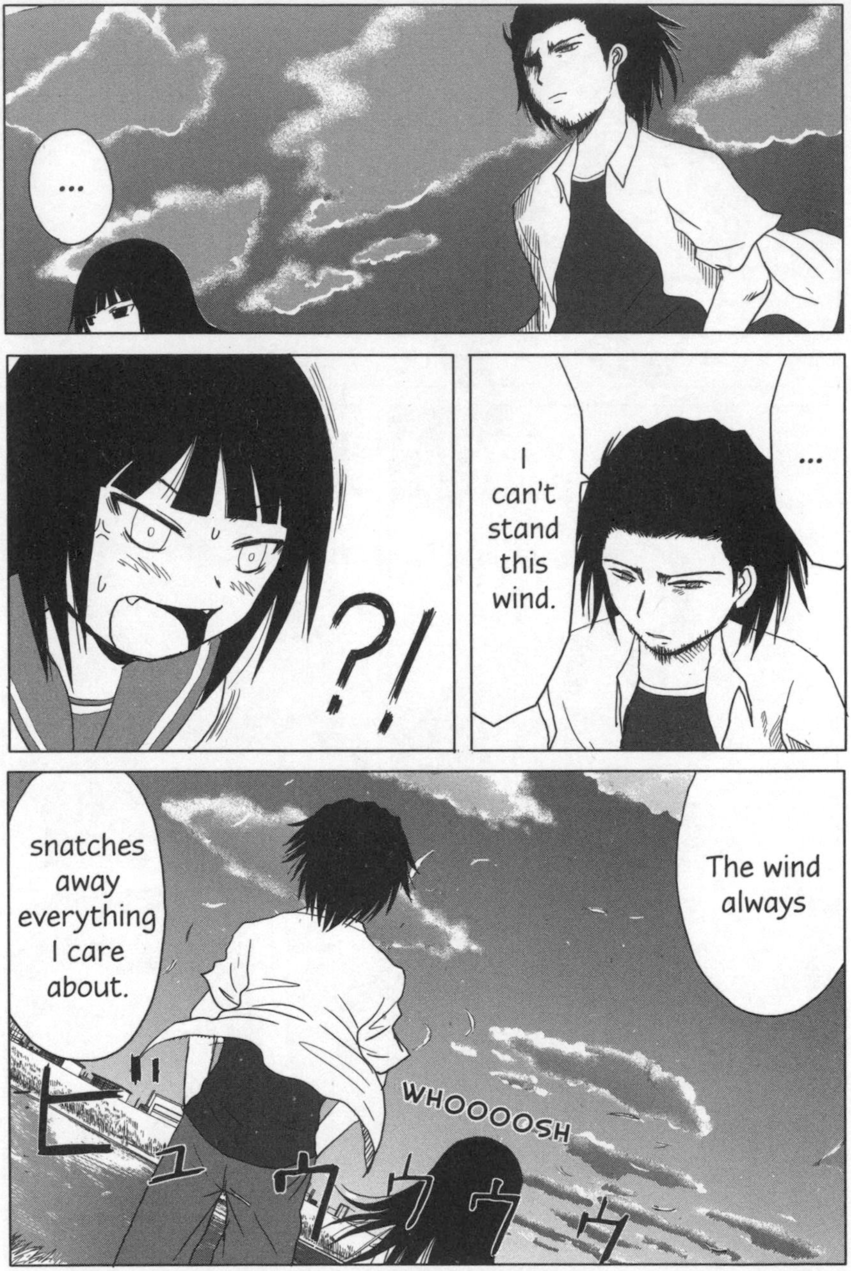
...
...
I can't stand this wind.
?!
The wind always
snatches away everything I care about.
WHOOOOSH
ビュウウウウ

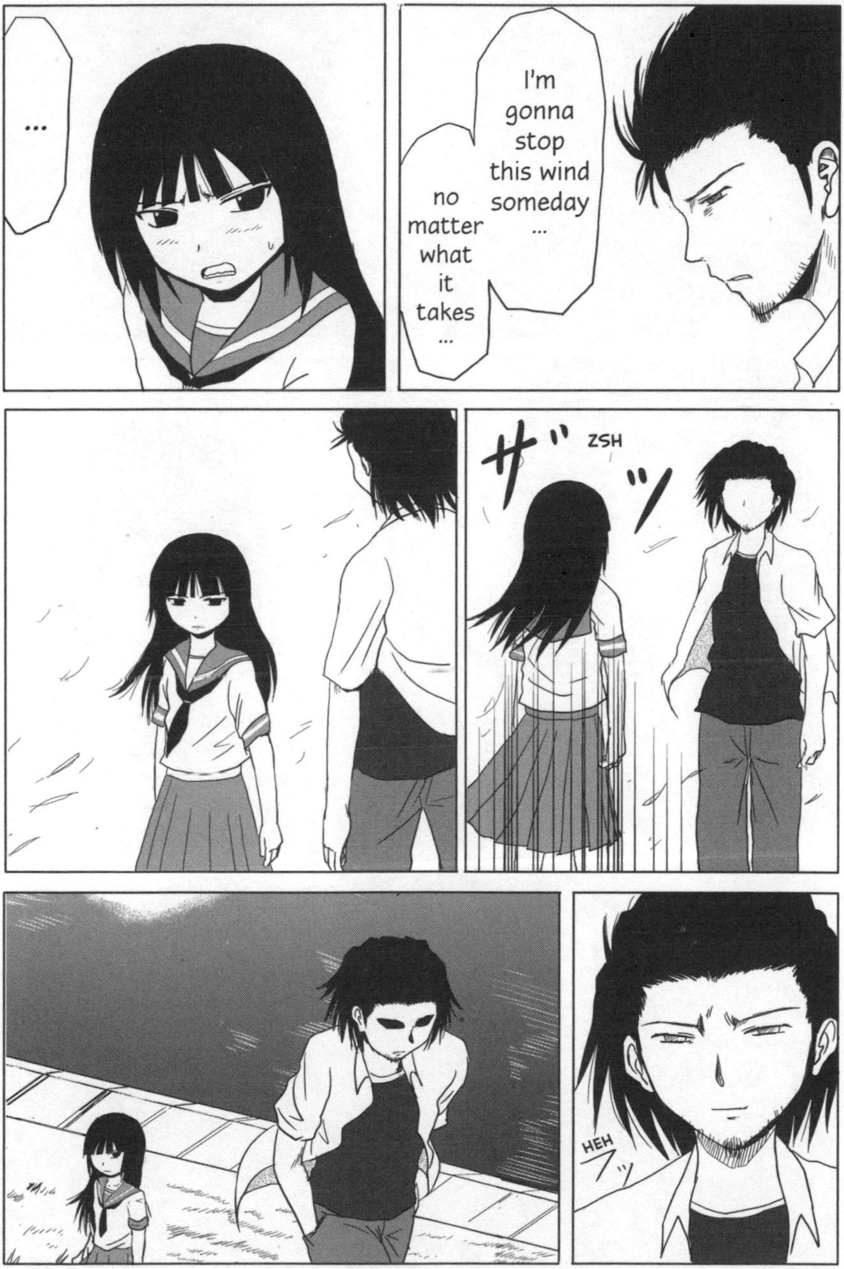
I'm gonna stop this wind someday ...
no matter what it takes ...
...
ZSH
HEH

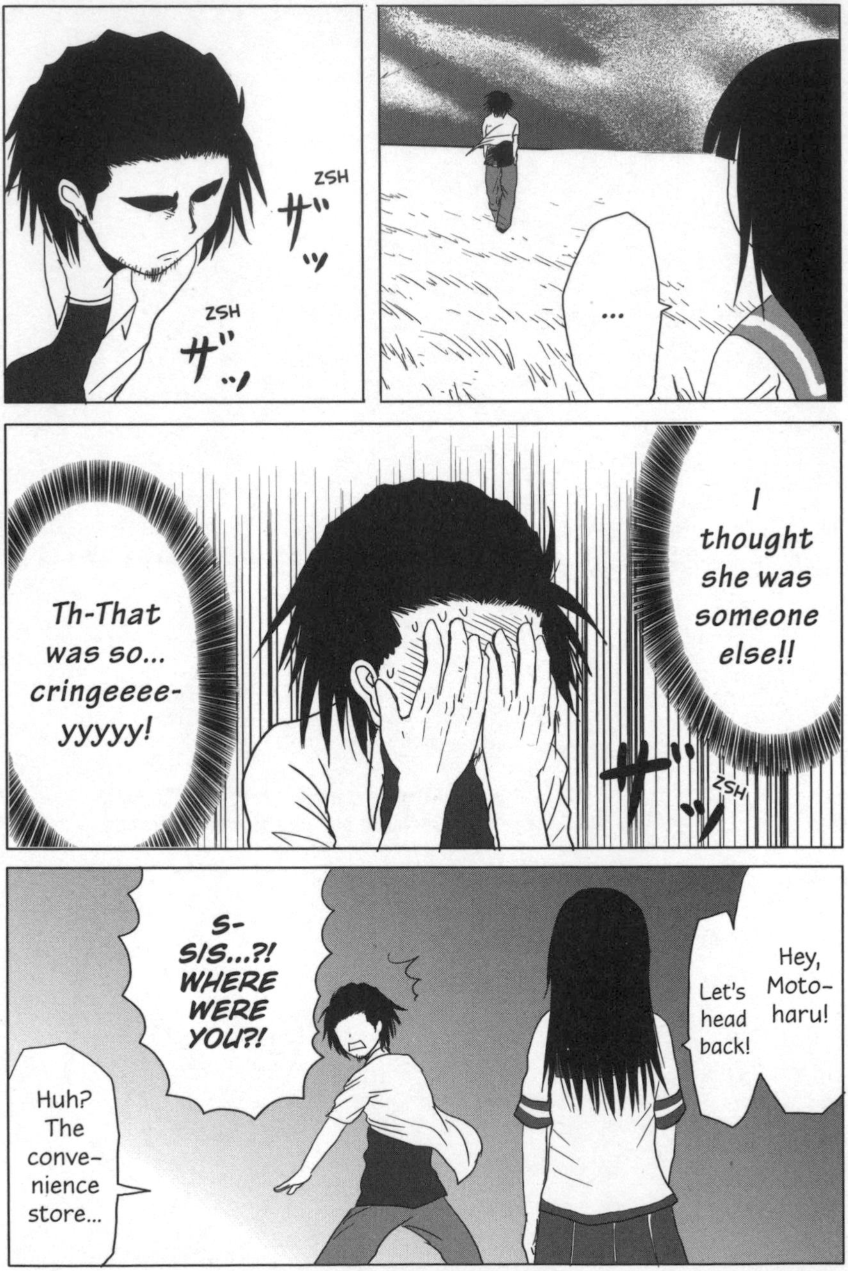
...
ZSH
ザッ
ZSH
ザッ
I thought she was someone else!!
Th-That was so... cringeeeee-yyyyy!
ザッ
ZSH
Hey, Moto-haru!
Let's head back!
S-SIS...?! WHERE WERE YOU?!
Huh? The conve-nience store...

- Attends Sanada West High School
- Sociable and has plenty of friends

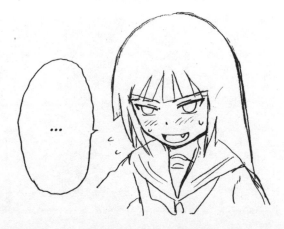

chapter 10:
high school boys and traditions

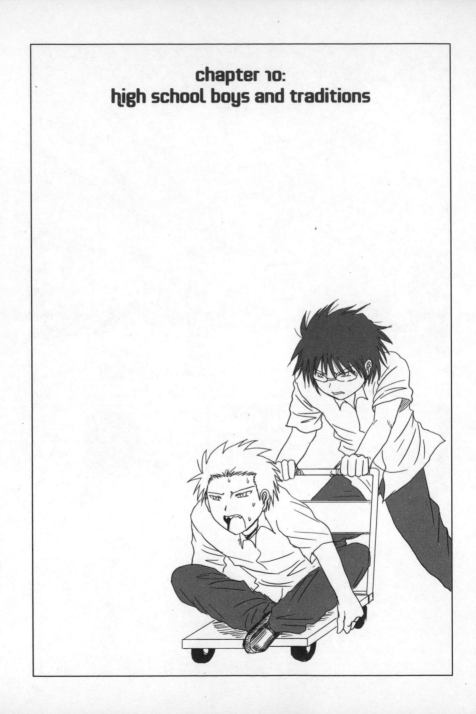

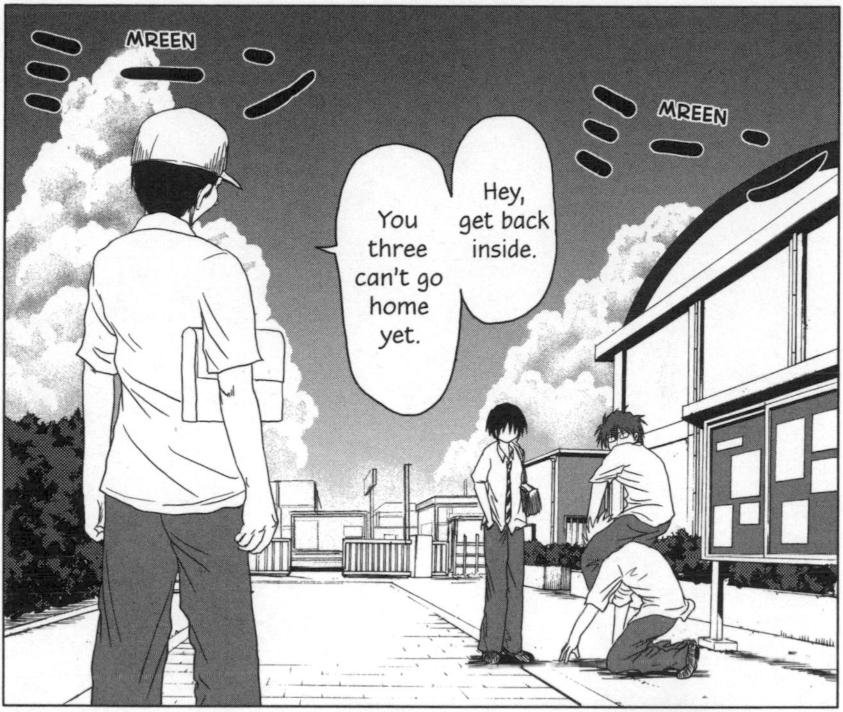
MREEN
MREEN
Hey, get back inside.
You three can't go home yet.

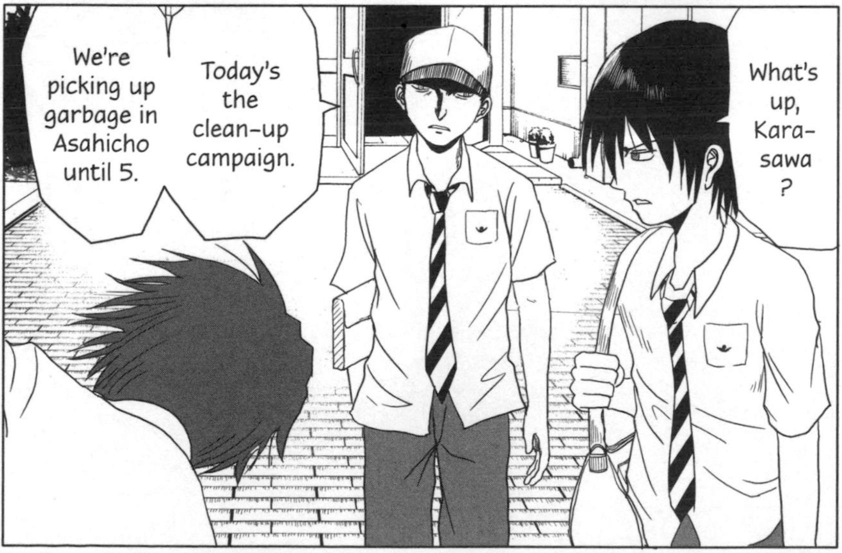
What's up, Kara-sawa?
Today's the clean-up campaign.
We're picking up garbage in Asahicho until 5.

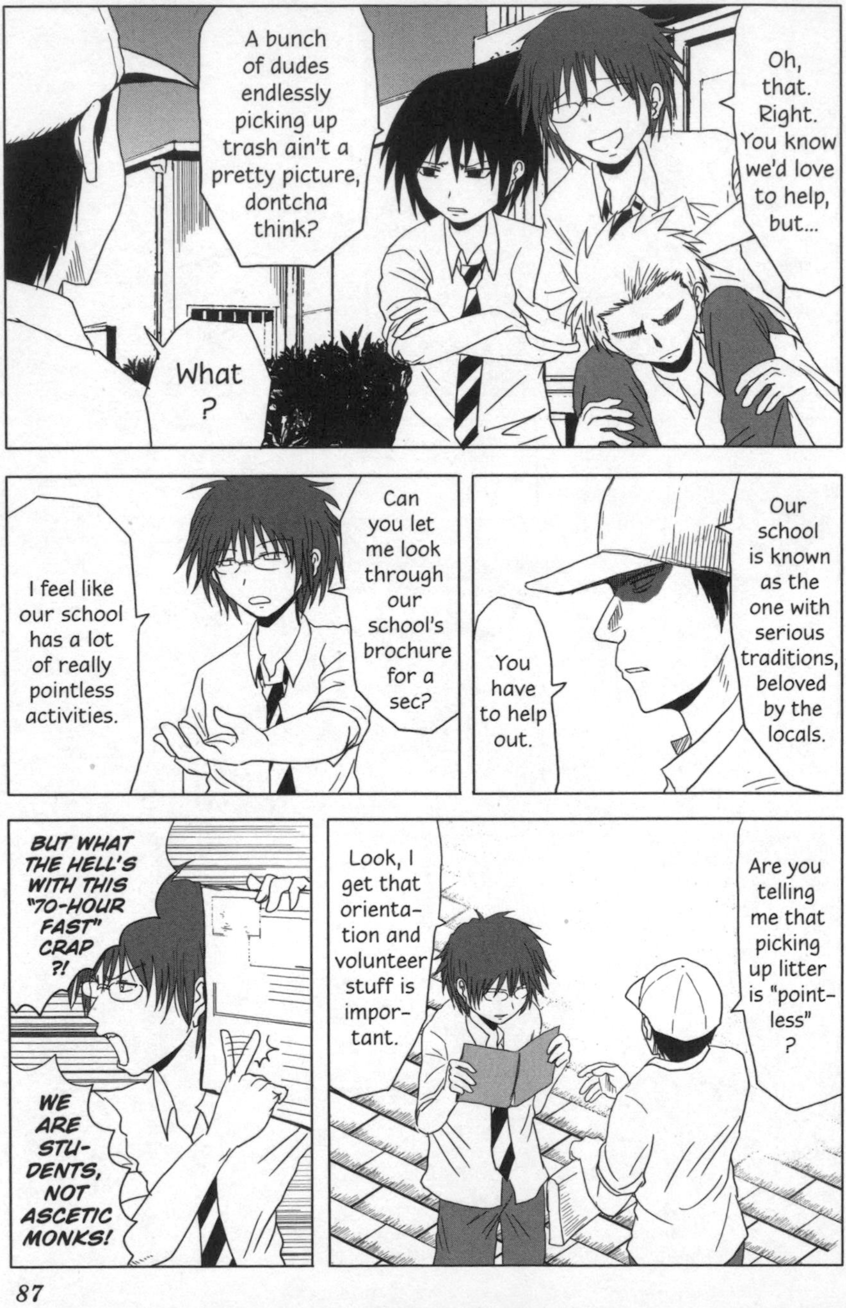
Oh, that. Right. You know we'd love to help, but...
A bunch of dudes endlessly picking up trash ain't a pretty picture, dontcha think?
What?
Our school is known as the one with serious traditions, beloved by the locals.
You have to help out.
Can you let me look through our school's brochure for a sec?
I feel like our school has a lot of really pointless activities.
Are you telling me that picking up litter is "pointless"?
Look, I get that orientation and volunteer stuff is important.
BUT WHAT THE HELL'S WITH THIS "70-HOUR FAST" CRAP?!
WE ARE STUDENTS, NOT ASCETIC MONKS!

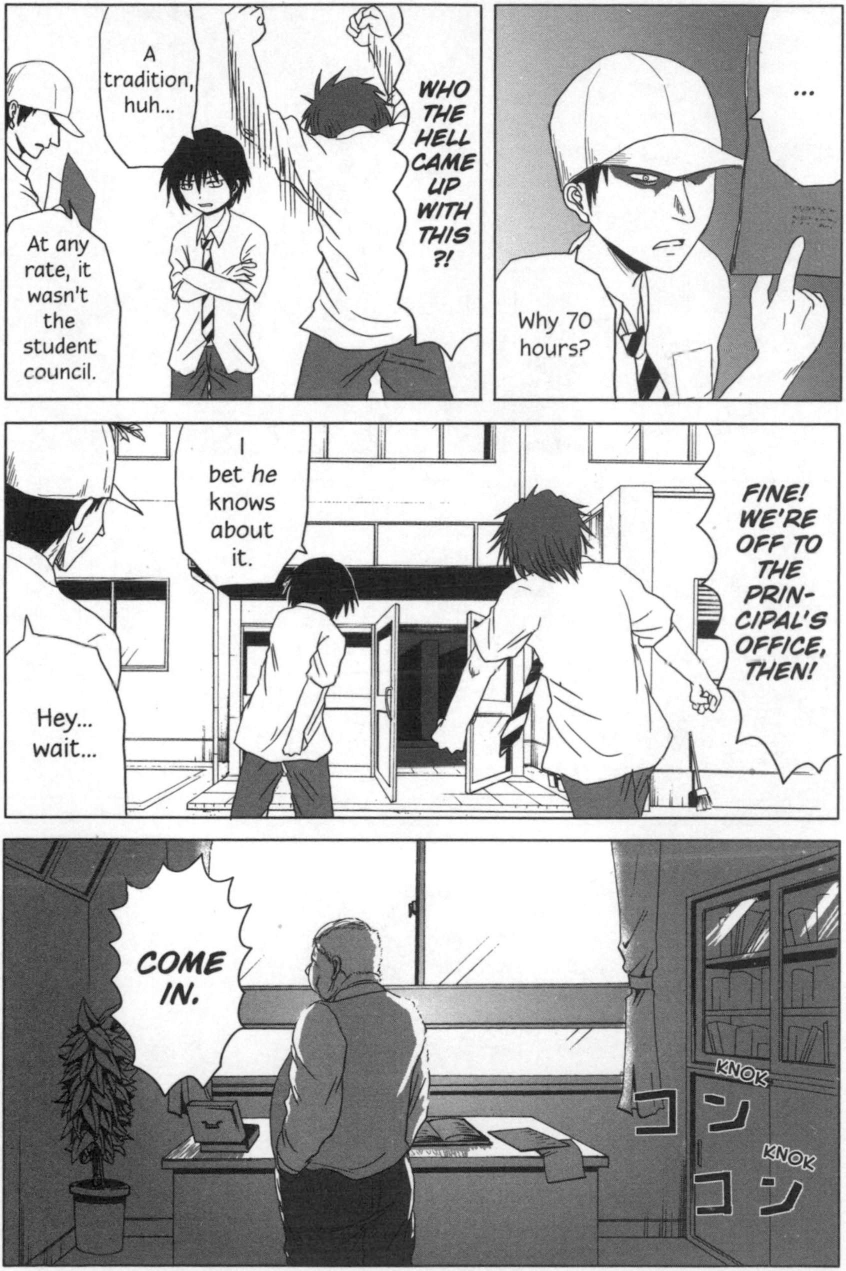
...
Why 70 hours?
WHO THE HELL CAME UP WITH THIS?!
A tradition, huh...
At any rate, it wasn't the student council.
FINE! WE'RE OFF TO THE PRIN-CIPAL'S OFFICE, THEN!
I bet *he* knows about it.
Hey... wait...
KNOK
コン
KNOK
コン
COME IN.

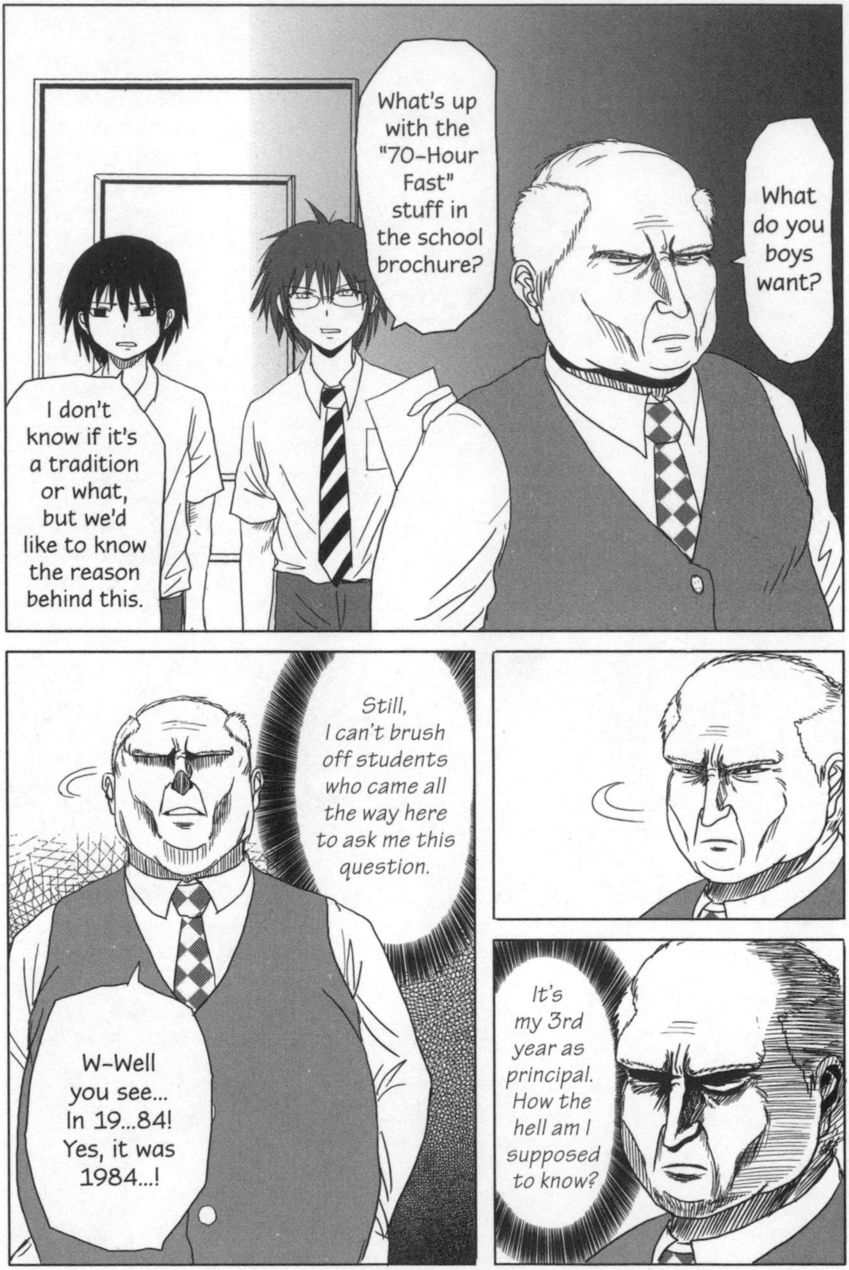
What do you boys want?
What's up with the "70-Hour Fast" stuff in the school brochure?
I don't know if it's a tradition or what, but we'd like to know the reason behind this.
It's my 3rd year as principal. How the hell am I supposed to know?
Still, I can't brush off students who came all the way here to ask me this question.
W-Well you see... In 19...84! Yes, it was 1984...!

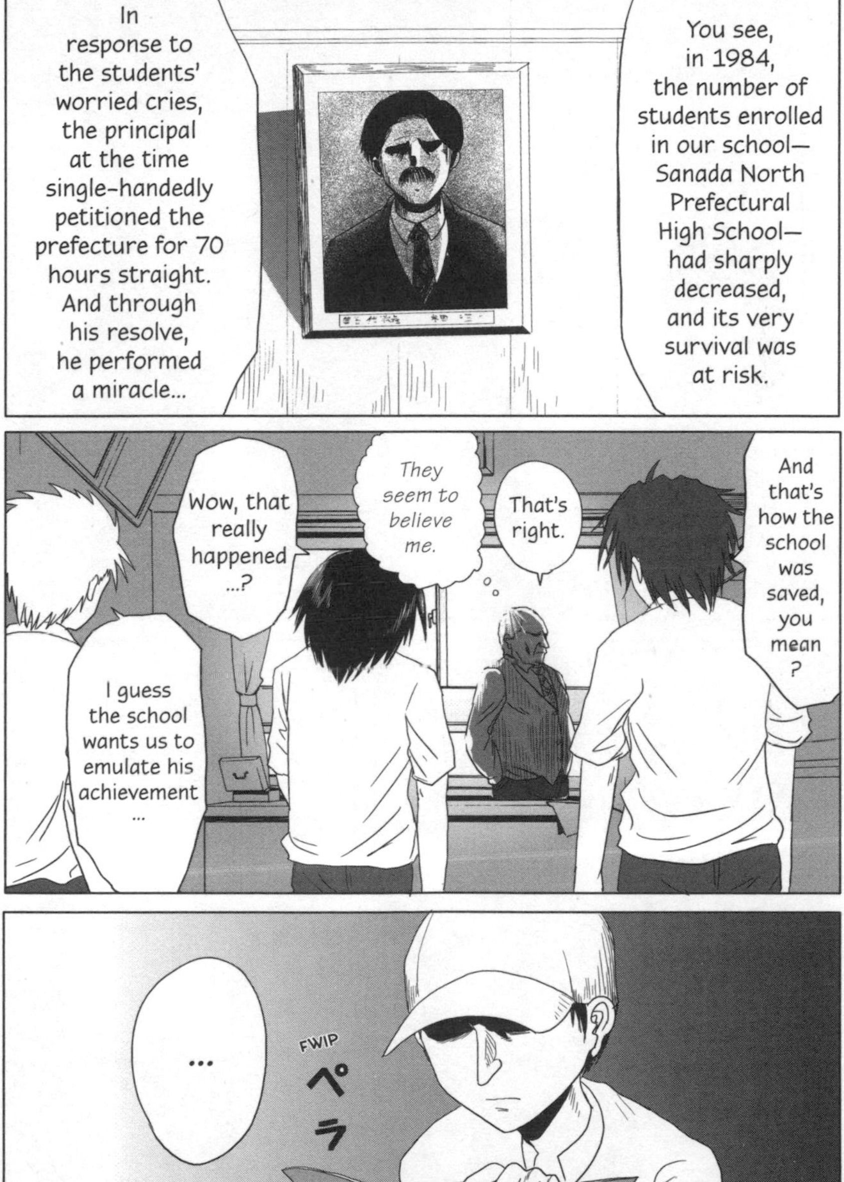
You see, in 1984, the number of students enrolled in our school—Sanada North Prefectural High School—had sharply decreased, and its very survival was at risk.
In response to the students' worried cries, the principal at the time single-handedly petitioned the prefecture for 70 hours straight. And through his resolve, he performed a miracle...
And that's how the school was saved, you mean?
That's right.
They seem to believe me.
Wow, that really happened ...?
I guess the school wants us to emulate his achievement ...
FWIP
ペラ
...

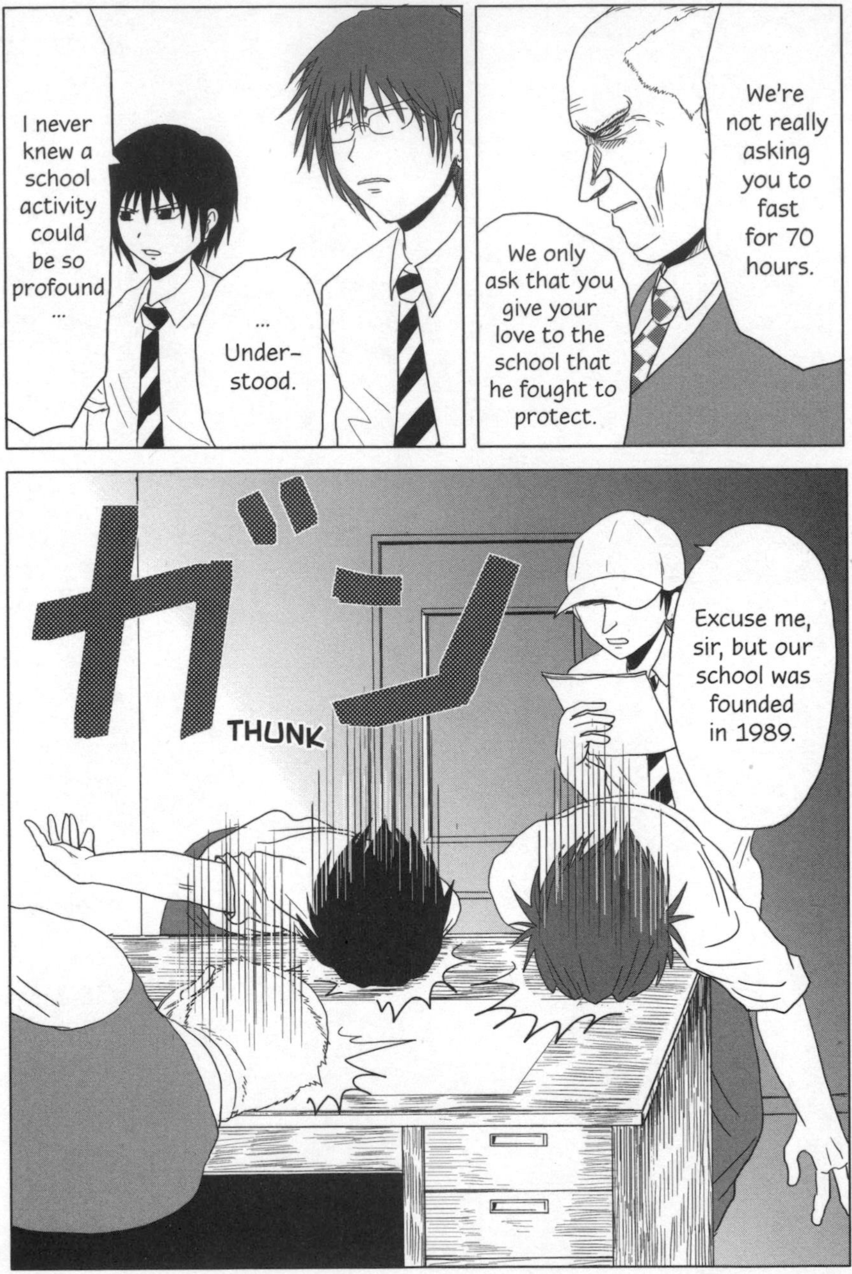
We're not really asking you to fast for 70 hours.
We only ask that you give your love to the school that he fought to protect.
... Under-stood.
I never knew a school activity could be so profound ...
Excuse me, sir, but our school was founded in 1989.
ガン
THUNK

the

daily

lives

of

1 high school boys

chapter 11:
high school boys and summer plans

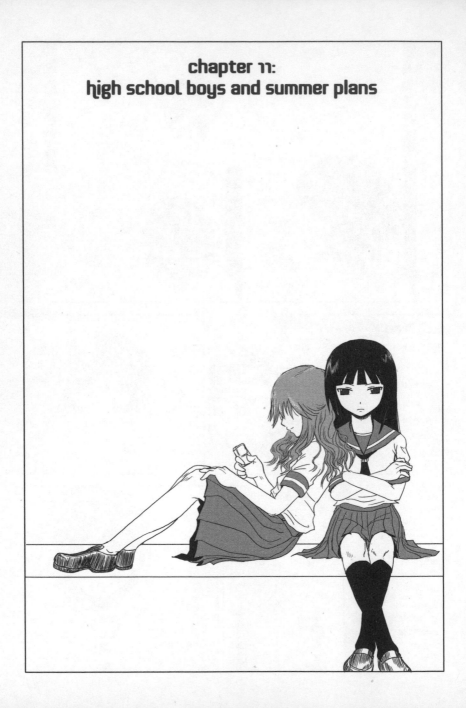

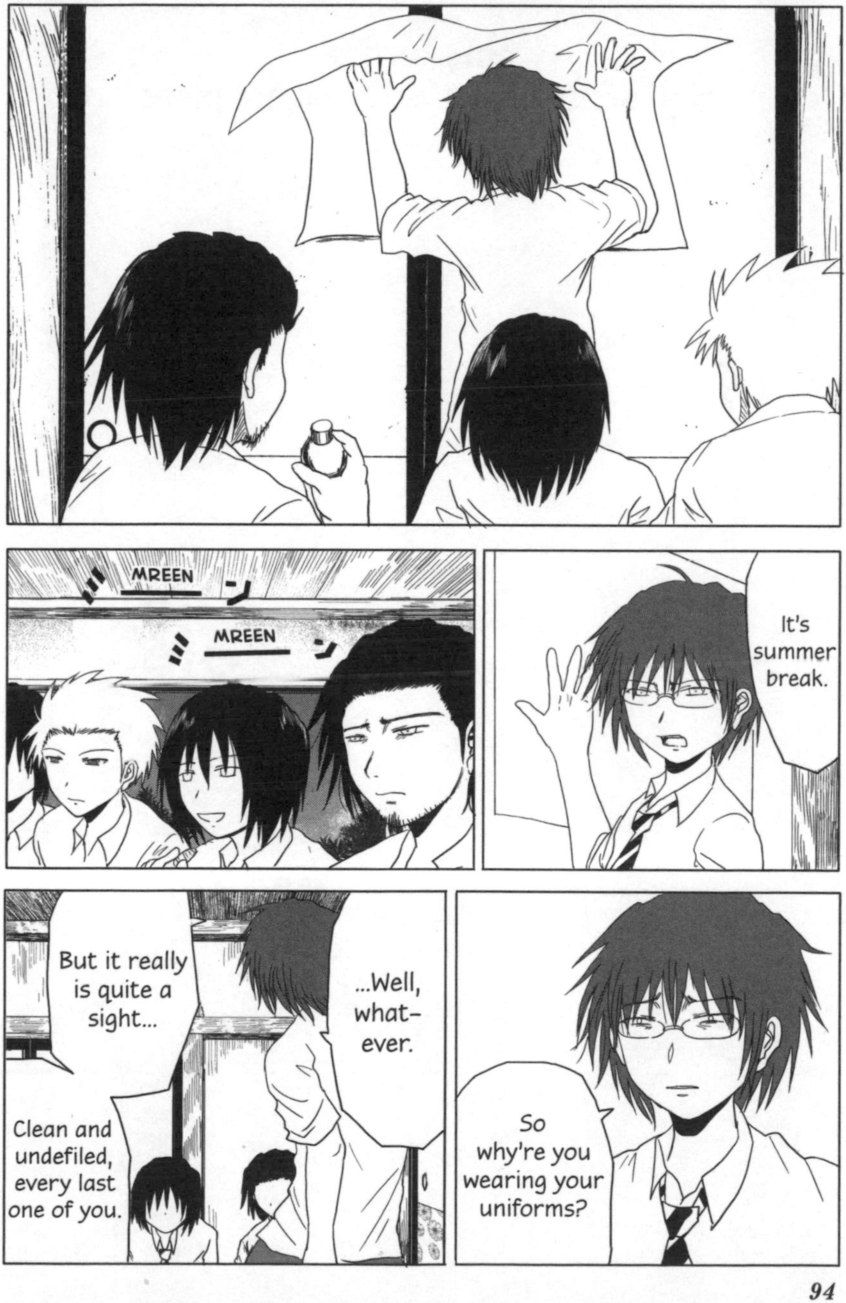
It's summer break.
MREEN
MREEN
So why're you wearing your uniforms?
...Well, whatever.
But it really is quite a sight...
Clean and undefiled, every last one of you.

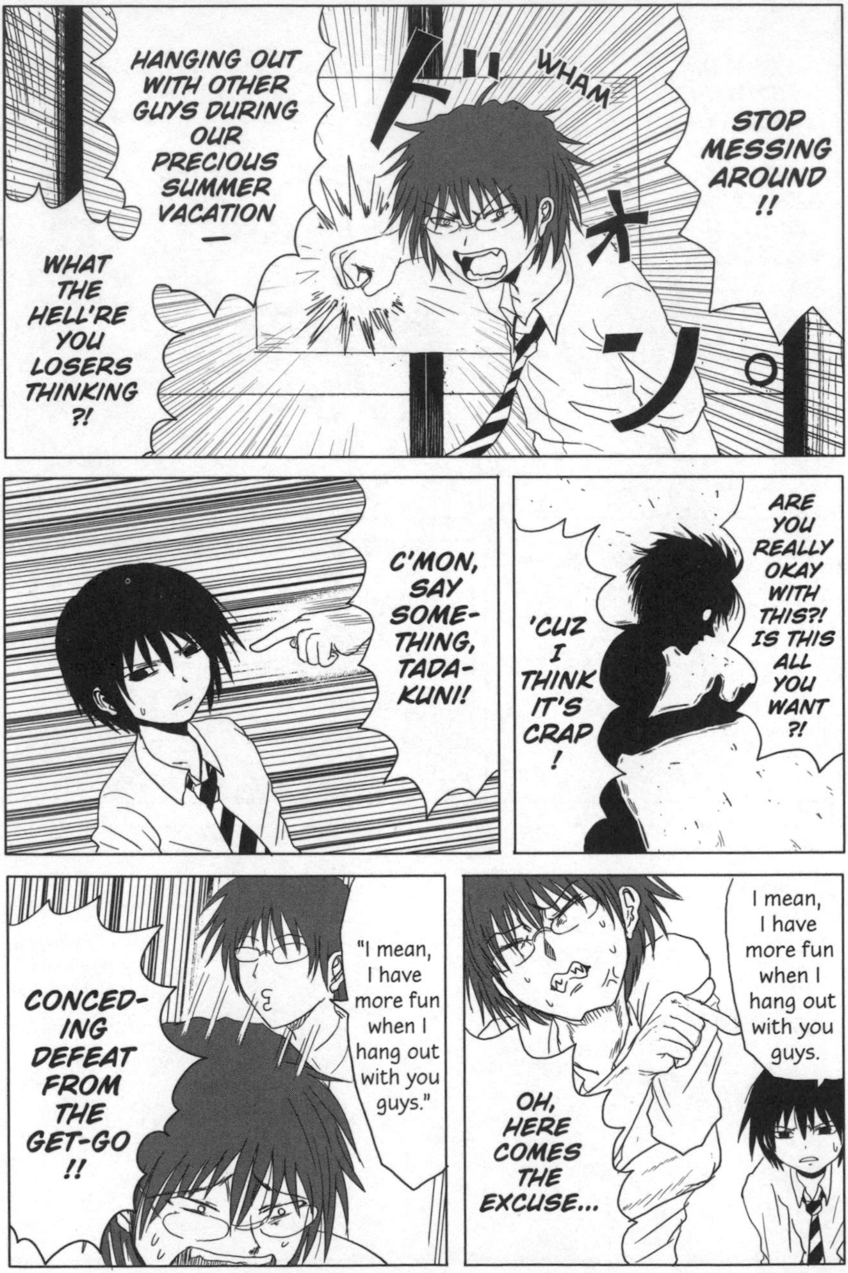
WHAM
ドッオーン。
STOP MESSING AROUND!!
HANGING OUT WITH OTHER GUYS DURING OUR PRECIOUS SUMMER VACATION—
WHAT THE HELL'RE YOU LOSERS THINKING?!
ARE YOU REALLY OKAY WITH THIS?! IS THIS ALL YOU WANT?!
'CUZ I THINK IT'S CRAP!
C'MON, SAY SOME-THING, TADA-KUNI!
I mean, I have more fun when I hang out with you guys.
OH, HERE COMES THE EXCUSE...
"I mean, I have more fun when I hang out with you guys."
CONCED-ING DEFEAT FROM THE GET-GO!!

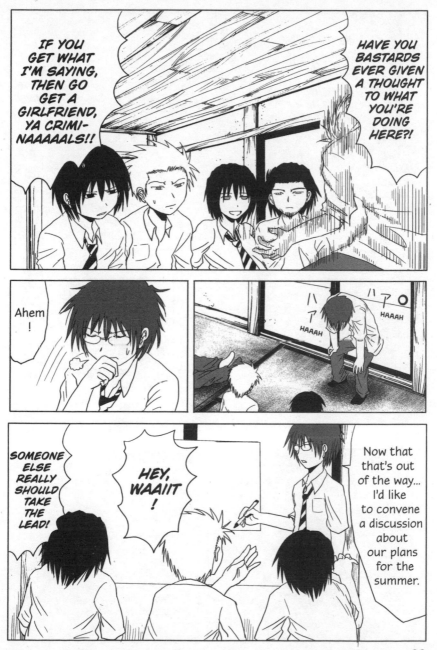

HAVE YOU BASTARDS EVER GIVEN A THOUGHT TO WHAT YOU'RE DOING HERE?!
IF YOU GET WHAT I'M SAYING, THEN GO GET A GIRLFRIEND, YA CRIMI-NAAAAALS!!
ハア
HAAAH
ハア
HAAAH
Ahem!
Now that that's out of the way... I'd like to convene a discussion about our plans for the summer.
HEY, WAAIIT!
SOMEONE ELSE REALLY SHOULD TAKE THE LEAD!

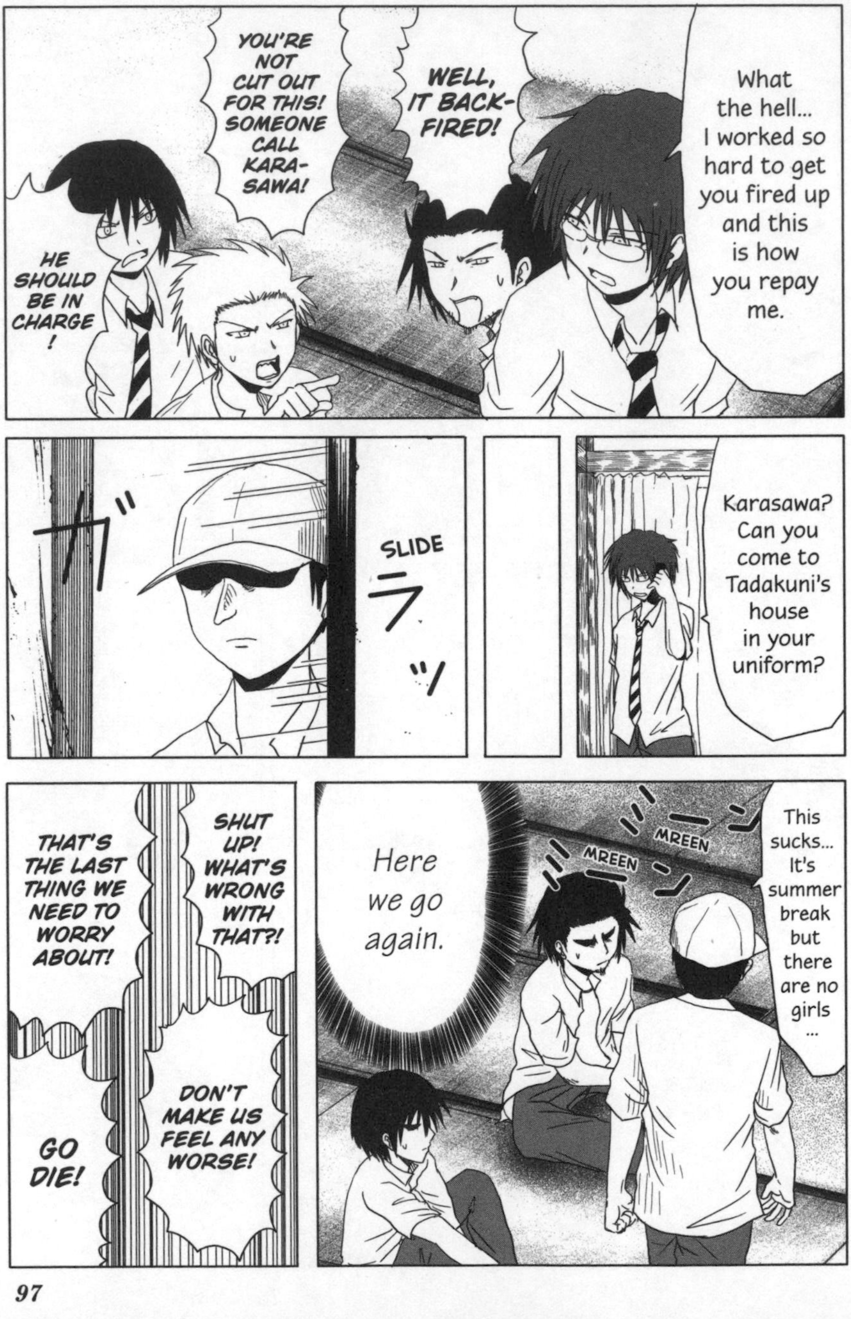
What the hell... I worked so hard to get you fired up and this is how you repay me.
WELL, IT BACK-FIRED!
YOU'RE NOT CUT OUT FOR THIS! SOMEONE CALL KARA-SAWA!
HE SHOULD BE IN CHARGE!
Karasawa? Can you come to Tadakuni's house in your uniform?
SLIDE
ガラッ
This sucks... It's summer break but there are no girls ...
MREEN
MREEN
Here we go again.
SHUT UP! WHAT'S WRONG WITH THAT?!
THAT'S THE LAST THING WE NEED TO WORRY ABOUT!
DON'T MAKE US FEEL ANY WORSE!
GO DIE!

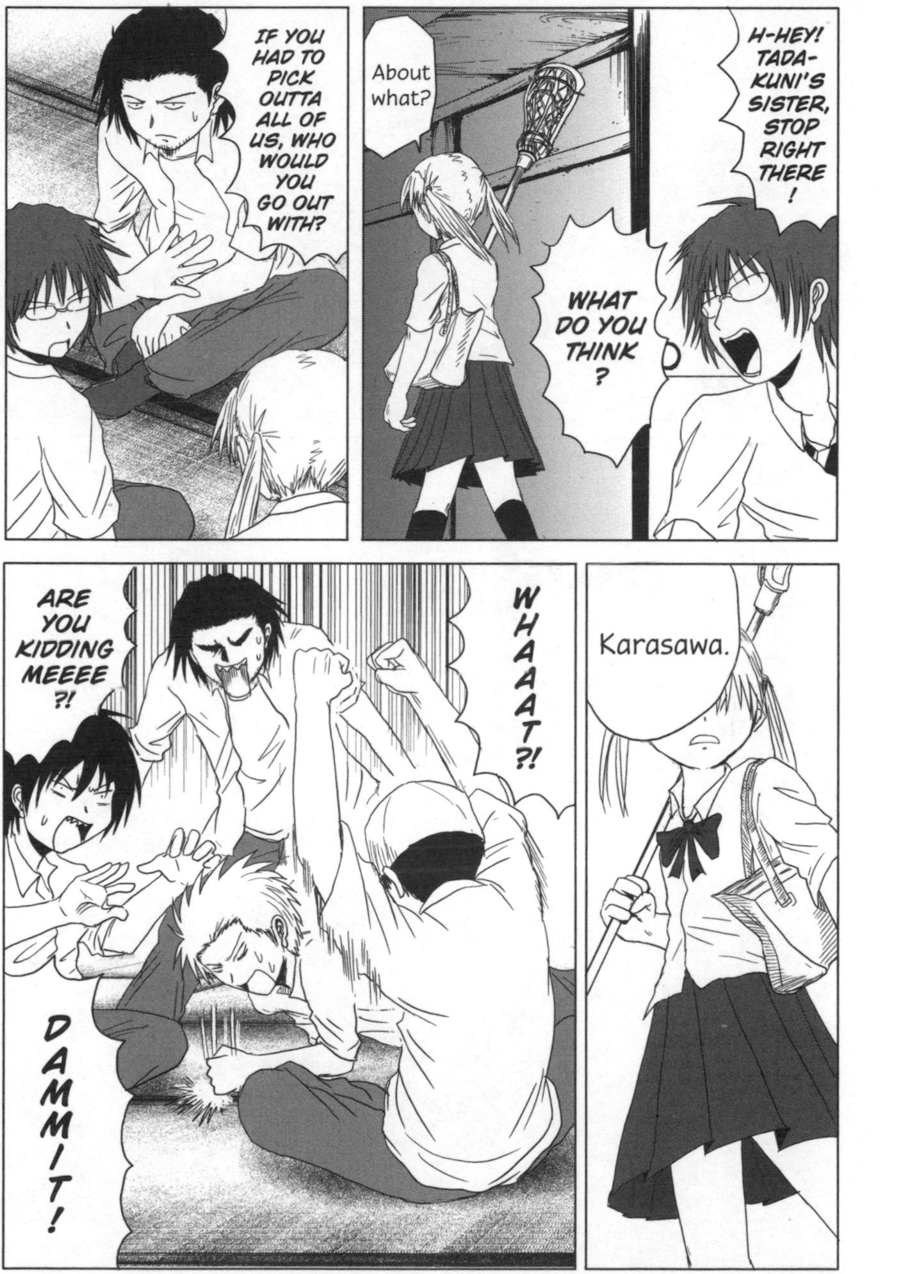
H-HEY! TADA-KUNI'S SISTER, STOP RIGHT THERE!
About what?
WHAT DO YOU THINK?
IF YOU HAD TO PICK OUTTA ALL OF US, WHO WOULD YOU GO OUT WITH?
Karasawa.
WHAAAAT?!
ARE YOU KIDDING MEEEE?!
DAMMIT!

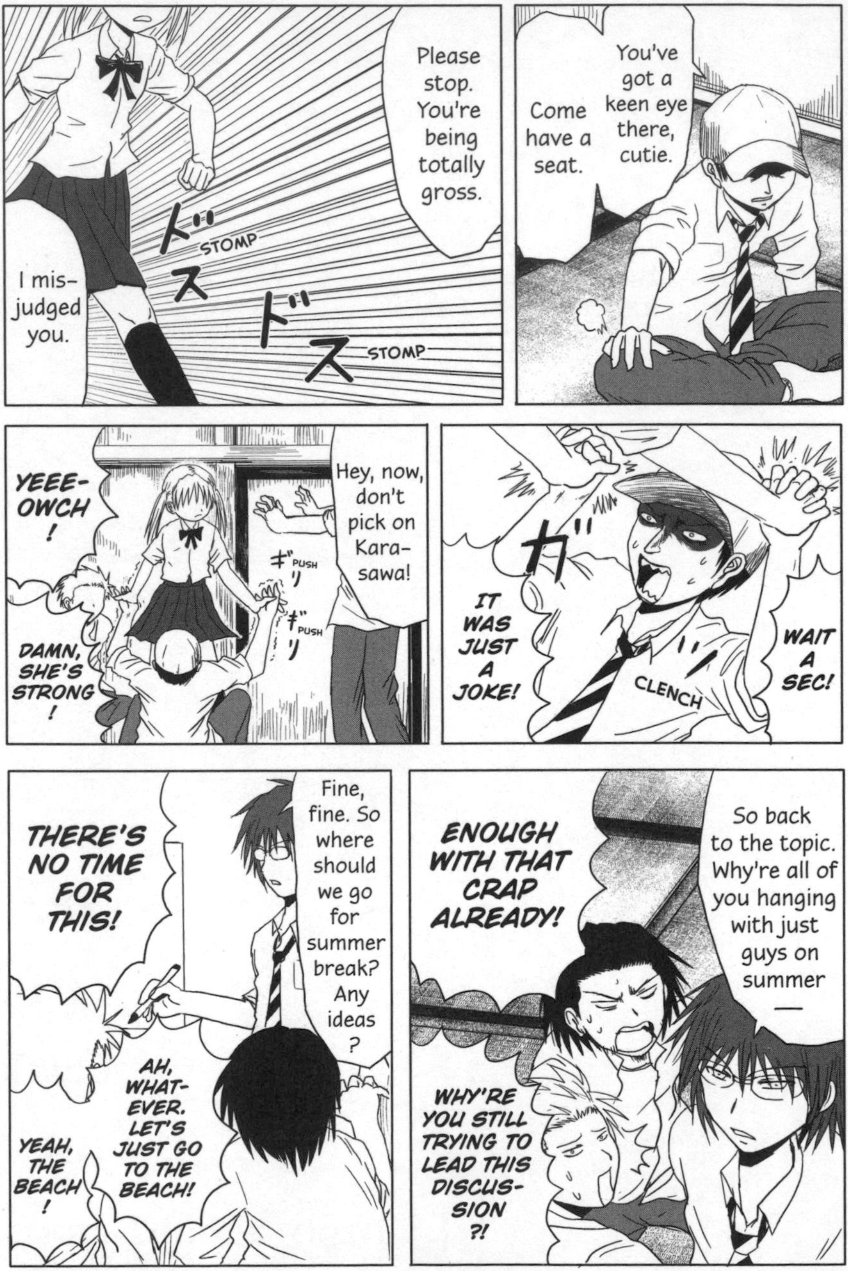
You've got a keen eye there, cutie.
Come have a seat.
Please stop. You're being totally gross.
ドス STOMP
ドス STOMP
I mis-judged you.
WAIT A SEC!
ガ
IT WAS JUST A JOKE!
CLENCH
Hey, now, don't pick on Kara-sawa!
ギリ PUSH
ギリ PUSH
YEEE-OWCH!
DAMN, SHE'S STRONG!
So back to the topic. Why're all of you hanging with just guys on summer—
ENOUGH WITH THAT CRAP ALREADY!
WHY'RE YOU STILL TRYING TO LEAD THIS DISCUS-SION?!
Fine, fine. So where should we go for summer break? Any ideas?
THERE'S NO TIME FOR THIS!
AH, WHAT-EVER. LET'S JUST GO TO THE BEACH!
YEAH, THE BEACH!

the

daily

lives

of

1 high school boys

chapter 12:
high school boys and the seaside shack

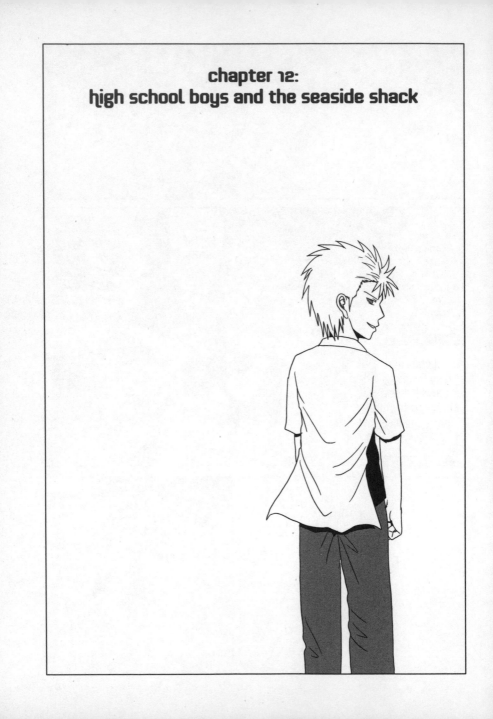

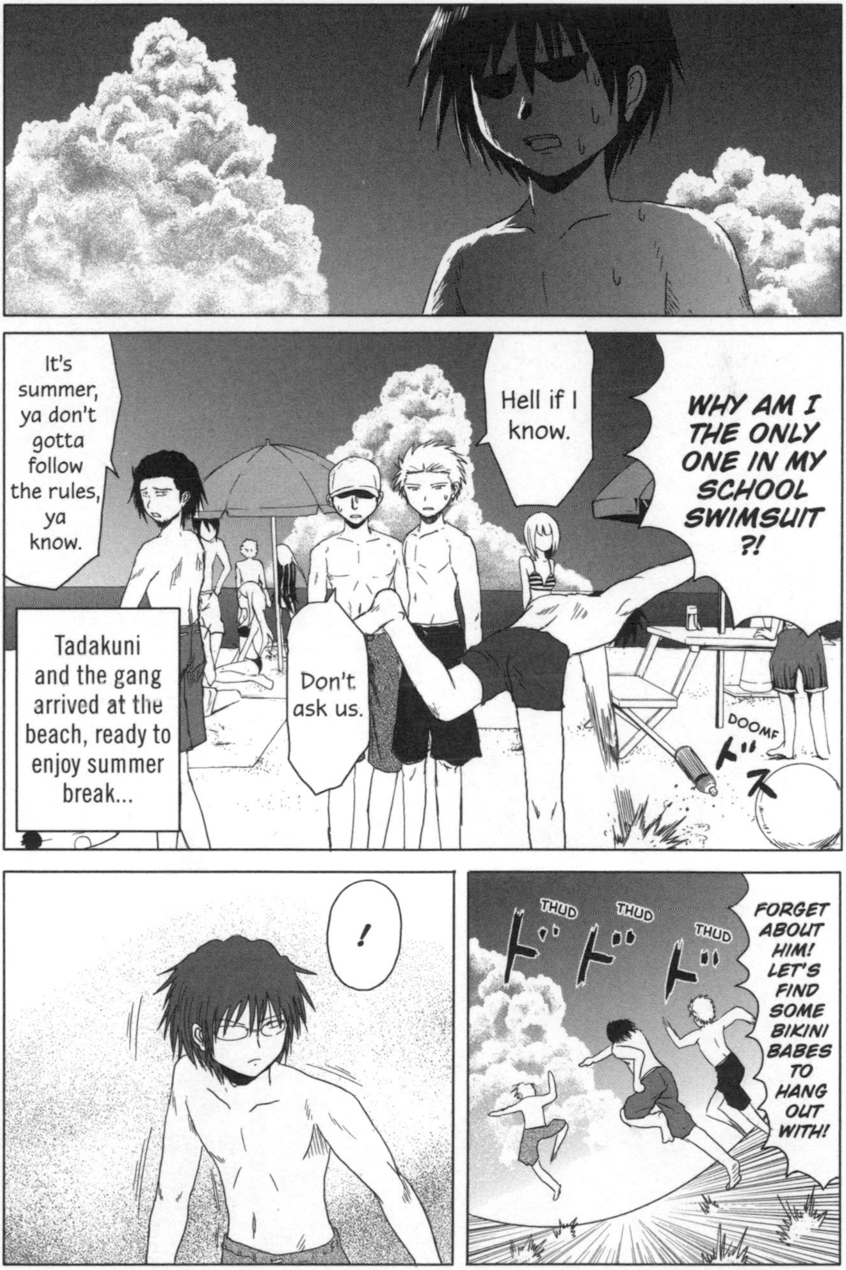
WHY AM I THE ONLY ONE IN MY SCHOOL SWIMSUIT?!
Hell if I know.
It's summer, ya don't gotta follow the rules, ya know.
Don't ask us.
Tadakuni and the gang arrived at the beach, ready to enjoy summer break...
DOOMF
ドス
THUD THUD THUD
ドドド
FORGET ABOUT HIM! LET'S FIND SOME BIKINI BABES TO HANG OUT WITH!
!

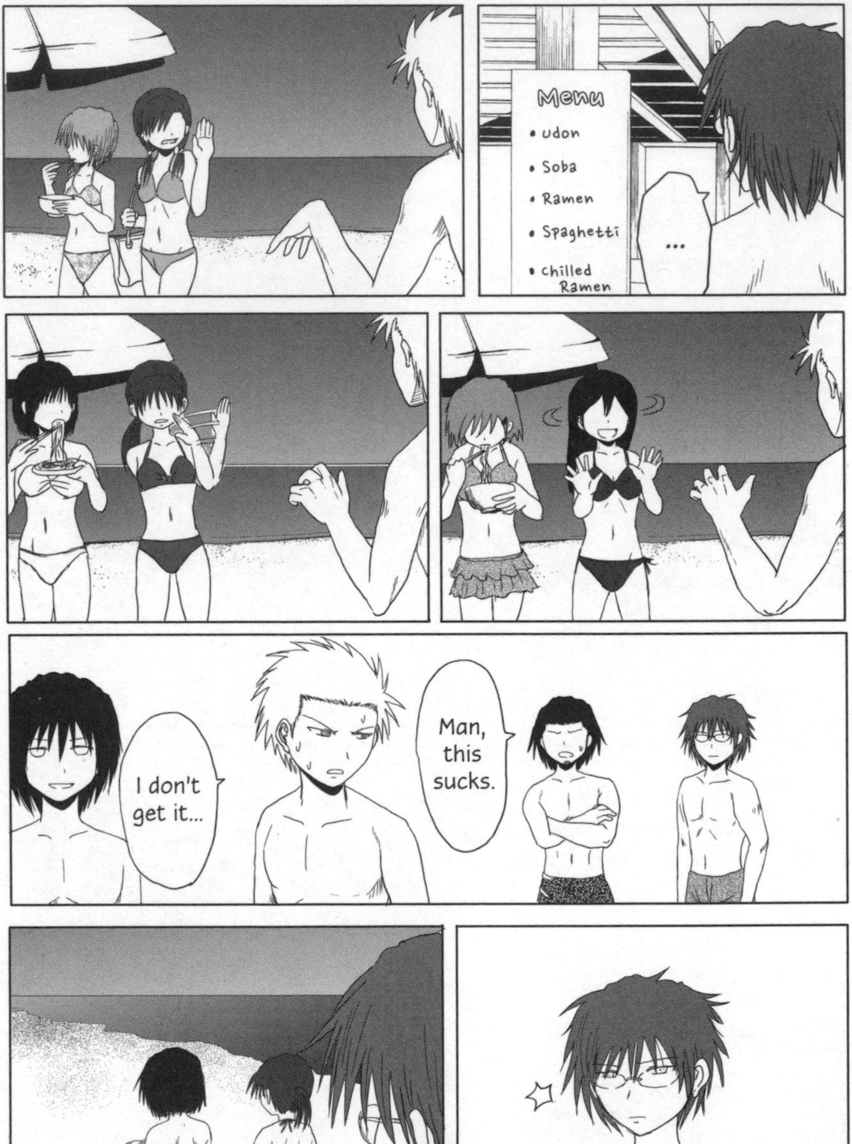
Menu
• udon
• Soba
• Ramen
• Spaghetti
• chilled Ramen
...
Man, this sucks.
I don't get it...

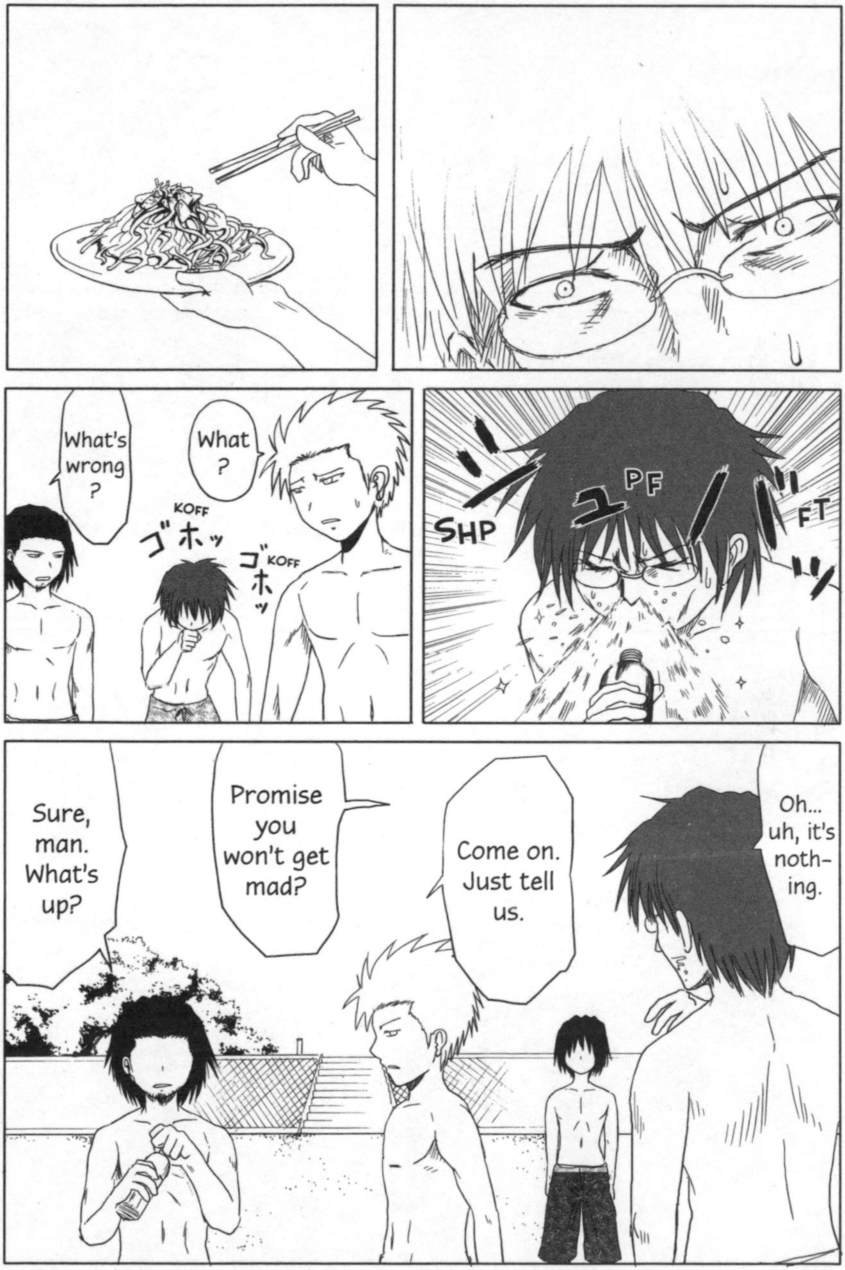
SHP
PF
FT
What?
What's wrong?
KOFF
ゴホッ
KOFF
ゴホッ
Oh... uh, it's nothing.
Come on. Just tell us.
Promise you won't get mad?
Sure, man. What's up?

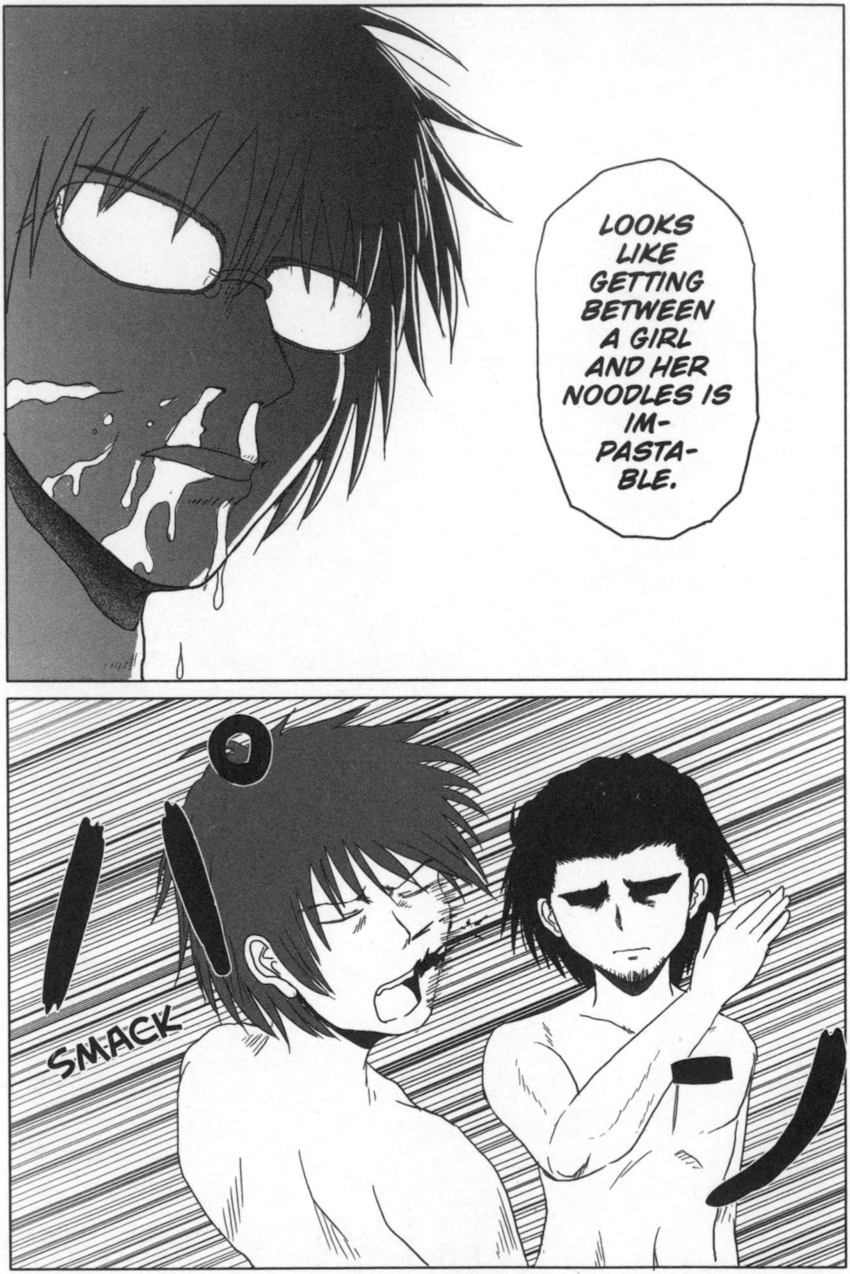
LOOKS LIKE GETTING BETWEEN A GIRL AND HER NOODLES IS IM-PASTA-BLE.
SMACK

the

daily

lives

of

1 high school boys

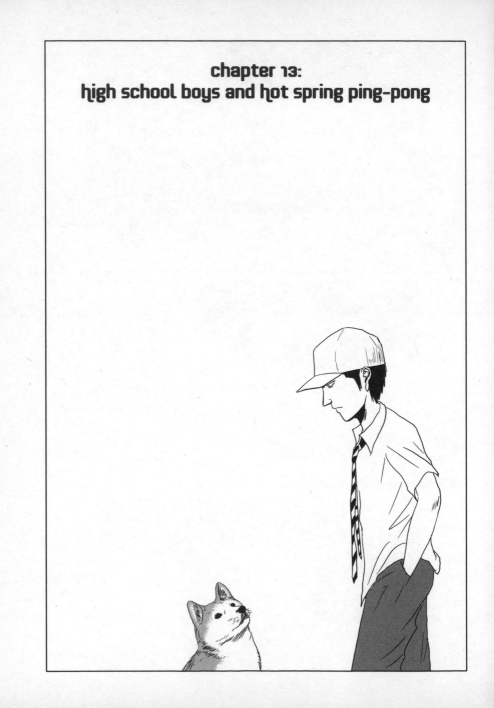

chapter 13:
high school boys and hot spring ping-pong

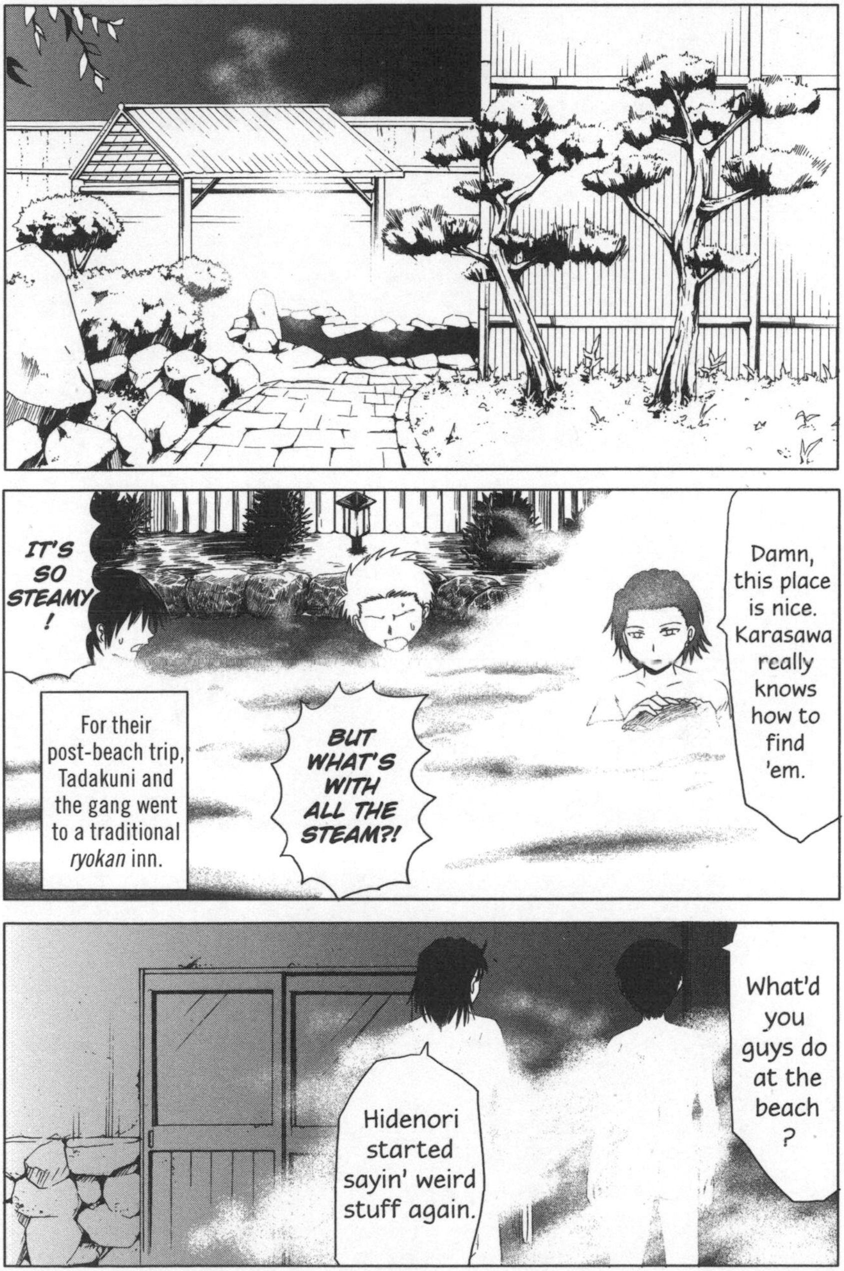
Damn, this place is nice. Karasawa really knows how to find 'em.
IT'S SO STEAMY!
BUT WHAT'S WITH ALL THE STEAM?!
For their post-beach trip, Tadakuni and the gang went to a traditional *ryokan* inn.
What'd you guys do at the beach?
Hidenori started sayin' weird stuff again.

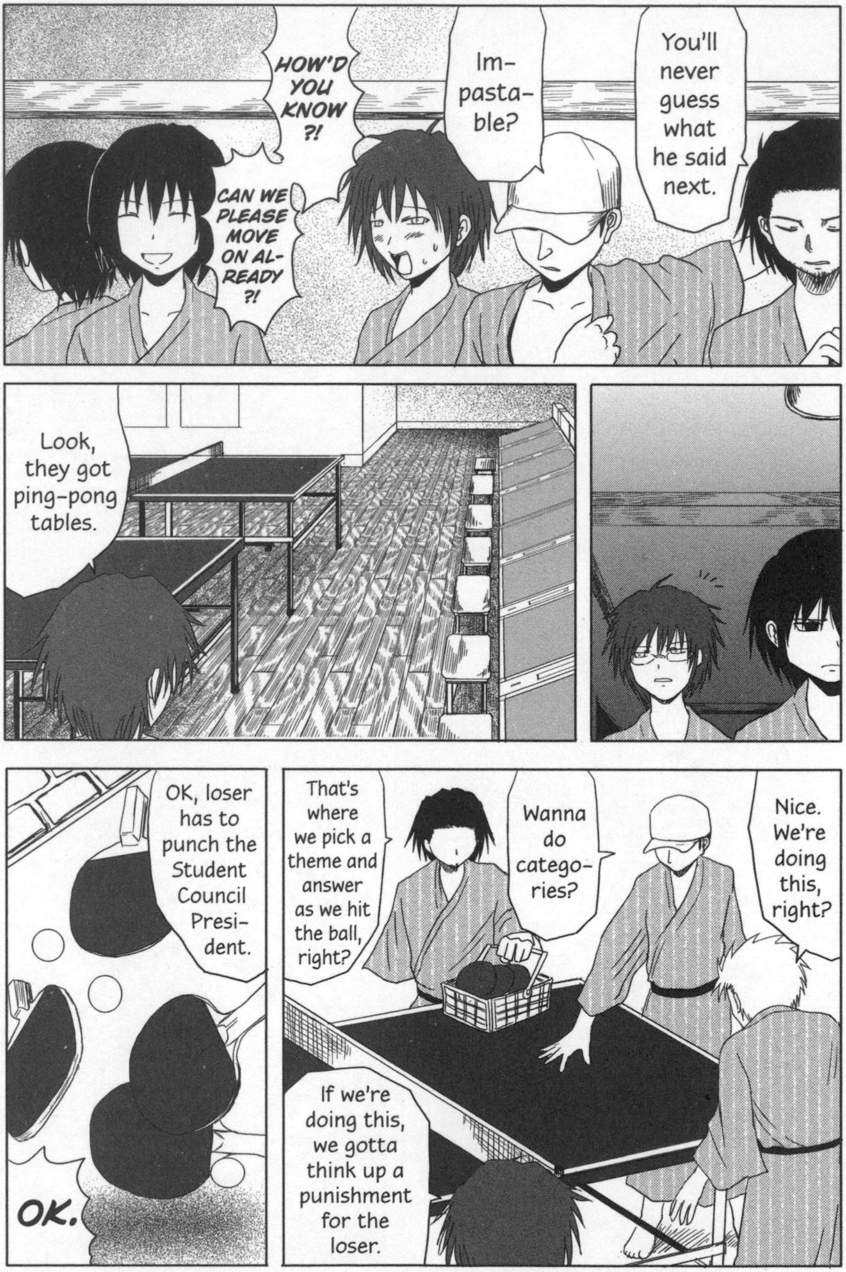

You'll never guess what he said next.
Im-pasta-ble?
HOW'D YOU KNOW?!
CAN WE PLEASE MOVE ON AL-READY?!
Look, they got ping-pong tables.
Nice. We're doing this, right?
Wanna do catego-ries?
That's where we pick a theme and answer as we hit the ball, right?
If we're doing this, we gotta think up a punishment for the loser.
OK, loser has to punch the Student Council Presi-dent.
OK.

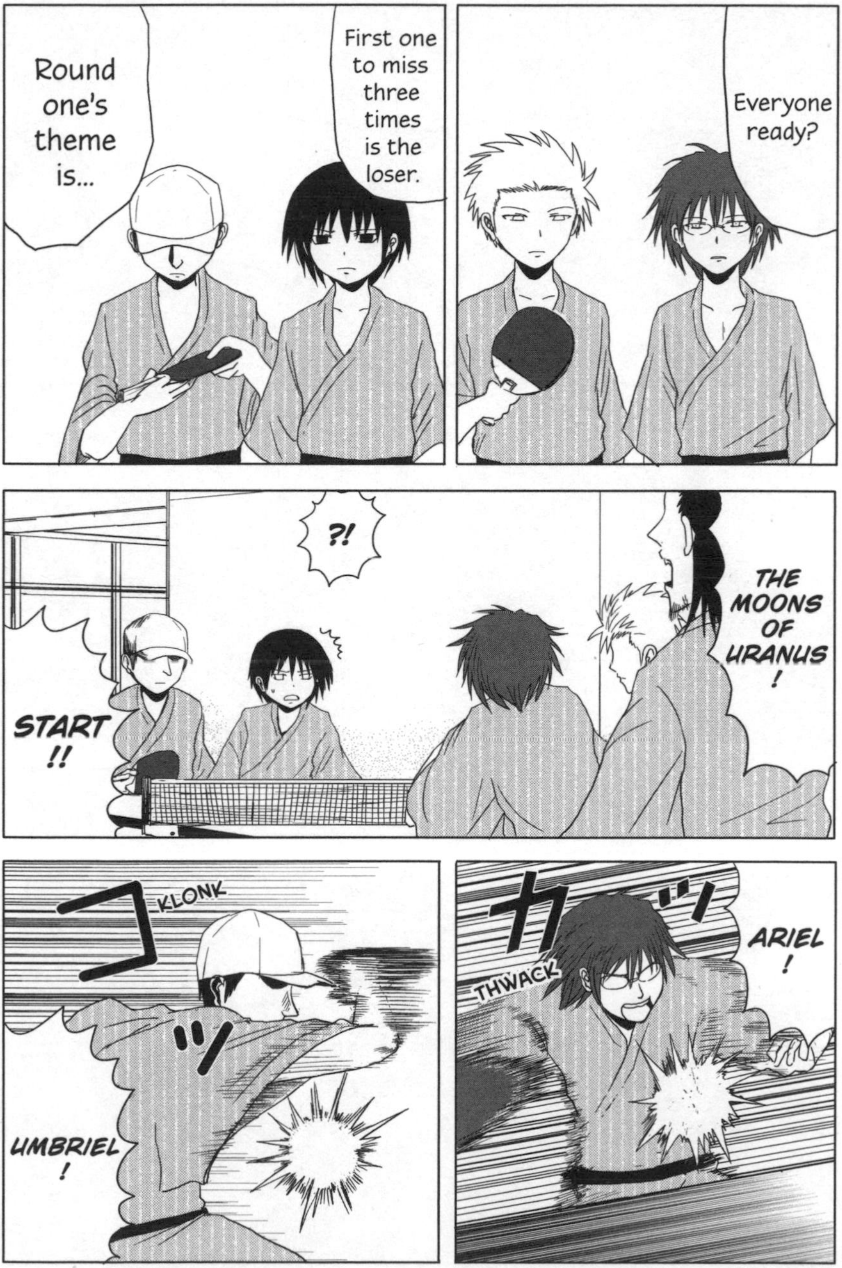
Everyone ready?
First one to miss three times is the loser.
Round one's theme is...
THE MOONS OF URANUS!
?!
START!!
ARIEL!
THWACK
KLONK
UMBRIEL!

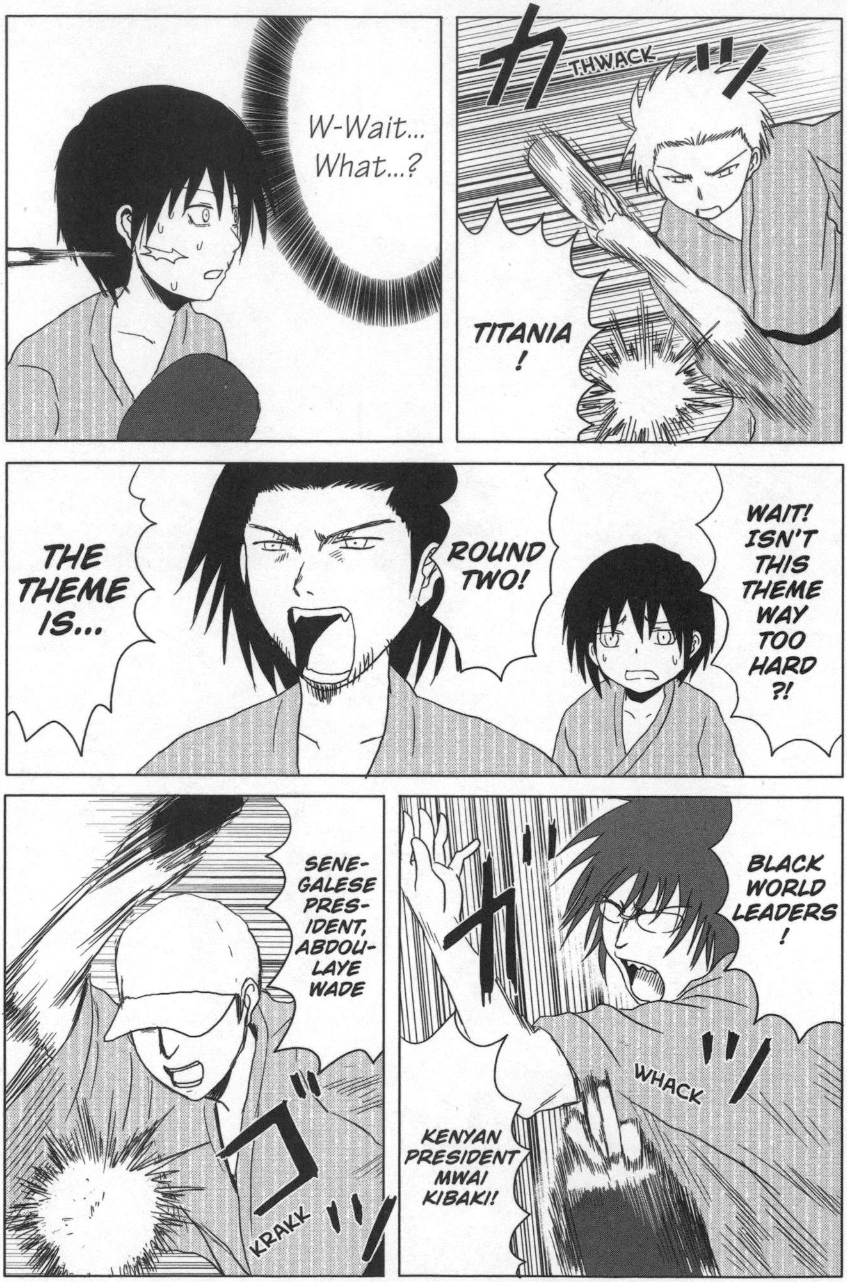
THWACK
TITANIA!
W-Wait... What...?
WAIT! ISN'T THIS THEME WAY TOO HARD?!
ROUND TWO!
THE THEME IS...
BLACK WORLD LEADERS!
WHACK
KENYAN PRESIDENT MWAI KIBAKI!
SENEGALESE PRESIDENT, ABDOULAYE WADE
KRAKK

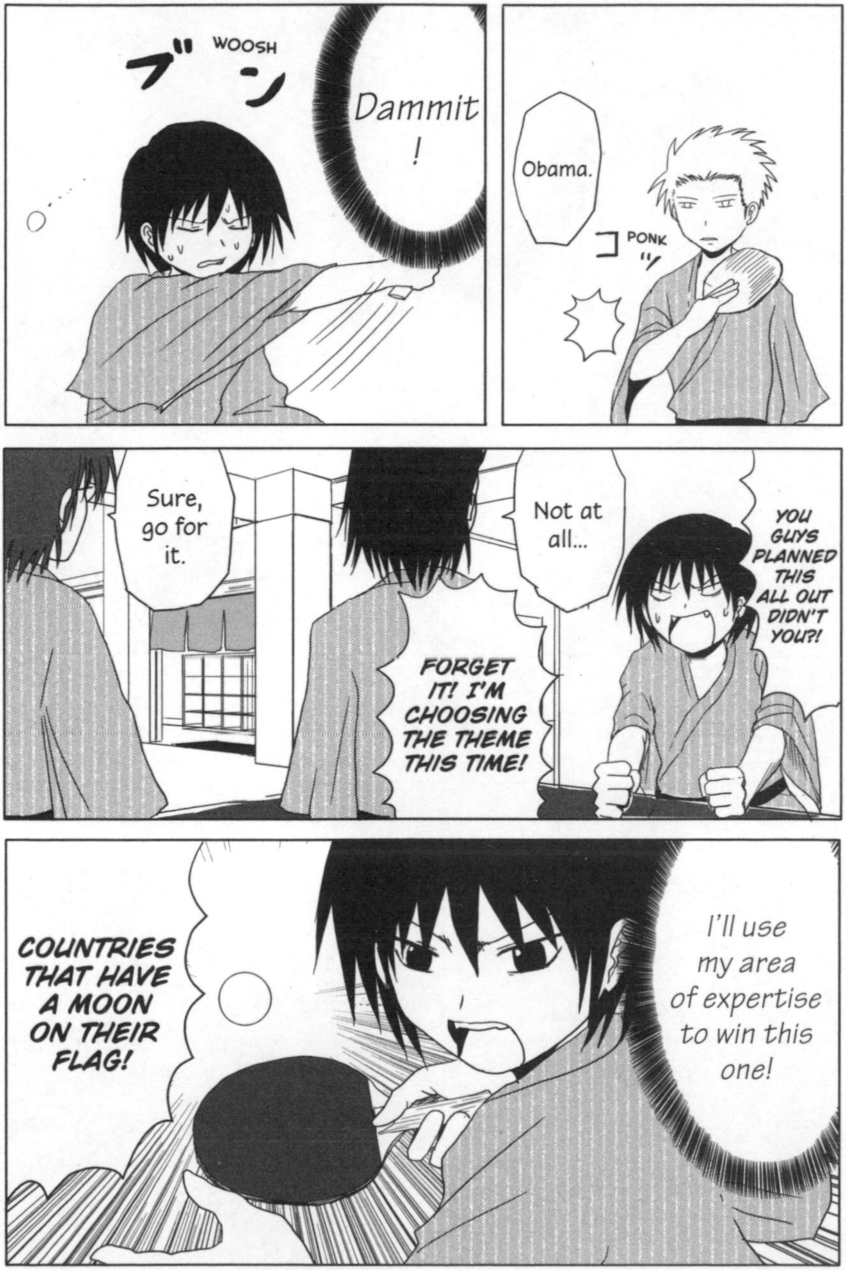
Obama.
PONK
WOOSH
Dammit!
YOU GUYS PLANNED THIS ALL OUT DIDN'T YOU?!
Not at all...
FORGET IT! I'M CHOOSING THE THEME THIS TIME!
Sure, go for it.
I'll use my area of expertise to win this one!
COUNTRIES THAT HAVE A MOON ON THEIR FLAG!

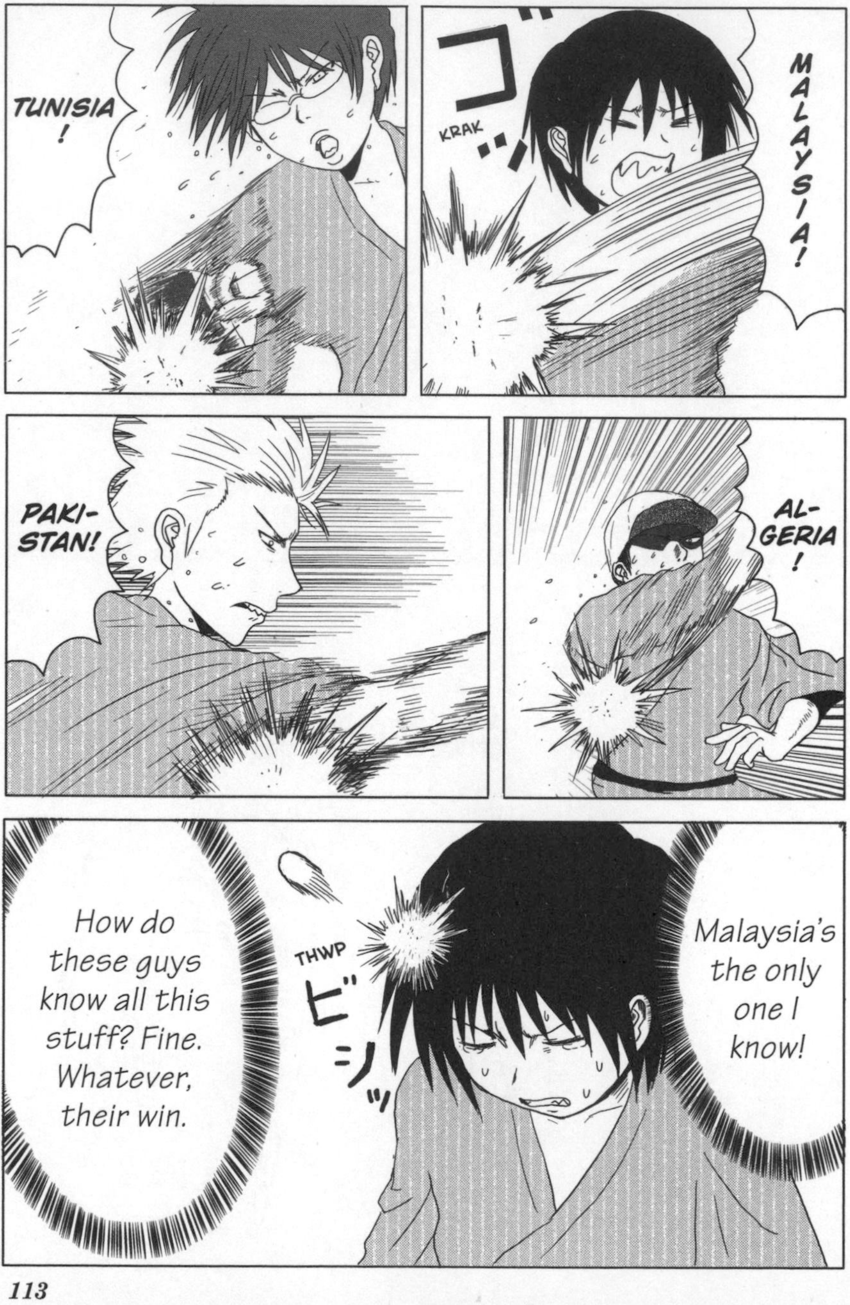
MALAYSIA!
ゴッ
KRAK
TUNISIA!
AL-GERIA!
PAKI-STAN!
Malaysia's the only one I know!
THWP
ビシッ
How do these guys know all this stuff? Fine. Whatever, their win.

At first, I drew him with a certain
lit tube of paper hanging out of his mouth.

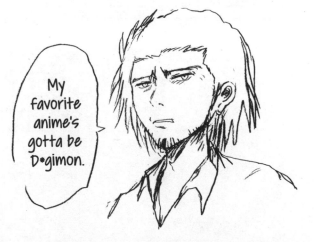

My
favorite
anime's
gotta be
D*gimon.

chapter 14:
high school boys and summer memories

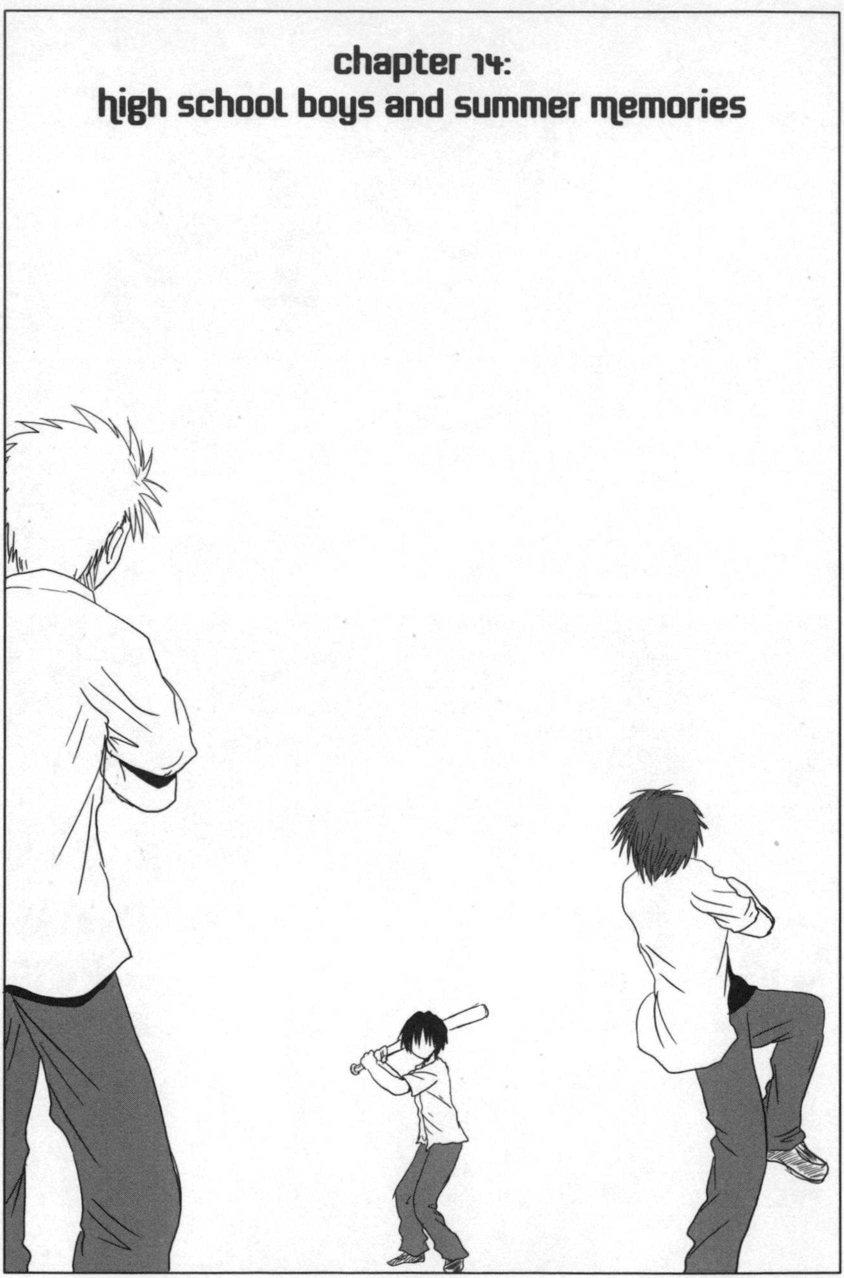

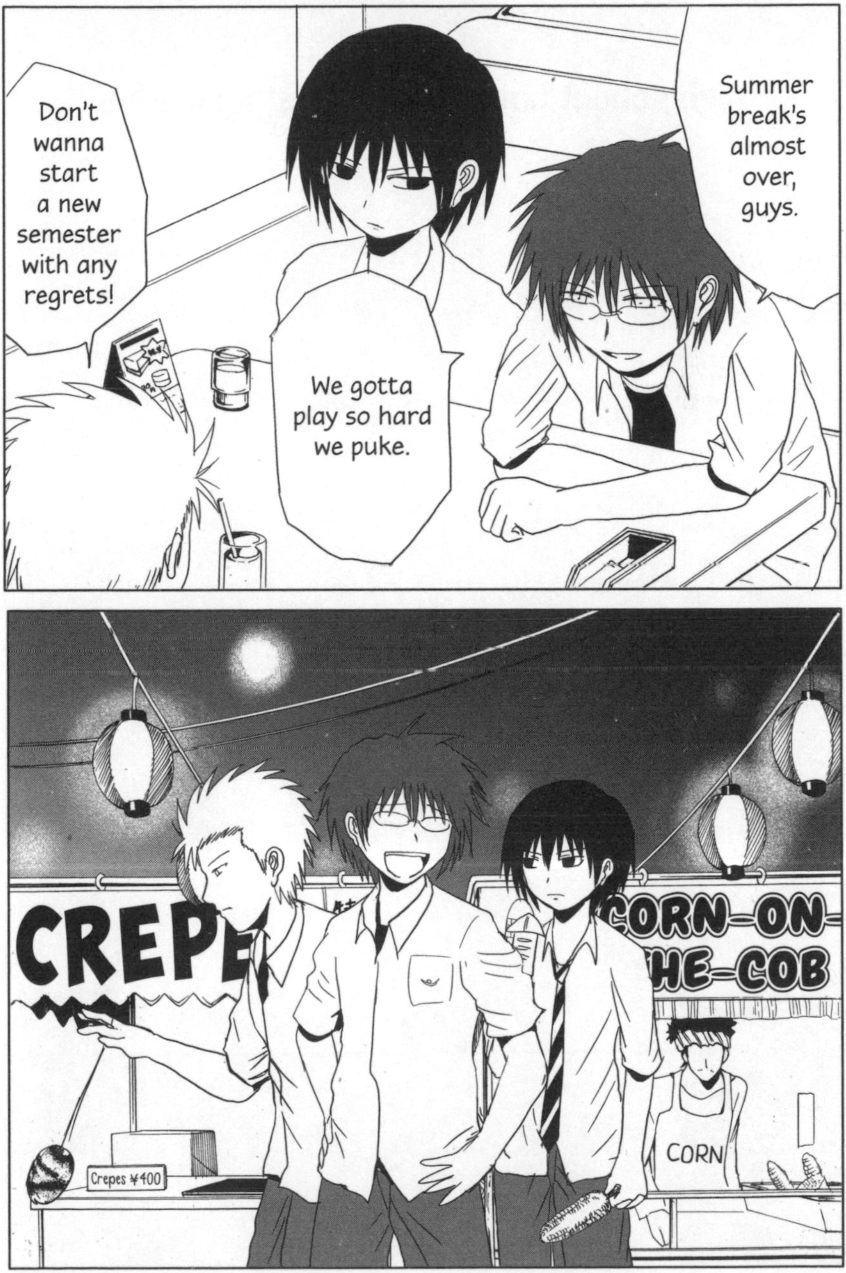
Summer break's almost over, guys.
Don't wanna start a new semester with any regrets!
We gotta play so hard we puke.
CORN-ON-
HE-COB
CORN
CREPE
Crepes ¥400

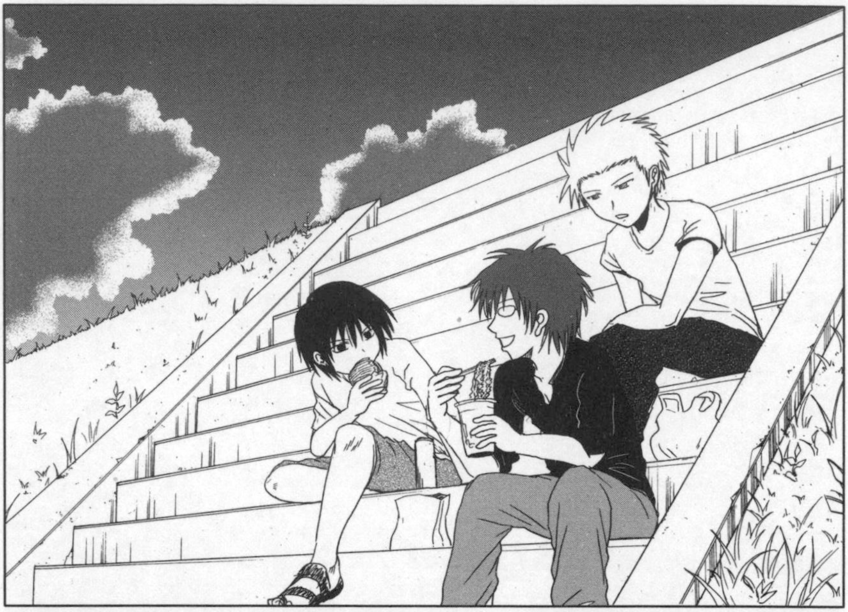
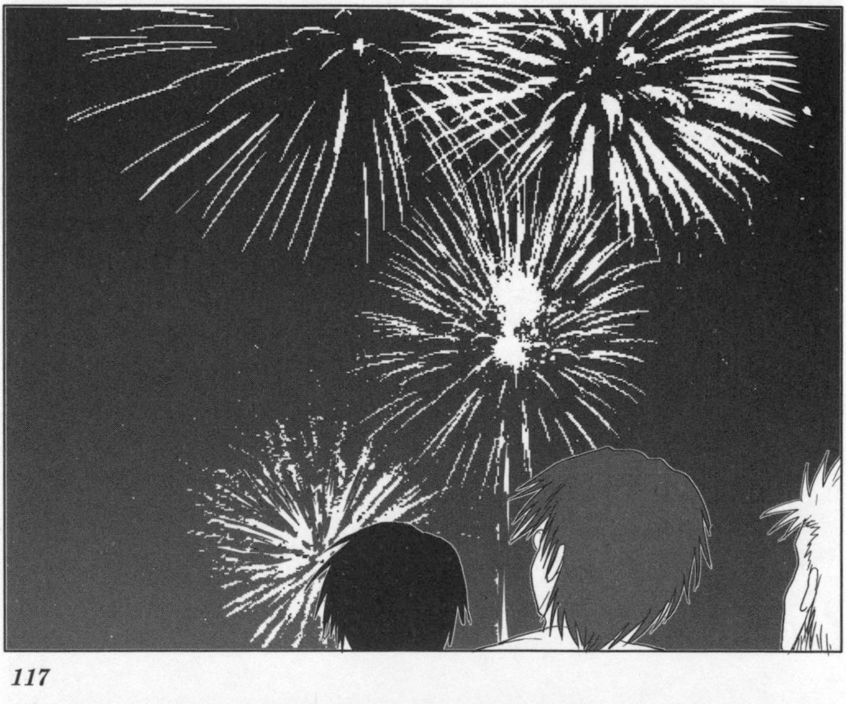

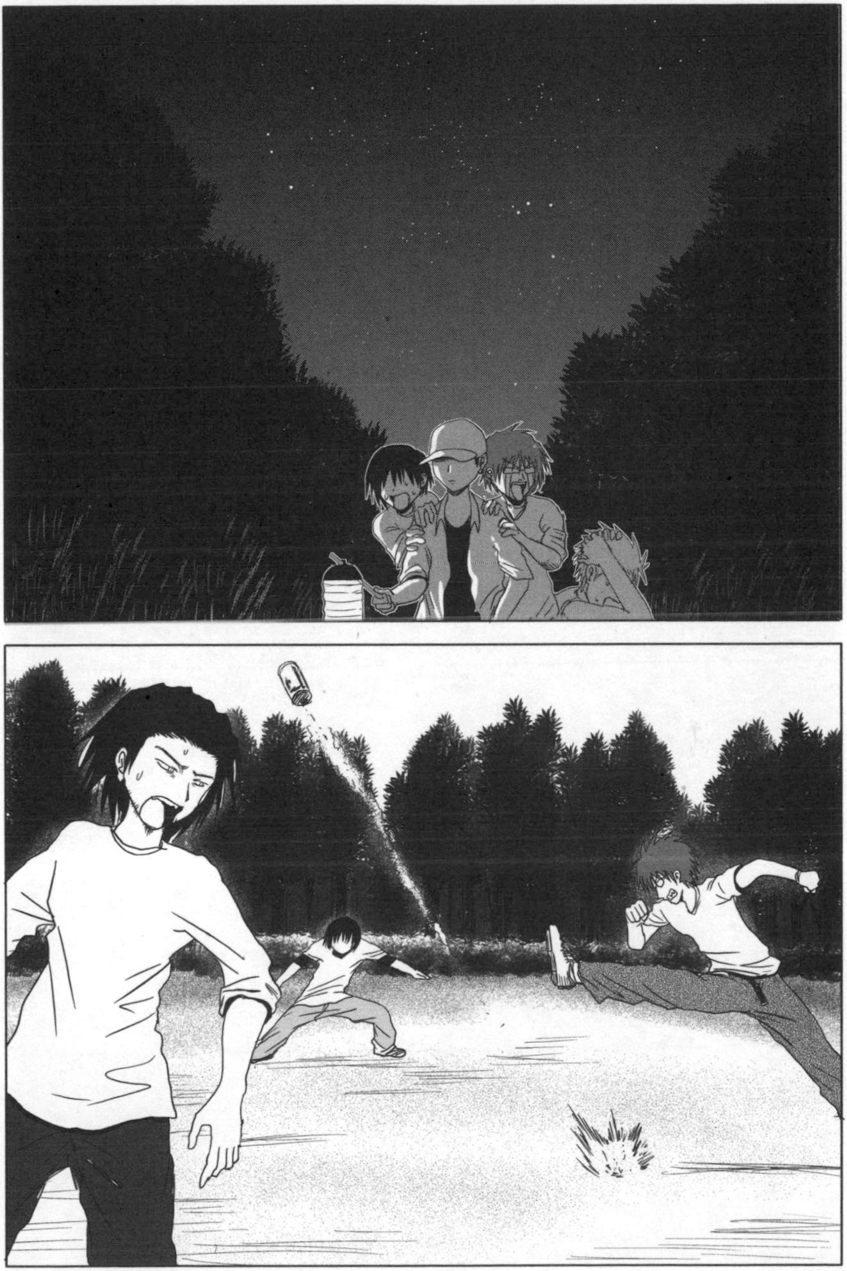

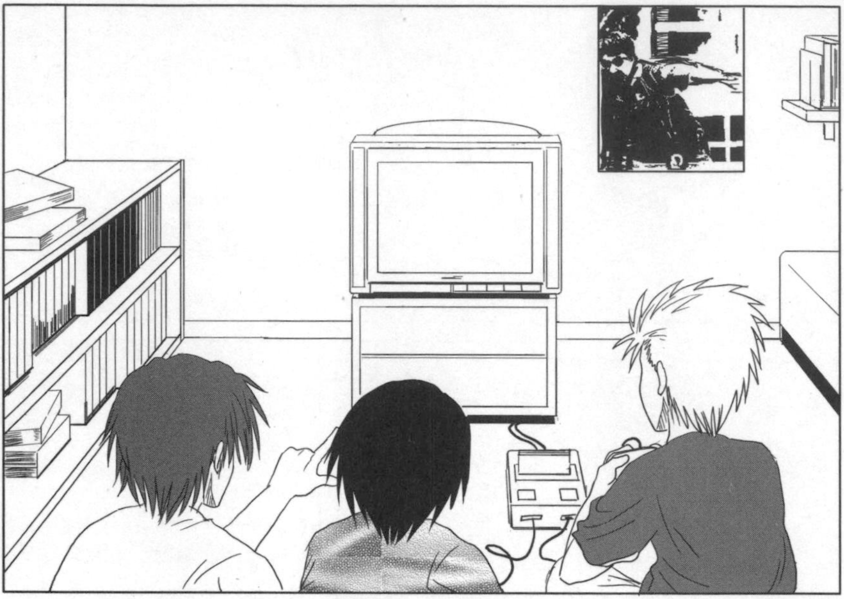

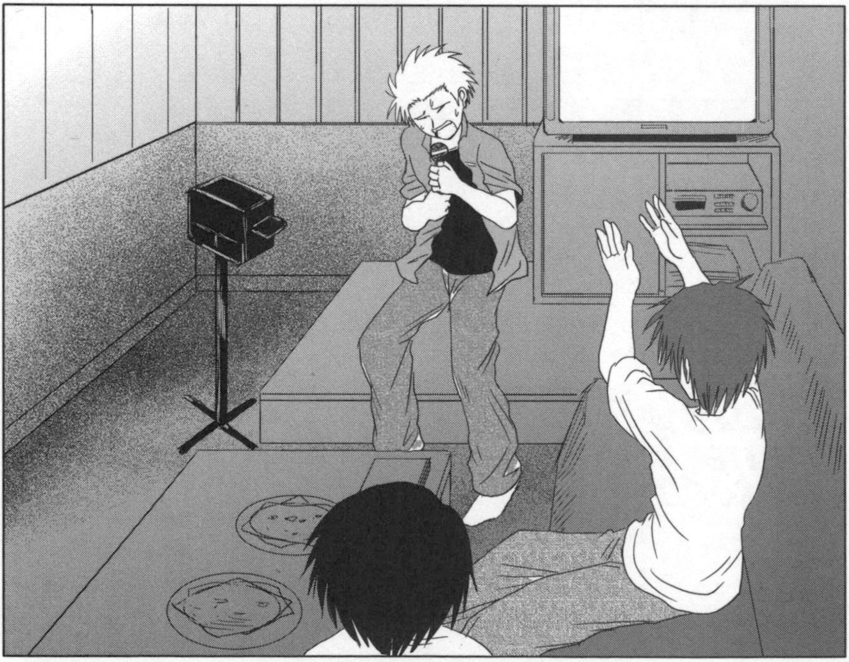

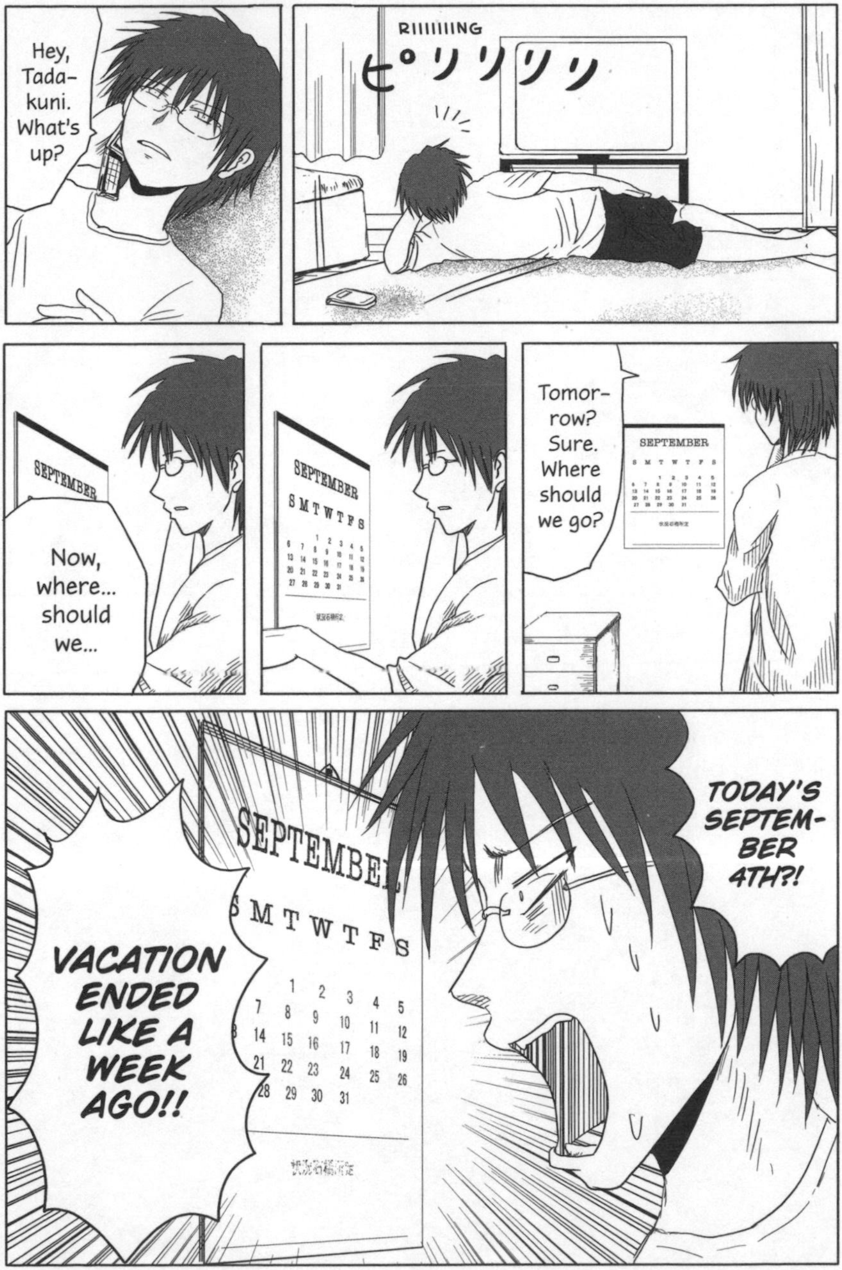
RIIIIIIING
ピリリリリ
Hey, Tada-kuni. What's up?
Tomor-row? Sure. Where should we go?
Now, where... should we...
TODAY'S SEPTEM-BER 4TH?!
VACATION ENDED LIKE A WEEK AGO!!

chapter 15:
high school boys and radio hosts

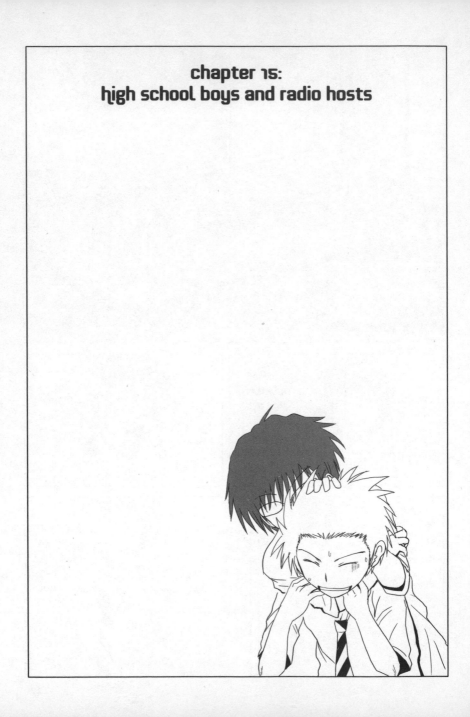

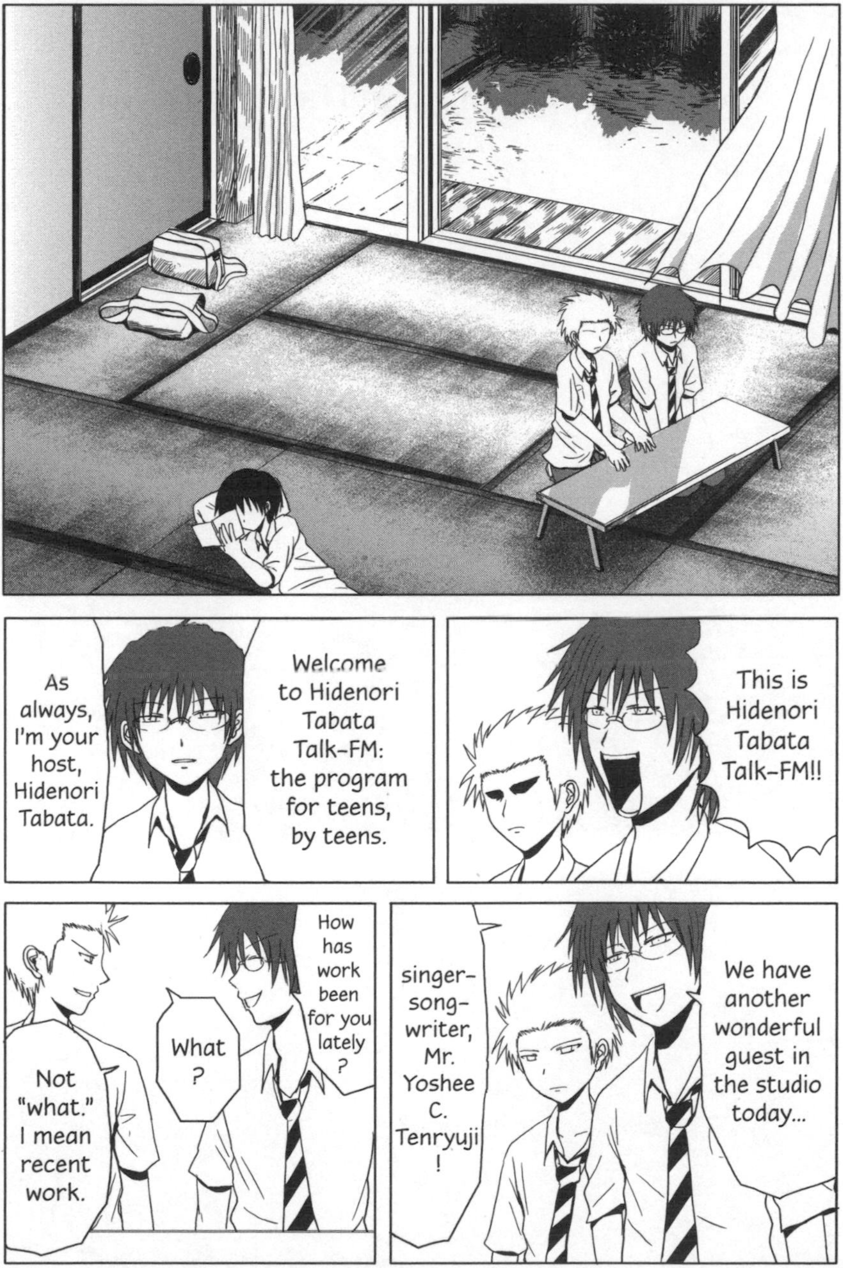
This is Hidenori Tabata Talk-FM!!
Welcome to Hidenori Tabata Talk-FM: the program for teens, by teens.
As always, I'm your host, Hidenori Tabata.
We have another wonderful guest in the studio today...
singer-songwriter, Mr. Yoshee C. Tenryuji!
How has work been for you lately?
What?
Not "what." I mean recent work.

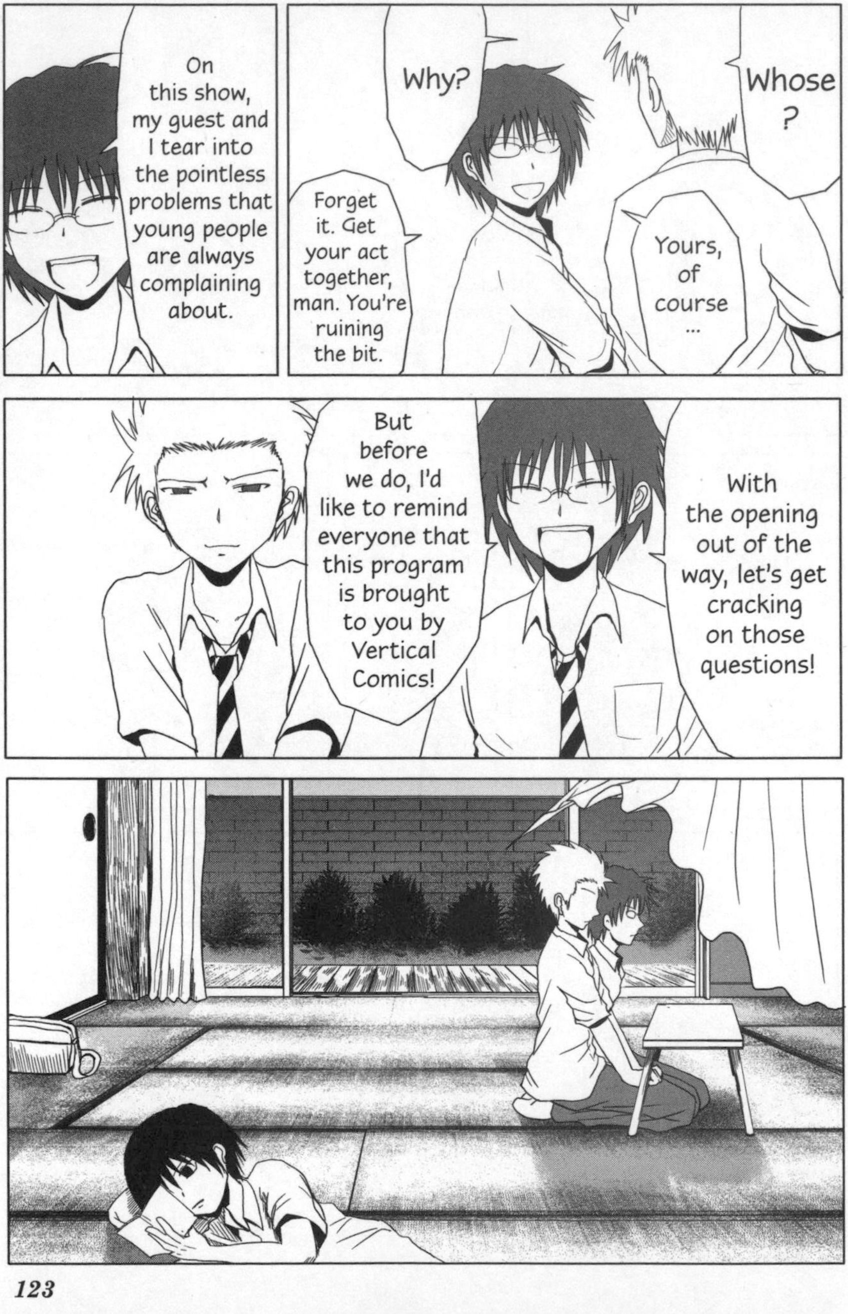
Whose?
Yours, of course...
Why?
Forget it. Get your act together, man. You're ruining the bit.
On this show, my guest and I tear into the pointless problems that young people are always complaining about.
With the opening out of the way, let's get cracking on those questions!
But before we do, I'd like to remind everyone that this program is brought to you by Vertical Comics!

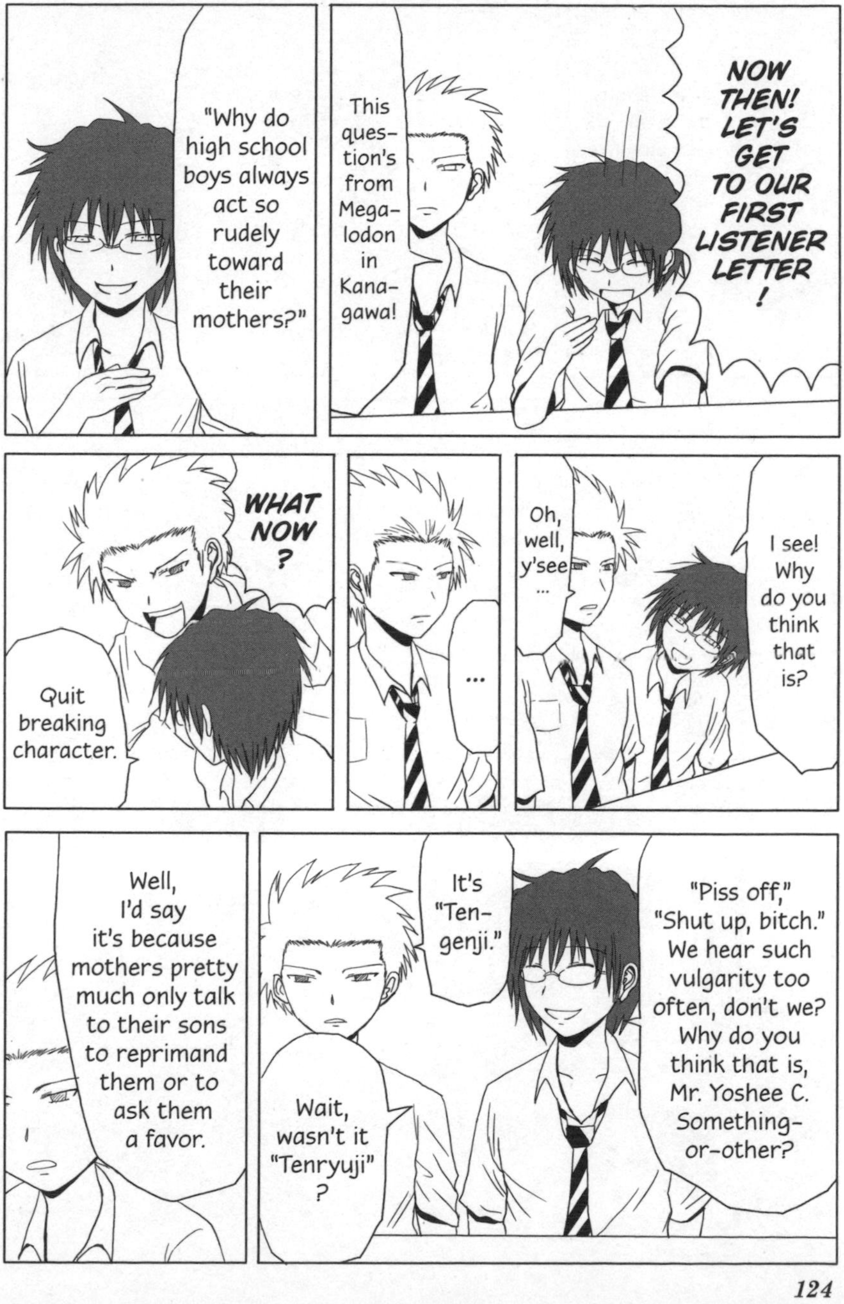
NOW THEN! LET'S GET TO OUR FIRST LISTENER LETTER!
This question's from Megalodon in Kanagawa!
"Why do high school boys always act so rudely toward their mothers?"
I see! Why do you think that is?
Oh, well, y'see ...
...
WHAT NOW?
Quit breaking character.
"Piss off," "Shut up, bitch." We hear such vulgarity too often, don't we? Why do you think that is, Mr. Yoshee C. Something-or-other?
It's "Tengenji."
Wait, wasn't it "Tenryuji"?
Well, I'd say it's because mothers pretty much only talk to their sons to reprimand them or to ask them a favor.

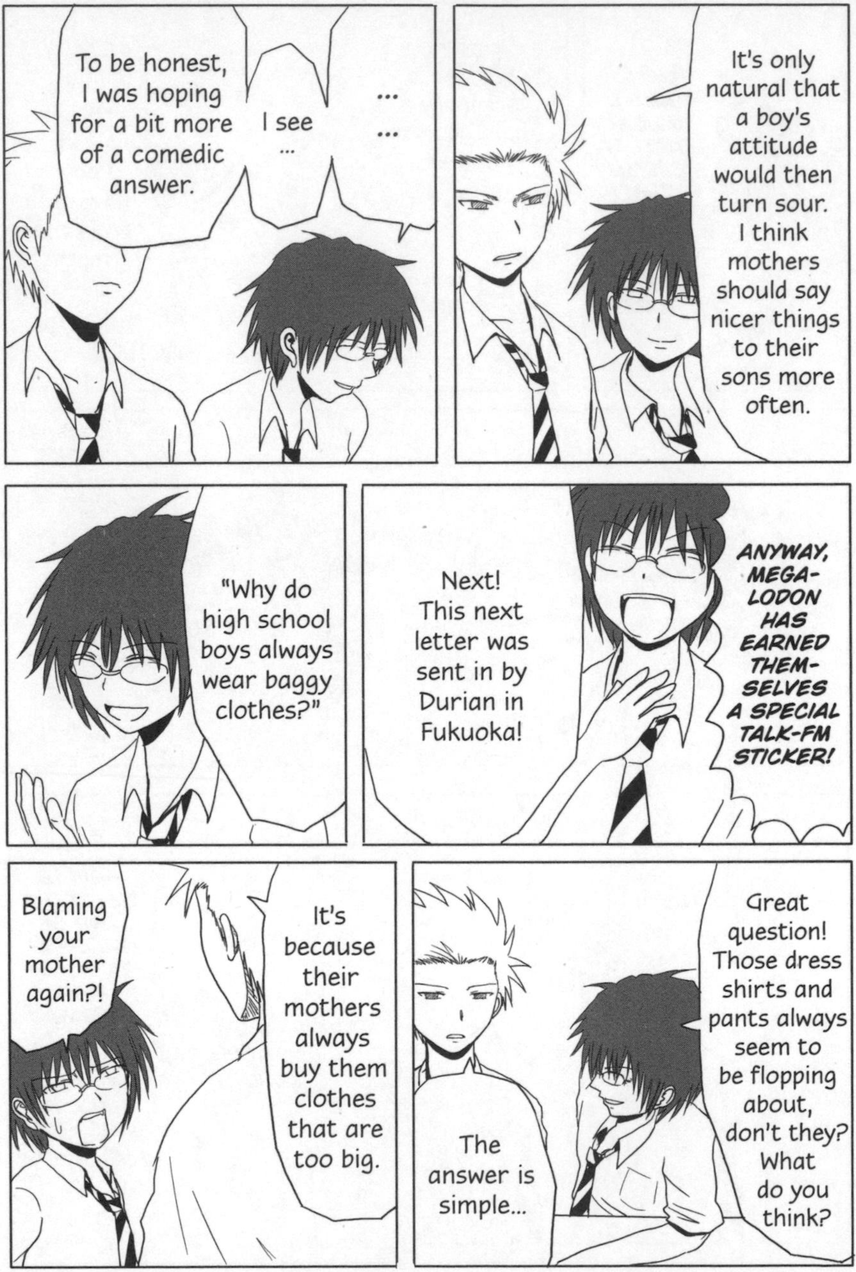
It's only natural that a boy's attitude would then turn sour. I think mothers should say nicer things to their sons more often.
... ...
I see ...
To be honest, I was hoping for a bit more of a comedic answer.
ANYWAY, MEGA-LODON HAS EARNED THEM-SELVES A SPECIAL TALK-FM STICKER!
Next! This next letter was sent in by Durian in Fukuoka!
"Why do high school boys always wear baggy clothes?"
Great question! Those dress shirts and pants always seem to be flopping about, don't they? What do you think?
The answer is simple...
It's because their mothers always buy them clothes that are too big.
Blaming your mother again?!

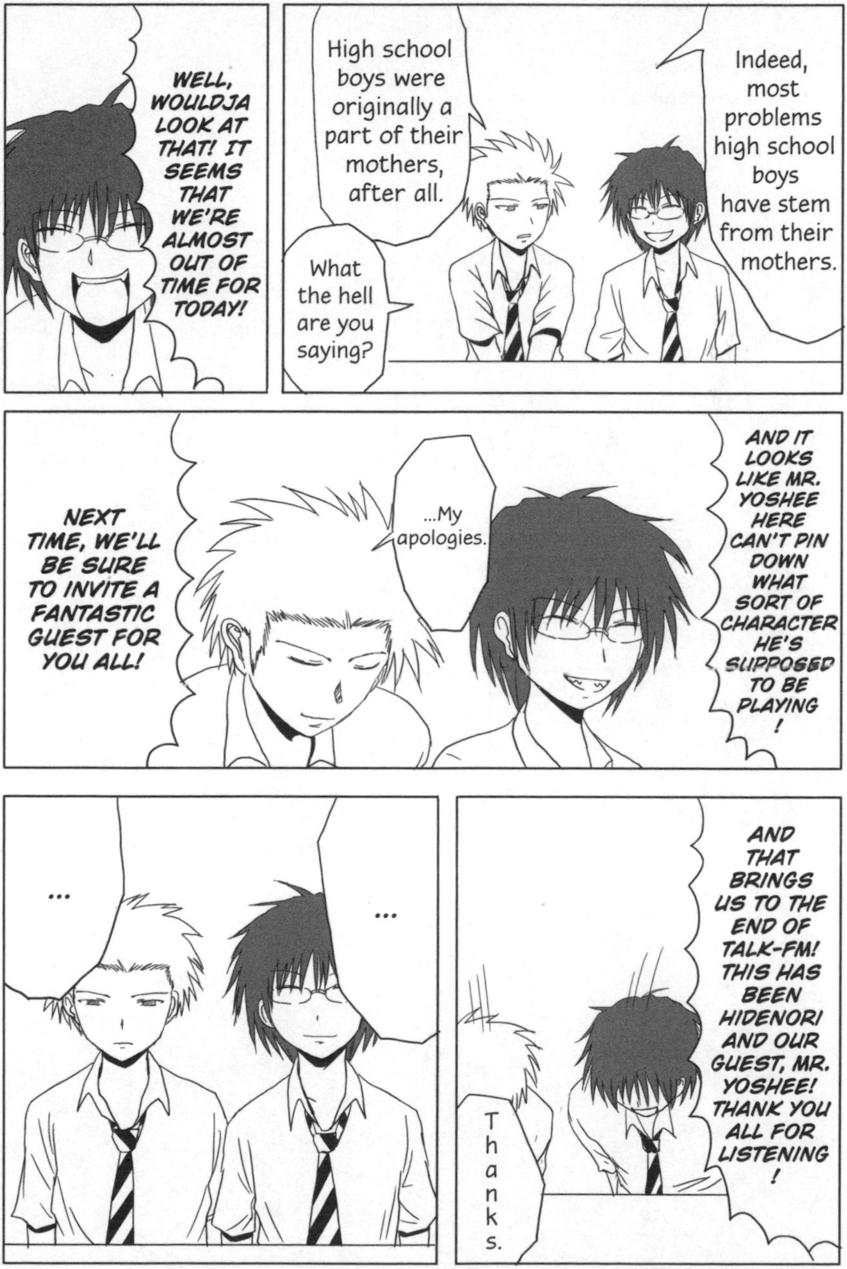
Indeed, most problems high school boys have stem from their mothers.
High school boys were originally a part of their mothers, after all.
What the hell are you saying?
WELL, WOULDJA LOOK AT THAT! IT SEEMS THAT WE'RE ALMOST OUT OF TIME FOR TODAY!
AND IT LOOKS LIKE MR. YOSHEE HERE CAN'T PIN DOWN WHAT SORT OF CHARACTER HE'S SUPPOSED TO BE PLAYING!
...My apologies.
NEXT TIME, WE'LL BE SURE TO INVITE A FANTASTIC GUEST FOR YOU ALL!
AND THAT BRINGS US TO THE END OF TALK-FM! THIS HAS BEEN HIDENORI AND OUR GUEST, MR. YOSHEE! THANK YOU ALL FOR LISTENING!
Thanks.
...
...

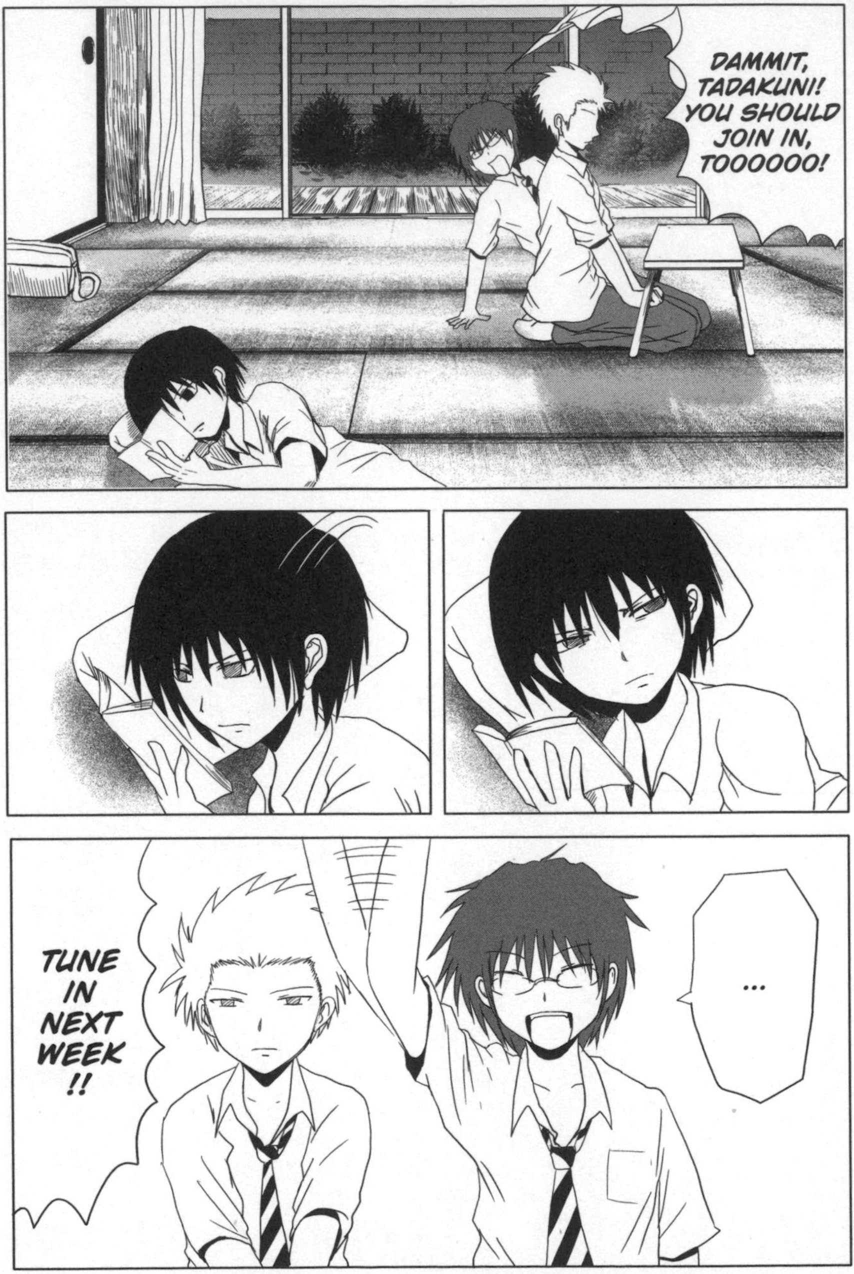
DAMMIT, TADAKUNI! YOU SHOULD JOIN IN, TOOOOOO!
...
TUNE IN NEXT WEEK!!

the

daily

lives

of

1 high school boys

I'm going to make the whole story about him.

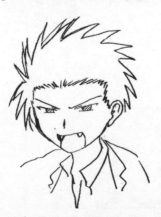

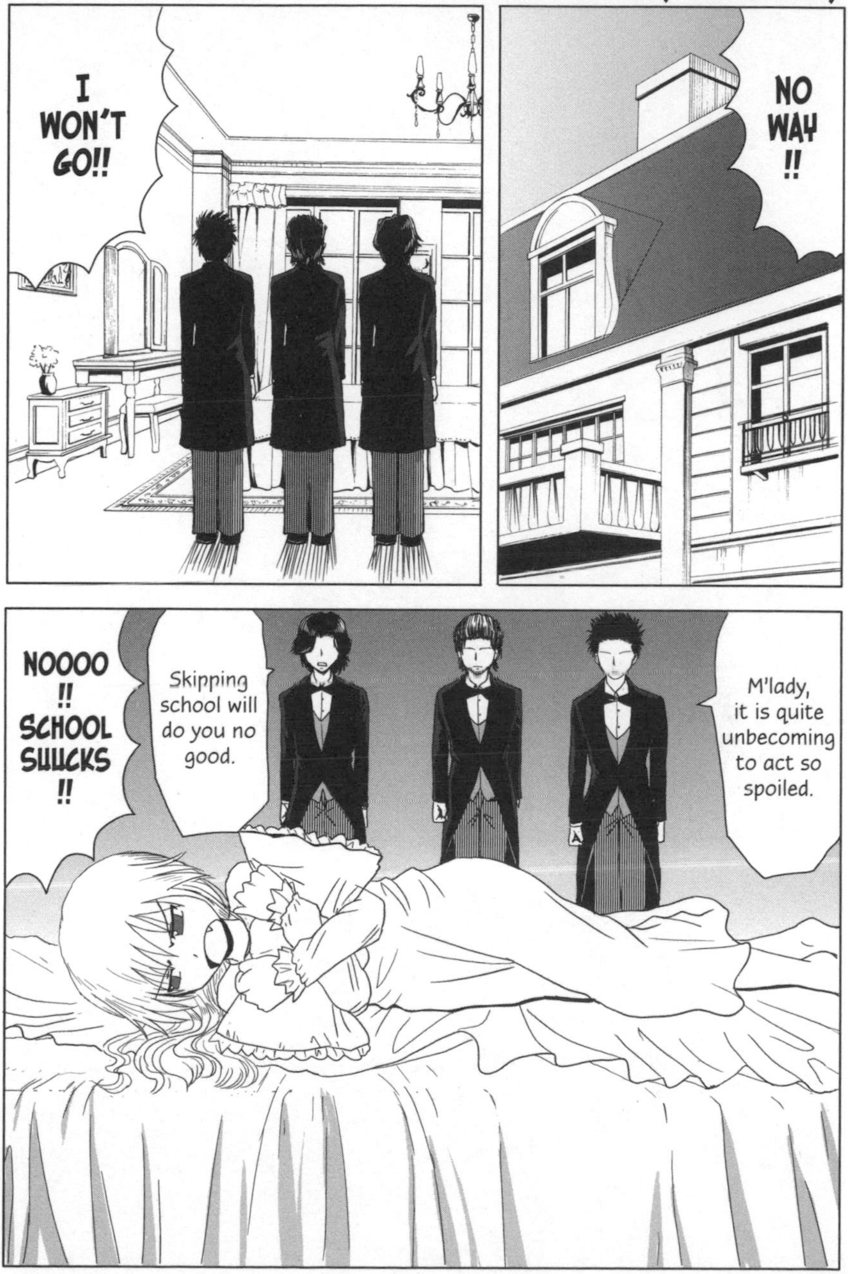
NO WAY !!
I WON'T GO!!
M'lady, it is quite unbecoming to act so spoiled.
Skipping school will do you no good.
NOOOO !! SCHOOL SUUCKS !!

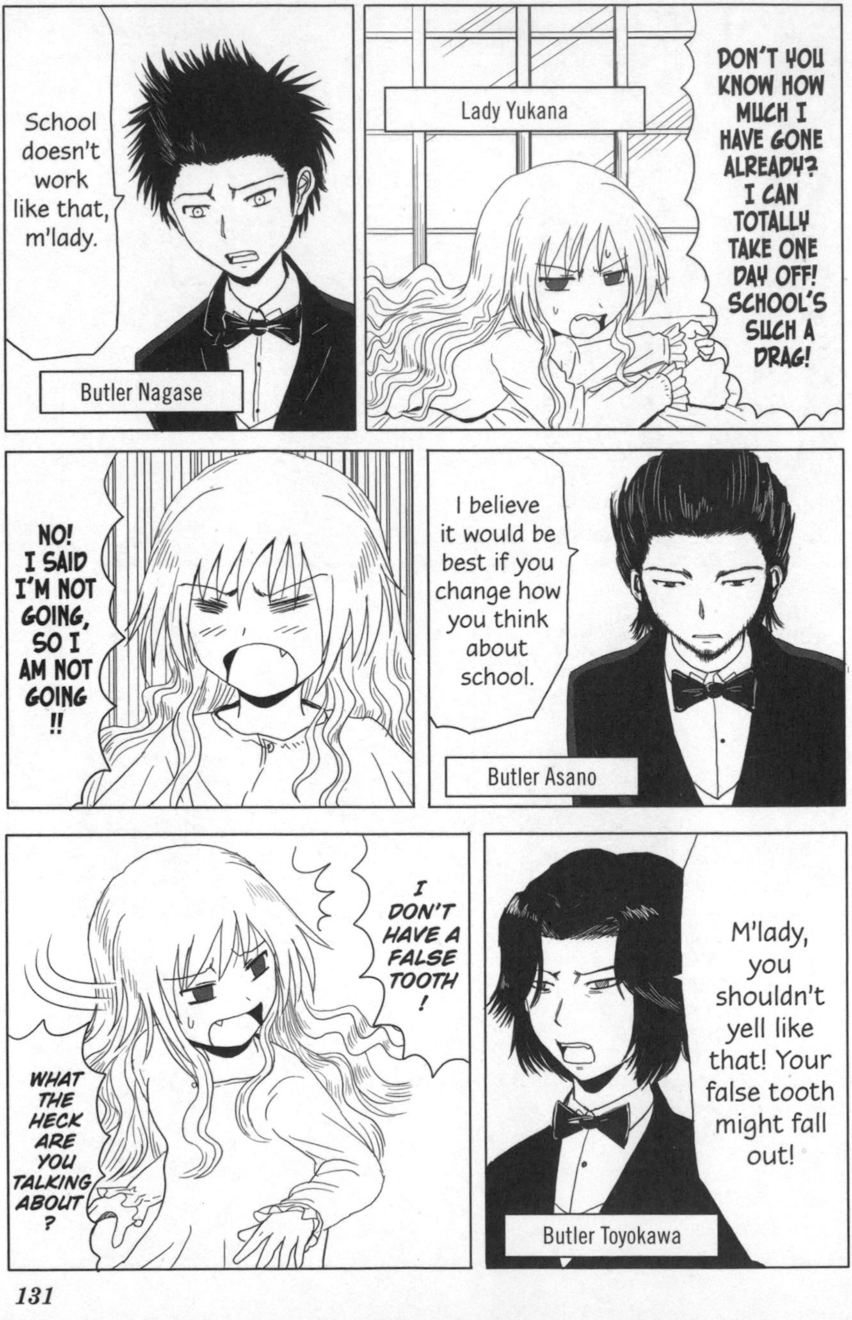
DON'T YOU KNOW HOW MUCH I HAVE GONE ALREADY? I CAN TOTALLY TAKE ONE DAY OFF! SCHOOL'S SUCH A DRAG!
Lady Yukana
School doesn't work like that, m'lady.
Butler Nagase
I believe it would be best if you change how you think about school.
Butler Asano
NO! I SAID I'M NOT GOING, SO I AM NOT GOING !!
M'lady, you shouldn't yell like that! Your false tooth might fall out!
Butler Toyokawa
I DON'T HAVE A FALSE TOOTH !
WHAT THE HECK ARE YOU TALKING ABOUT ?

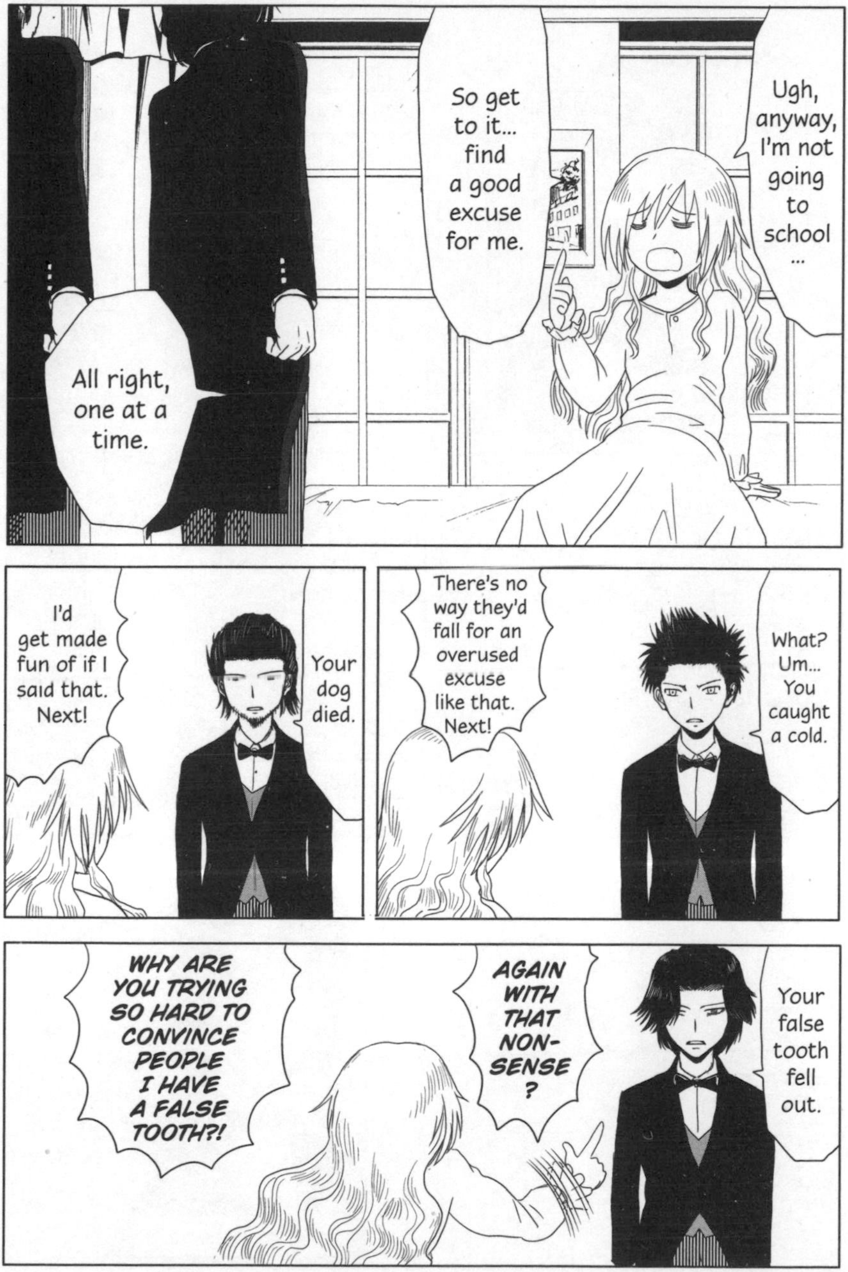
Ugh, anyway, I'm not going to school ...
So get to it... find a good excuse for me.
All right, one at a time.
What? Um... You caught a cold.
There's no way they'd fall for an overused excuse like that. Next!
Your dog died.
I'd get made fun of if I said that. Next!
Your false tooth fell out.
AGAIN WITH THAT NON-SENSE?
WHY ARE YOU TRYING SO HARD TO CONVINCE PEOPLE I HAVE A FALSE TOOTH?!

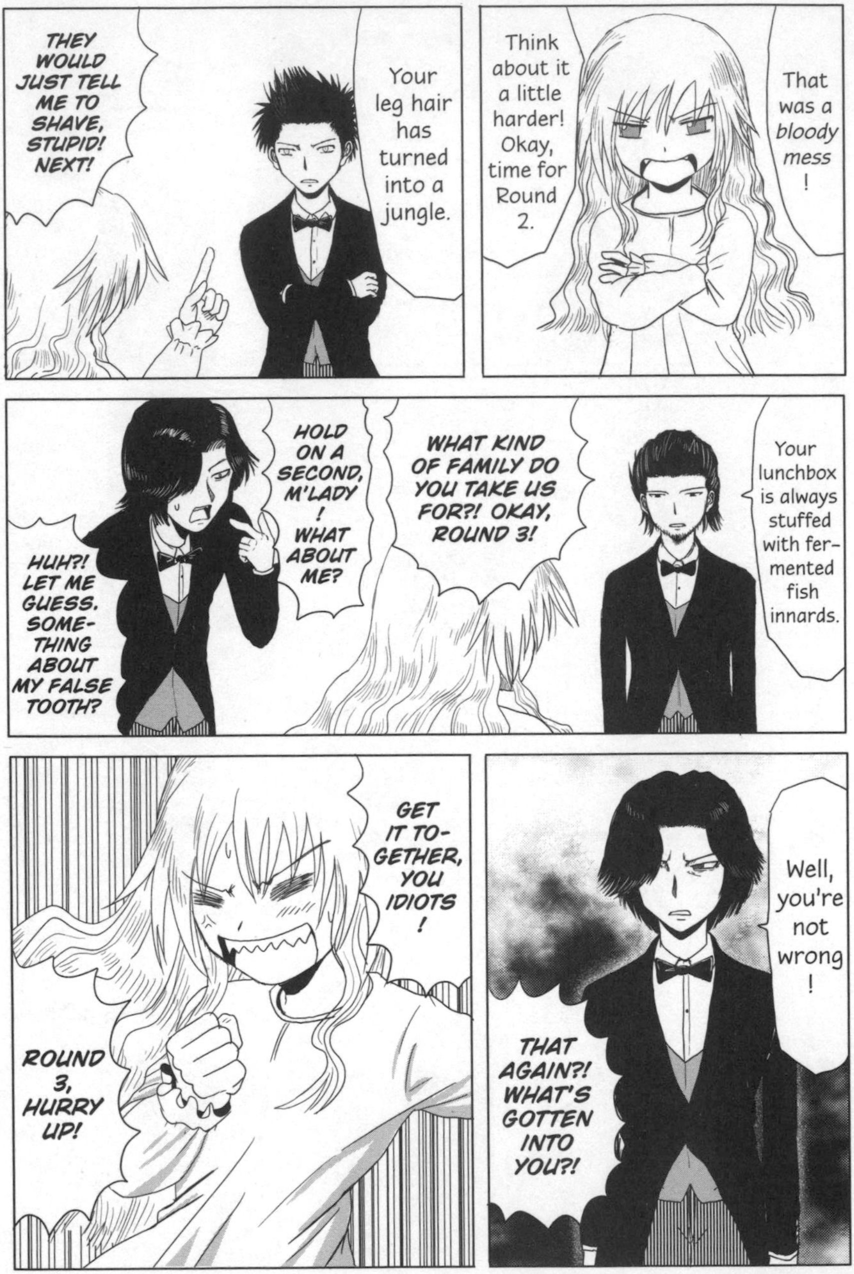
That was a bloody mess!
Think about it a little harder! Okay, time for Round 2.
Your leg hair has turned into a jungle.
THEY WOULD JUST TELL ME TO SHAVE, STUPID! NEXT!
Your lunchbox is always stuffed with fermented fish innards.
WHAT KIND OF FAMILY DO YOU TAKE US FOR?! OKAY, ROUND 3!
HOLD ON A SECOND, M'LADY! WHAT ABOUT ME?
HUH?! LET ME GUESS. SOMETHING ABOUT MY FALSE TOOTH?
Well, you're not wrong!
THAT AGAIN?! WHAT'S GOTTEN INTO YOU?!
GET IT TOGETHER, YOU IDIOTS!
ROUND 3, HURRY UP!

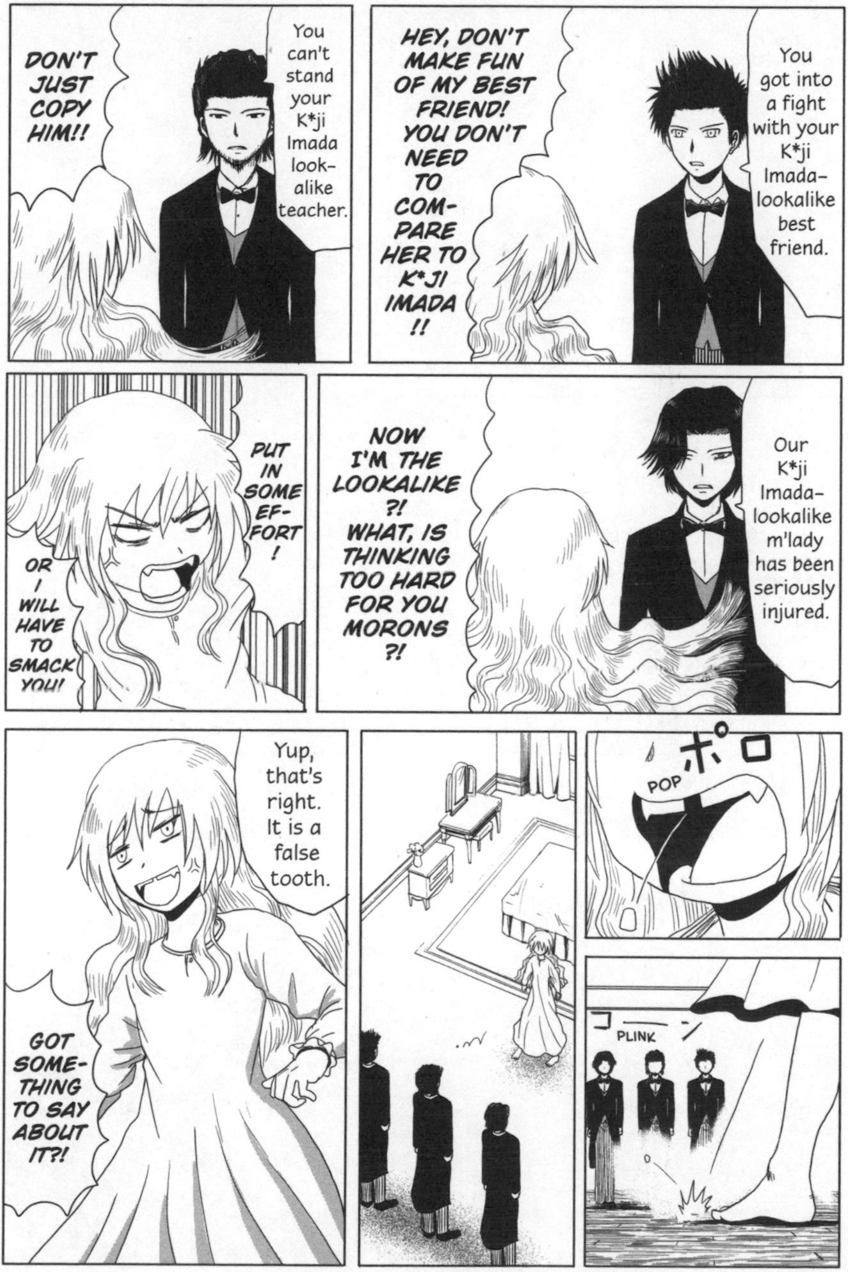
You got into a fight with your K*ji Imada-lookalike best friend.
HEY, DON'T MAKE FUN OF MY BEST FRIEND! YOU DON'T NEED TO COM-PARE HER TO K*JI IMADA!!
You can't stand your K*ji Imada look-alike teacher.
DON'T JUST COPY HIM!!
Our K*ji Imada-lookalike m'lady has been seriously injured.
NOW I'M THE LOOKALIKE?! WHAT, IS THINKING TOO HARD FOR YOU MORONS?!
PUT IN SOME EF-FORT!
OR I WILL HAVE TO SMACK YOU!
ポロ
POP
コーン
PLINK
Yup, that's right. It is a false tooth.
GOT SOME-THING TO SAY ABOUT IT?!

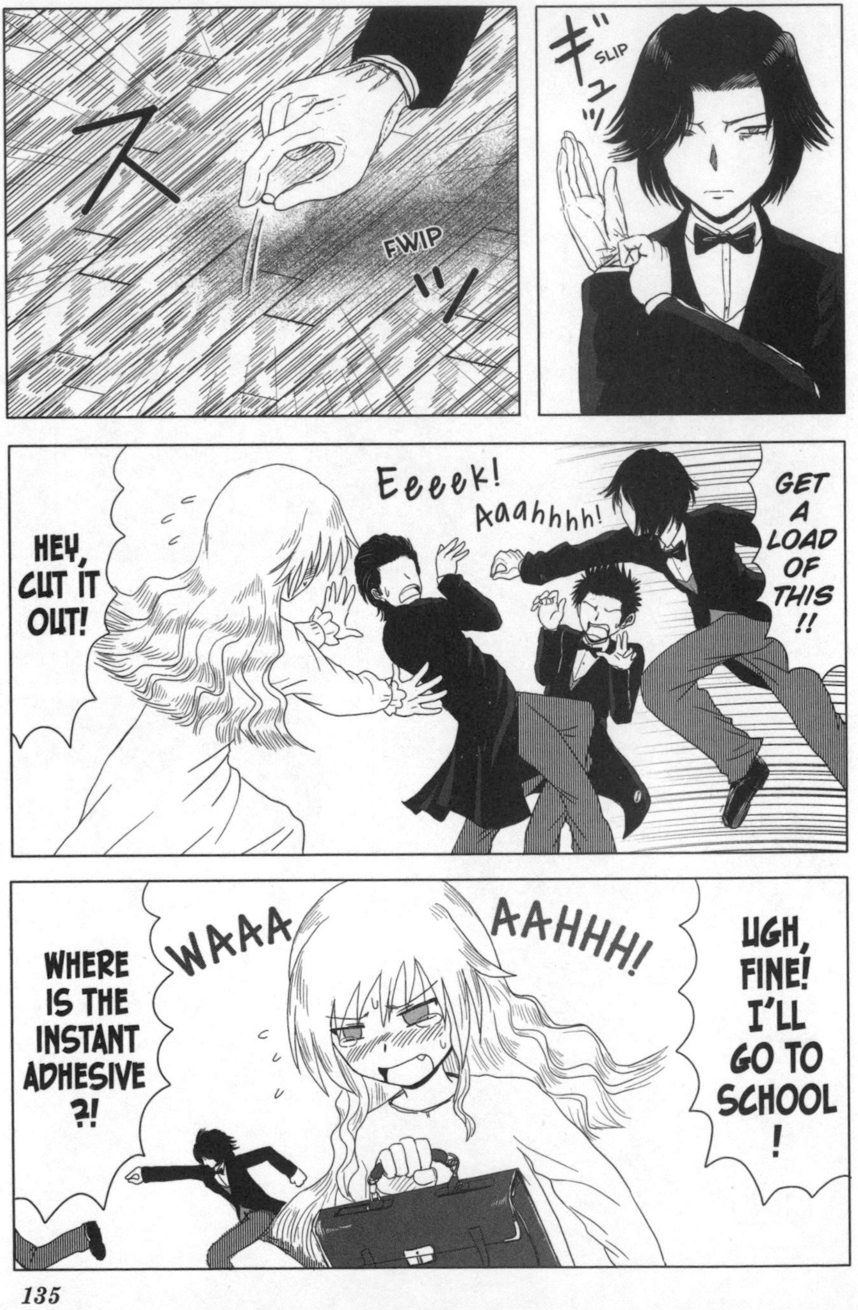

ギュッ
SLIP
ス
FWIP
ッ
GET A LOAD OF THIS!!
Eeeek!
Aaahhhh!
HEY, CUT IT OUT!
UGH, FINE! I'LL GO TO SCHOOL!
WAAAAHHHH!
WHERE IS THE INSTANT ADHESIVE?!

special one-shot: ***high school girls are bizarre***

Main Characters:

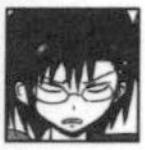

Yanagin

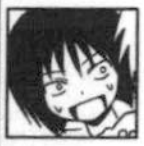

Habara

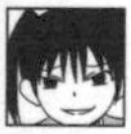

Ikushima

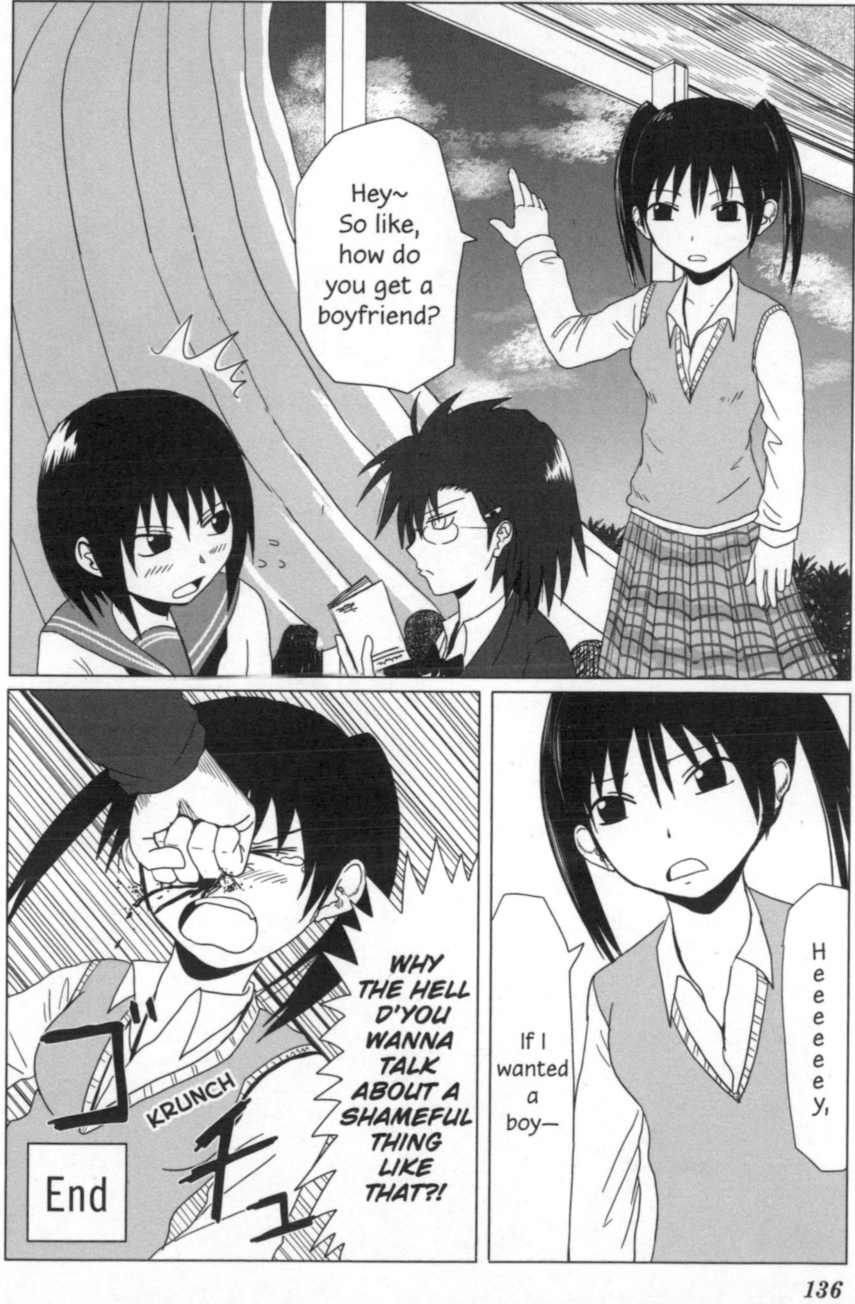
Hey~ So like, how do you get a boyfriend?
Heeeeeeey,
If I wanted a boy—
WHY THE HELL D'YOU WANNA TALK ABOUT A SHAMEFUL THING LIKE THAT?!
KRUNCH
ゴッチュ
End

chapter 2: uniforms

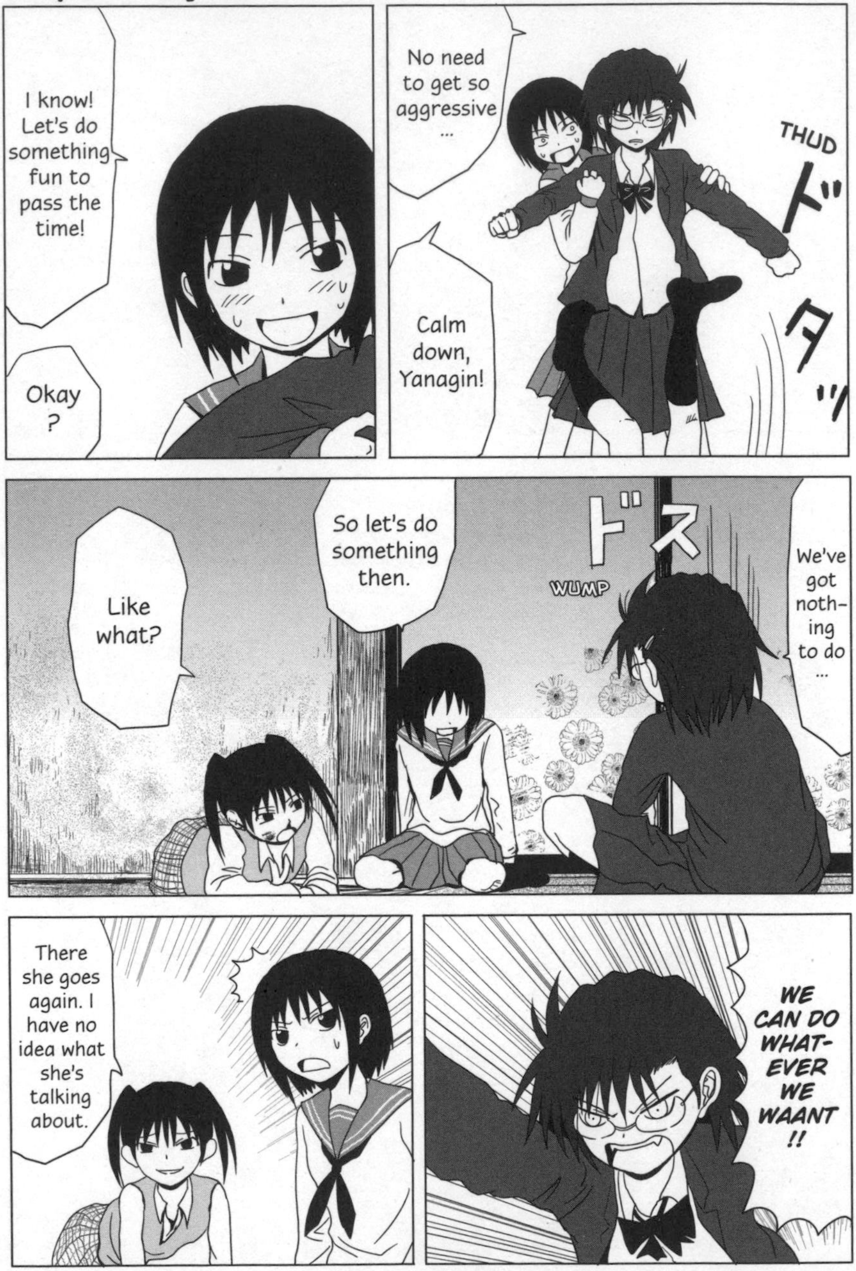

No need to get so aggressive ...
THUD
ドタッ
Calm down, Yanagin!
I know! Let's do something fun to pass the time!
Okay ?
We've got noth-ing to do ...
ドス
WUMP
So let's do something then.
Like what?
WE CAN DO WHAT-EVER WE WAANT !!
There she goes again. I have no idea what she's talking about.

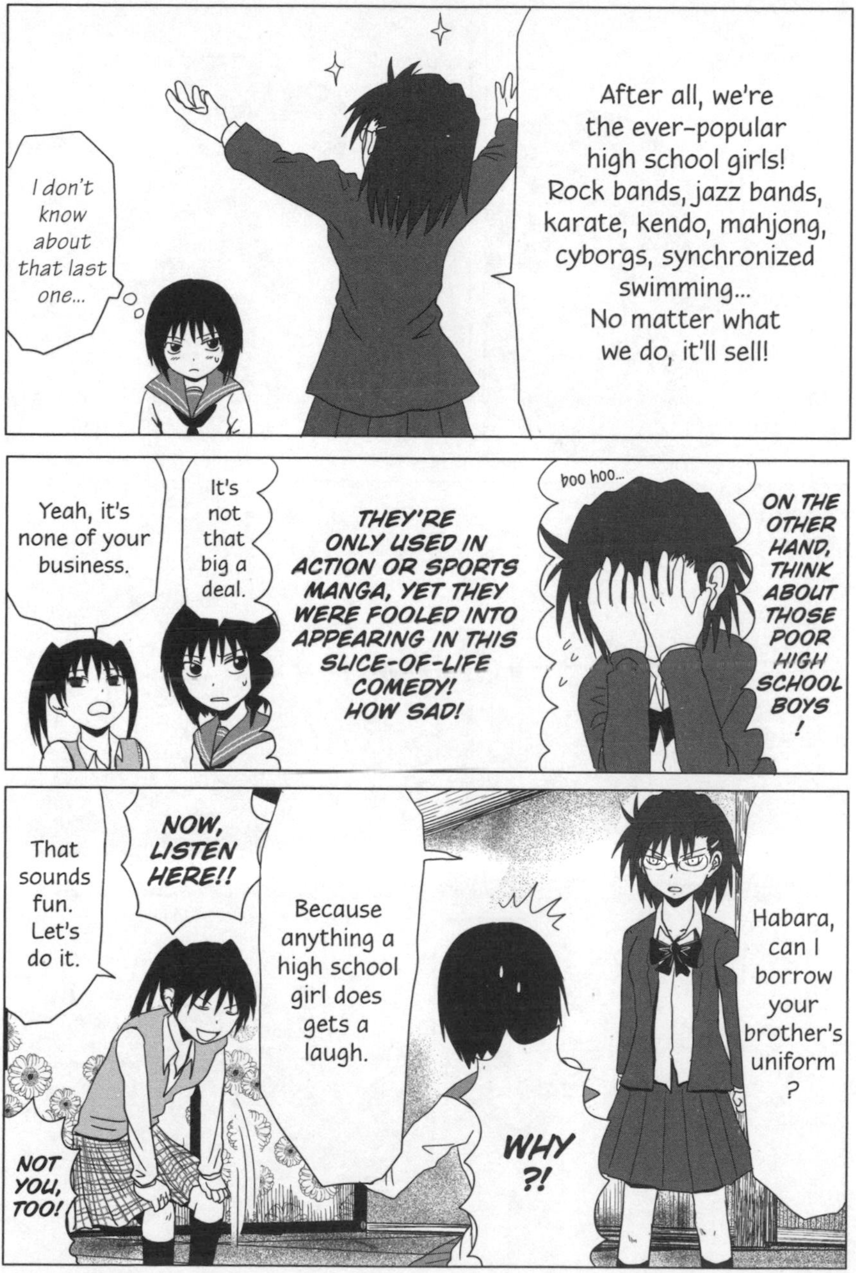
After all, we're the ever-popular high school girls! Rock bands, jazz bands, karate, kendo, mahjong, cyborgs, synchronized swimming... No matter what we do, it'll sell!
I don't know about that last one...
ON THE OTHER HAND, THINK ABOUT THOSE POOR HIGH SCHOOL BOYS!
boo hoo...
THEY'RE ONLY USED IN ACTION OR SPORTS MANGA, YET THEY WERE FOOLED INTO APPEARING IN THIS SLICE-OF-LIFE COMEDY! HOW SAD!
It's not that big a deal.
Yeah, it's none of your business.
Habara, can I borrow your brother's uniform?
WHY?!
Because anything a high school girl does gets a laugh.
NOW, LISTEN HERE!!
That sounds fun. Let's do it.
NOT YOU, TOO!

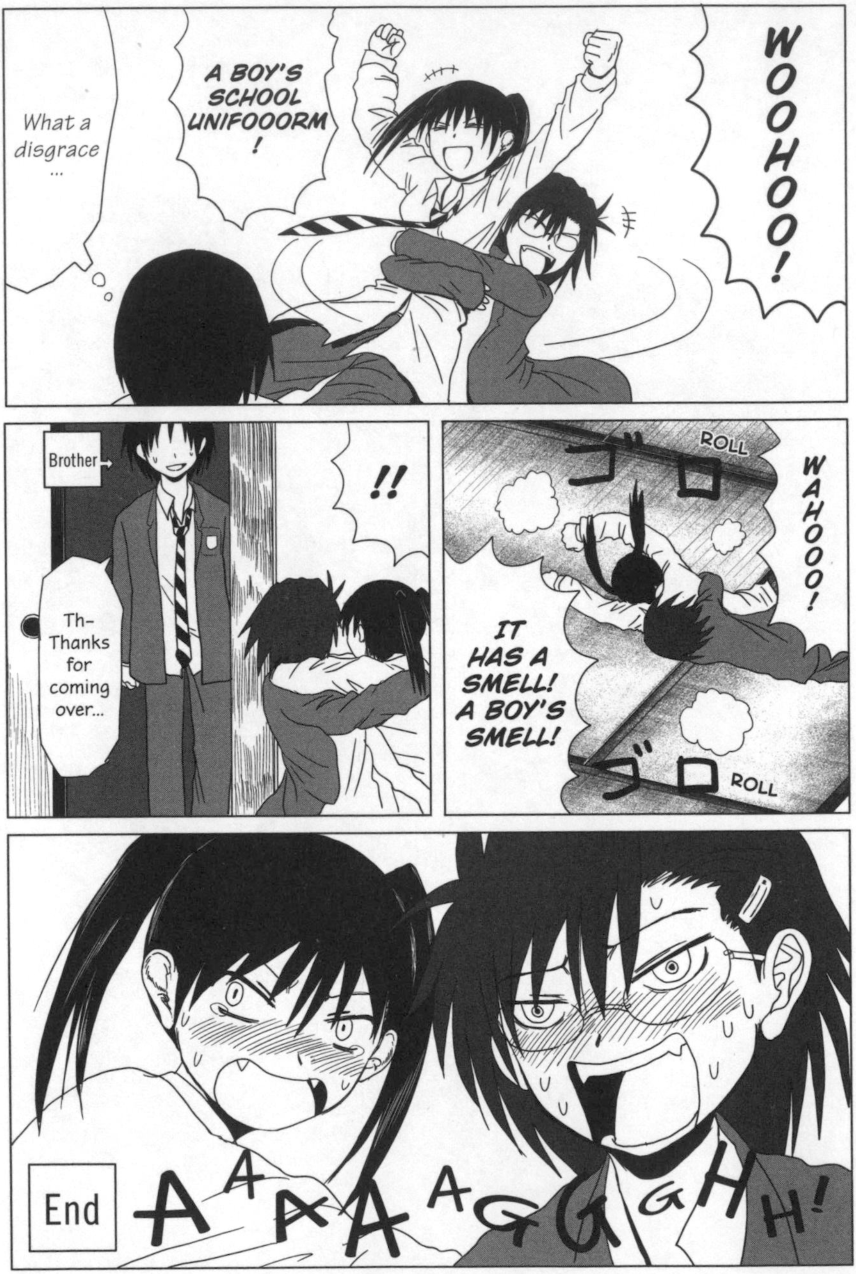

WOOHOOO!
A BOY'S SCHOOL UNIFOOORM!
What a disgrace ...
ゴロ
ROLL
WAHOOOO!
IT HAS A SMELL! A BOY'S SMELL!
ゴロ
ROLL
!!
Brother
Th- Thanks for coming over...
AAAAAGGGHH!
End

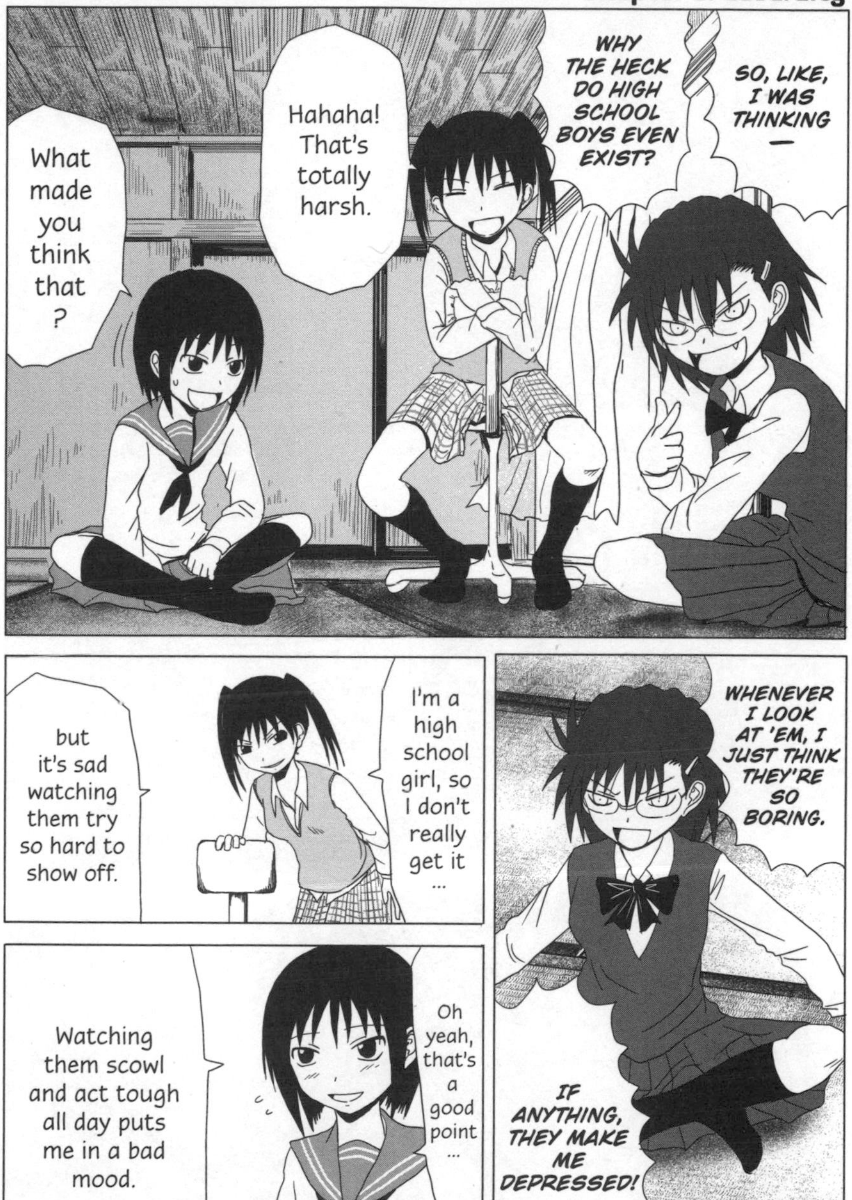
SO, LIKE, I WAS THINKING —
WHY THE HECK DO HIGH SCHOOL BOYS EVEN EXIST?
Hahaha! That's totally harsh.
What made you think that?
WHENEVER I LOOK AT 'EM, I JUST THINK THEY'RE SO BORING.
IF ANYTHING, THEY MAKE ME DEPRESSED!
I'm a high school girl, so I don't really get it ...
but it's sad watching them try so hard to show off.
Oh yeah, that's a good point ...
Watching them scowl and act tough all day puts me in a bad mood.

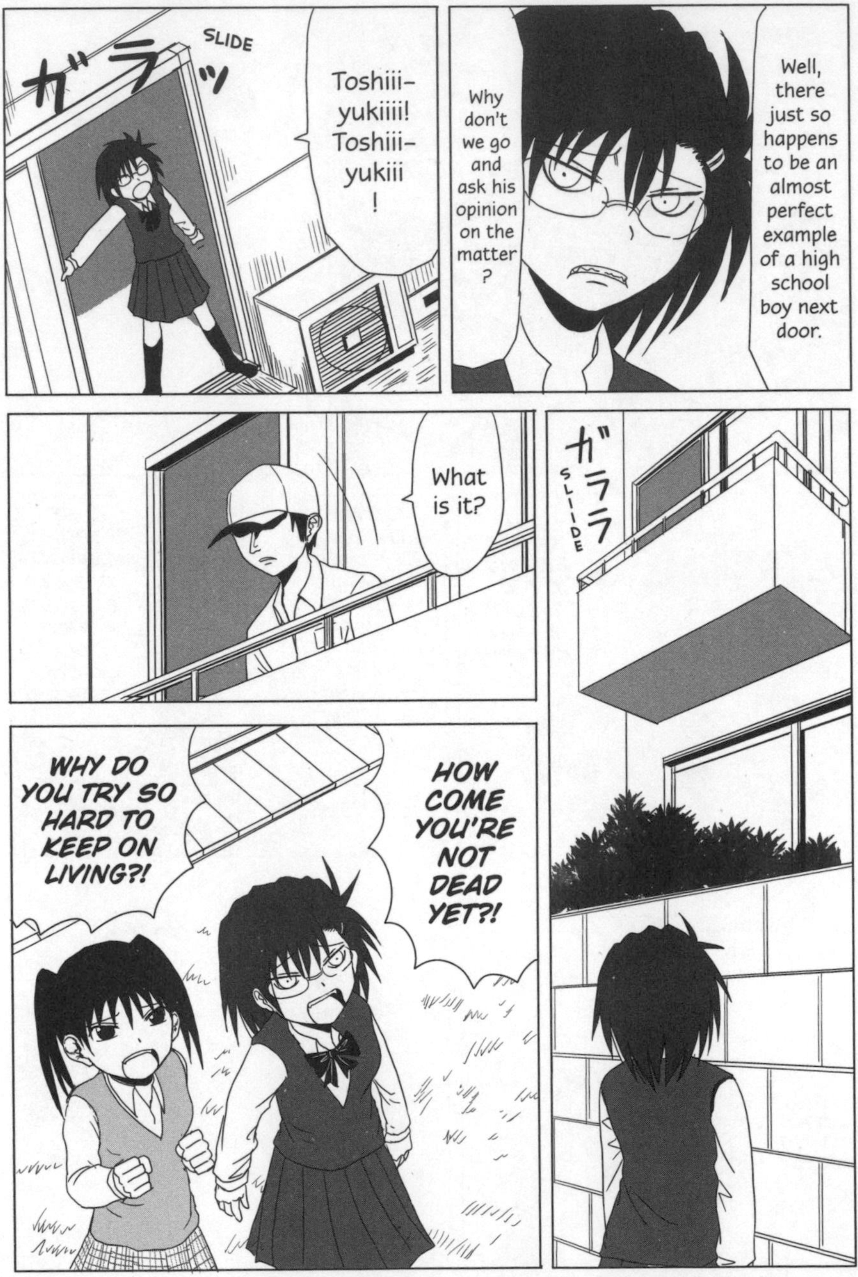
Well, there just so happens to be an almost perfect example of a high school boy next door.
Why don't we go and ask his opinion on the matter?
ガラッ
SLIDE
Toshiii-yukiiii! Toshiii-yukiii!
ガララ
SLIIDE
What is it?
HOW COME YOU'RE NOT DEAD YET?!
WHY DO YOU TRY SO HARD TO KEEP ON LIVING?!

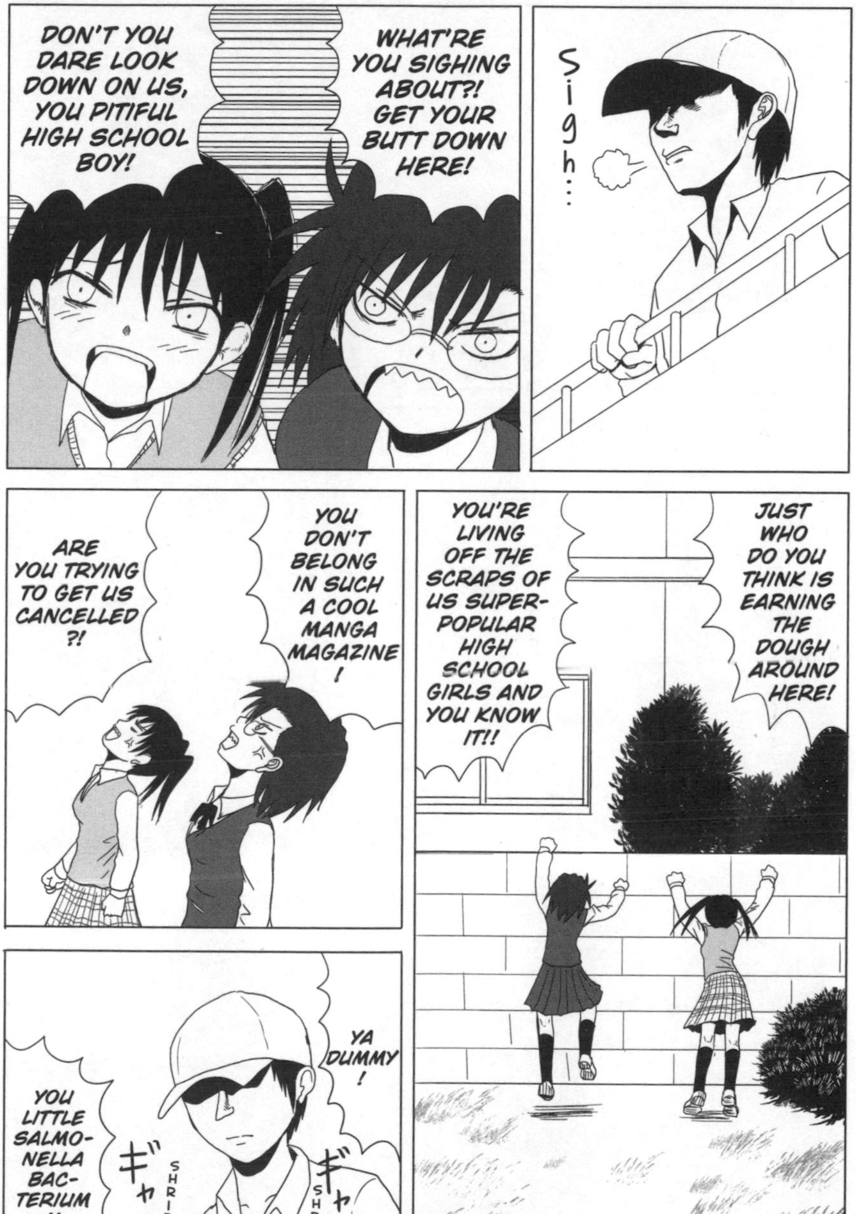
Sigh...
WHAT'RE YOU SIGHING ABOUT?! GET YOUR BUTT DOWN HERE!
DON'T YOU DARE LOOK DOWN ON US, YOU PITIFUL HIGH SCHOOL BOY!
JUST WHO DO YOU THINK IS EARNING THE DOUGH AROUND HERE!
YOU'RE LIVING OFF THE SCRAPS OF US SUPER-POPULAR HIGH SCHOOL GIRLS AND YOU KNOW IT!!
YOU DON'T BELONG IN SUCH A COOL MANGA MAGAZINE!
ARE YOU TRYING TO GET US CANCELLED?!
YA DUMMY!
ギャー
SHRIEK
ギャー
SHRIEK
YOU LITTLE SALMONELLA BACTERIUM!!

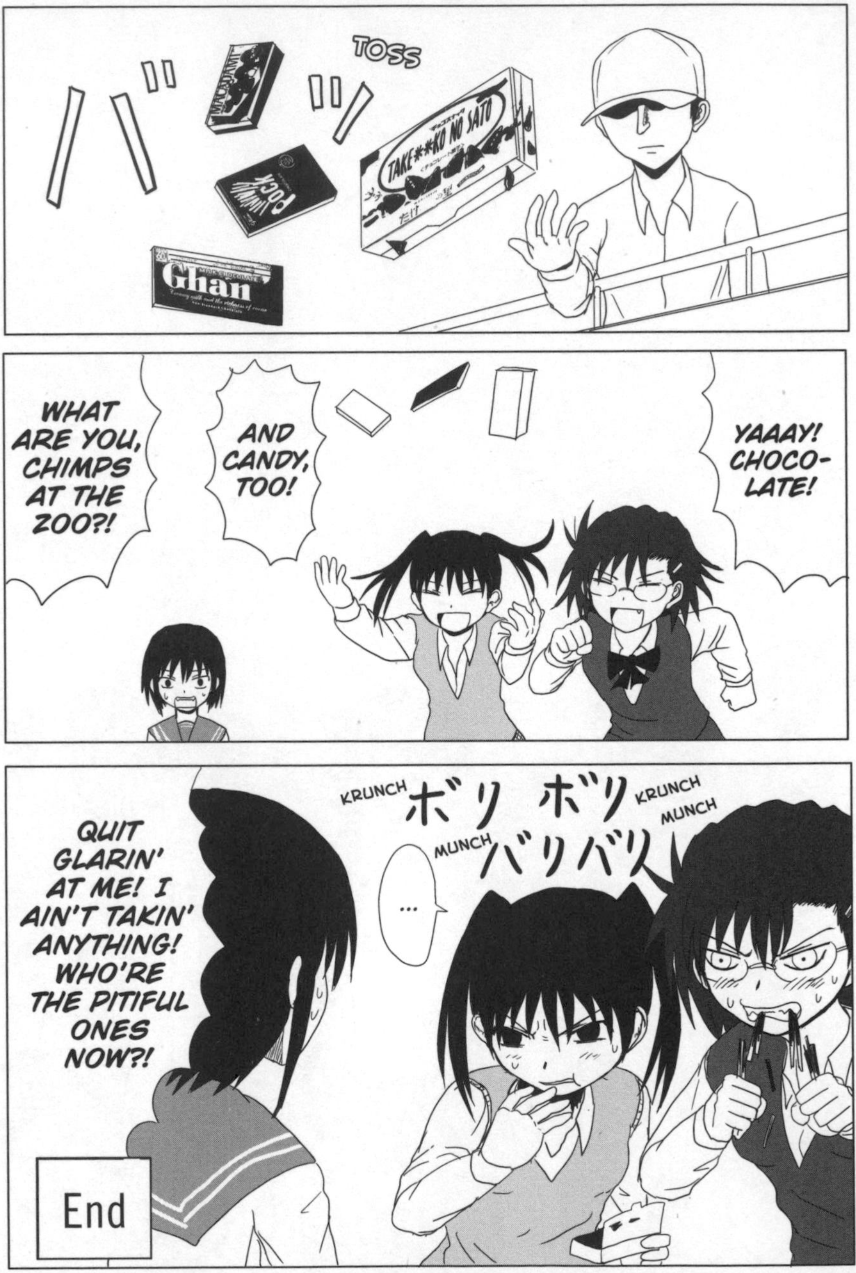

TOSS
バッ
TAKE**KO NO SATO
POCK
Ghan
MILK CHOCOLATE
YAAAY! CHOCOLATE!
AND CANDY, TOO!
WHAT ARE YOU, CHIMPS AT THE ZOO?!
KRUNCH ボリ ボリ KRUNCH
MUNCH バリバリ MUNCH
...
QUIT GLARIN' AT ME! I AIN'T TAKIN' ANYTHING! WHO'RE THE PITIFUL ONES NOW?!
End

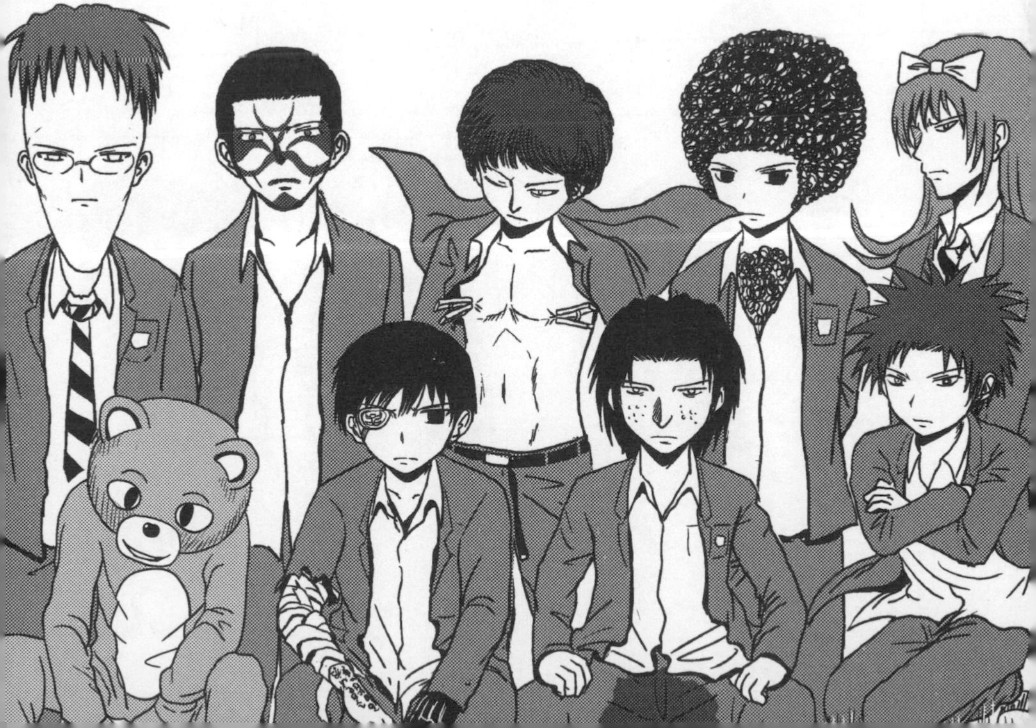

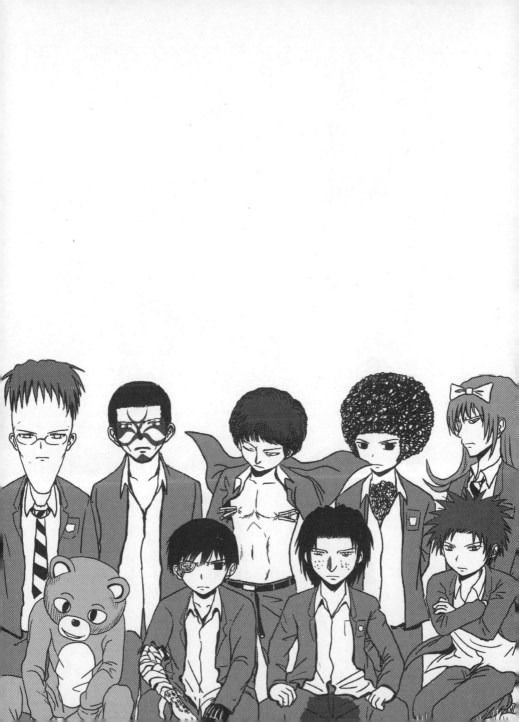

the daily lives of high school boys 1

yasunobu yamauchi

Sanada North High School
2-A Group Photo

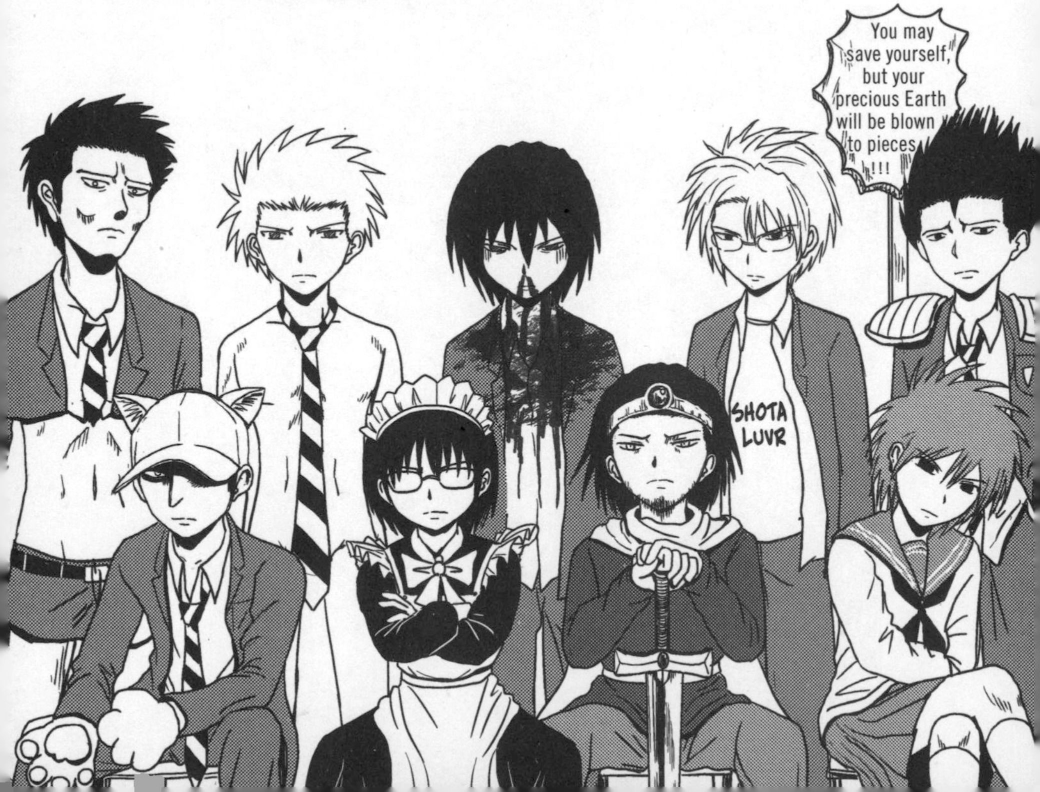
You may save yourself, but your precious Earth will be blown to pieces!!!
SHOTA LUVR

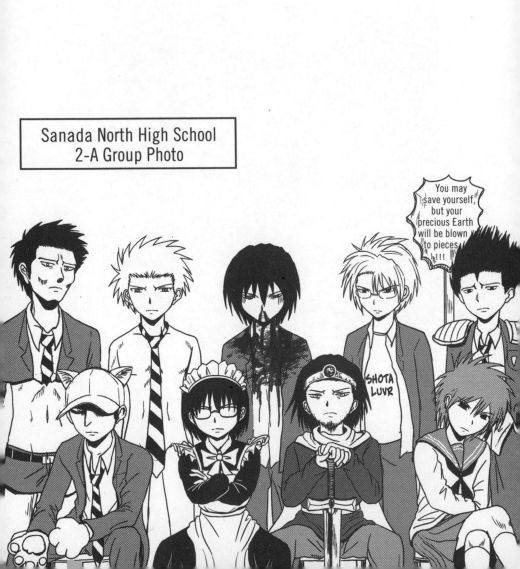

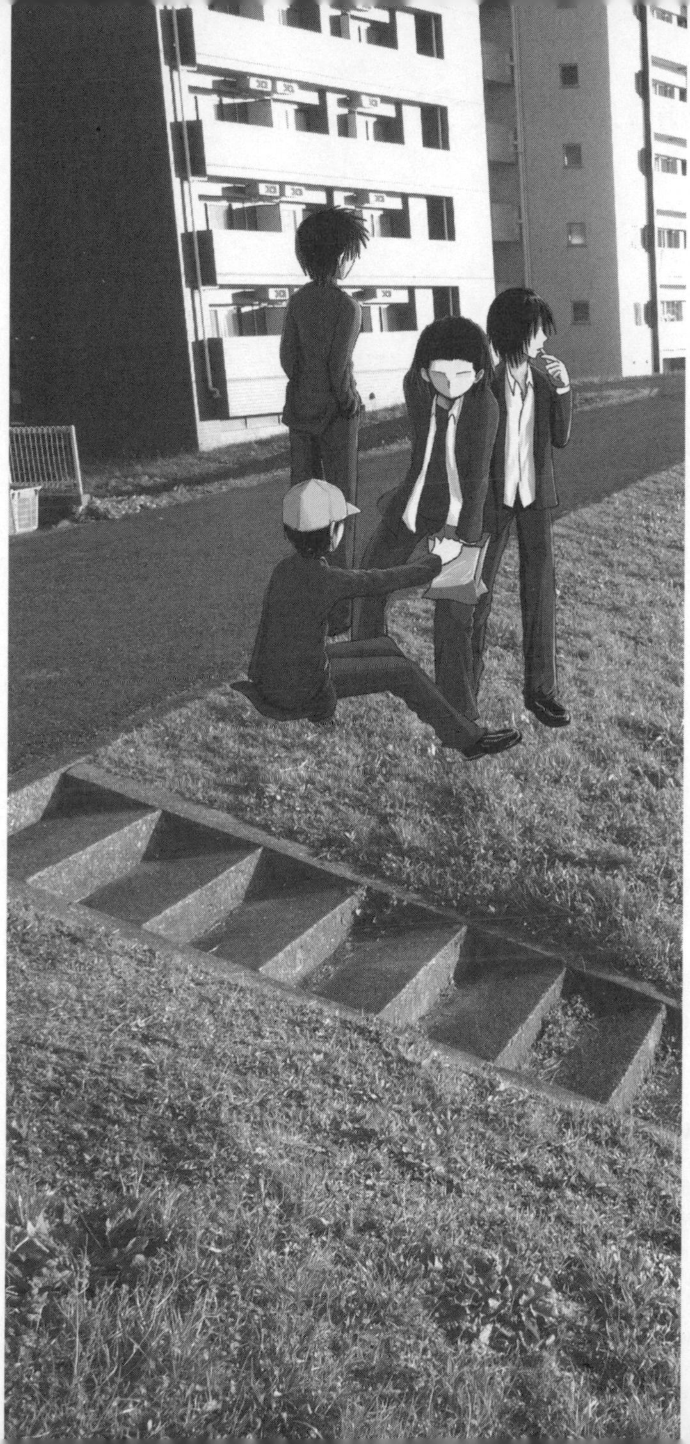

yasunobu
yamauchi

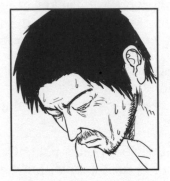

This is the first
time my manga has
been published.

I'd like to dedicate
this to all the fans
who've supported
this manga, to my
editor for putting
up with me, and
to the friends who
helped me come up
with material for
this series.

From the creator of *nichijou*, this surreal-slapstick series revolves around a penniless college student, Midori Nagumo, who lives in an ordinary city filled with not-quite-ordinary people. And as this reckless girl runs about, she sets the city in motion.

Midori is in a bit of a bind. She is in debt, and her landlady is trying to shake her down for unpaid rent. Her best friend refuses to loan her cash since she's wised up to her tricks.

Maybe some bullying would help. Or a bit of petty theft? Neither is sustainable. Maybe getting a job would settle things... But working means less time for fun adventures in the big city...

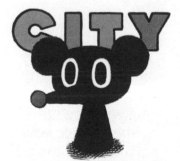

Volumes 1-8
Available Now!

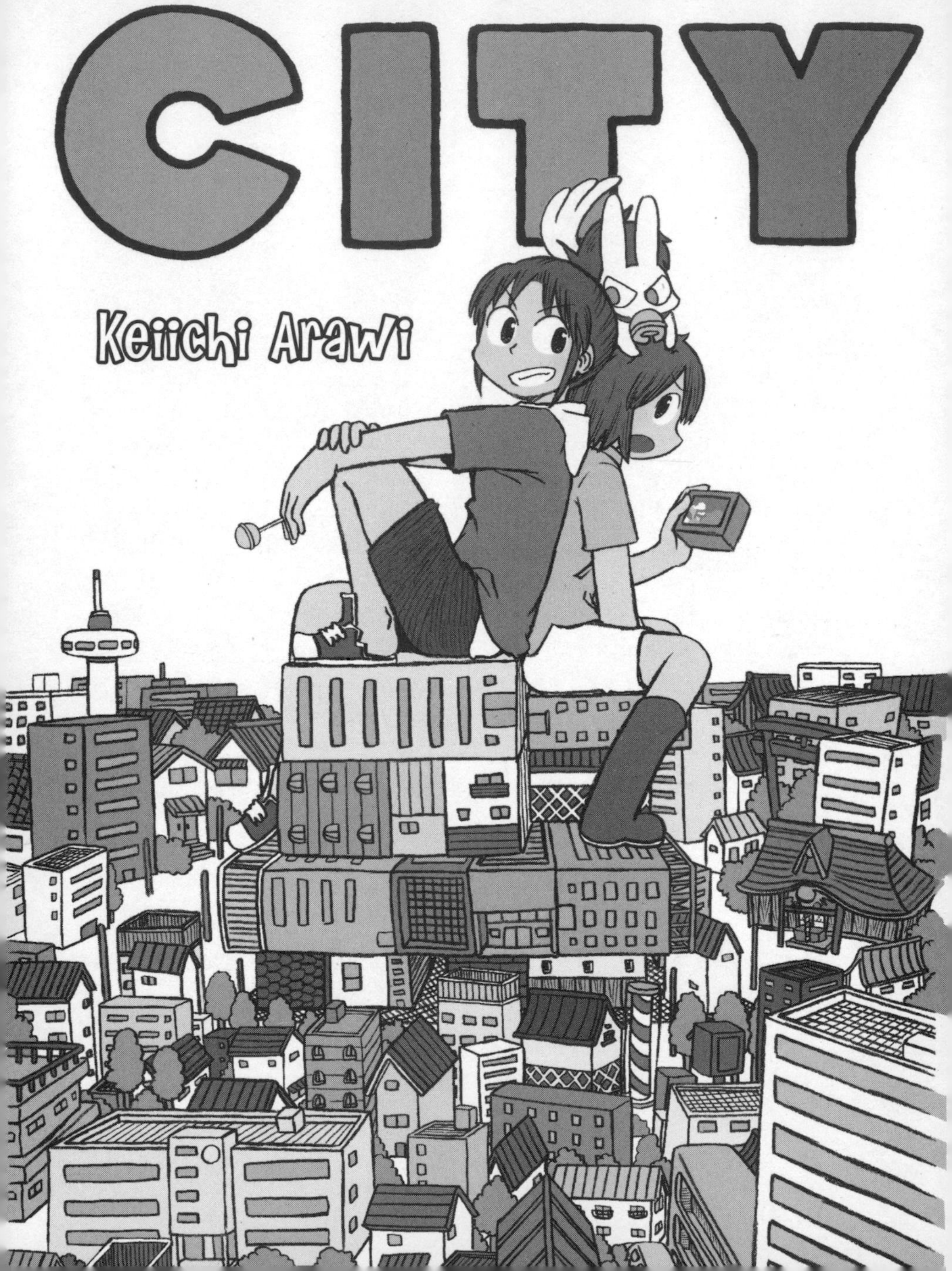
CITY
Keiichi Arawi

The Delinquent Housewife!
by Nemu Yoko

Tohru Komukai and his bride-to-be, Komugi, move in with his family just until they find a place of their own. Or, that was the plan, until Tohru suddenly leaves for a long-term business trip overseas, leaving Komugi to fend for herself on her in-laws' turf. While Komugi is pretty, considerate and appears to be an ideal housewife, the truth is she doesn't know how to do a lick of housework, and can't cook at all. Also, she has a secret past as a member of an all-girls *bosozoku* biker gang! The only member of the family to learn these secrets is Dai, Tohru's younger brother, and he helps Komugi keep up appearances until she can learn how to hold her own as a domestic goddess...

ALL VOLUMES AVAILABLE NOW!

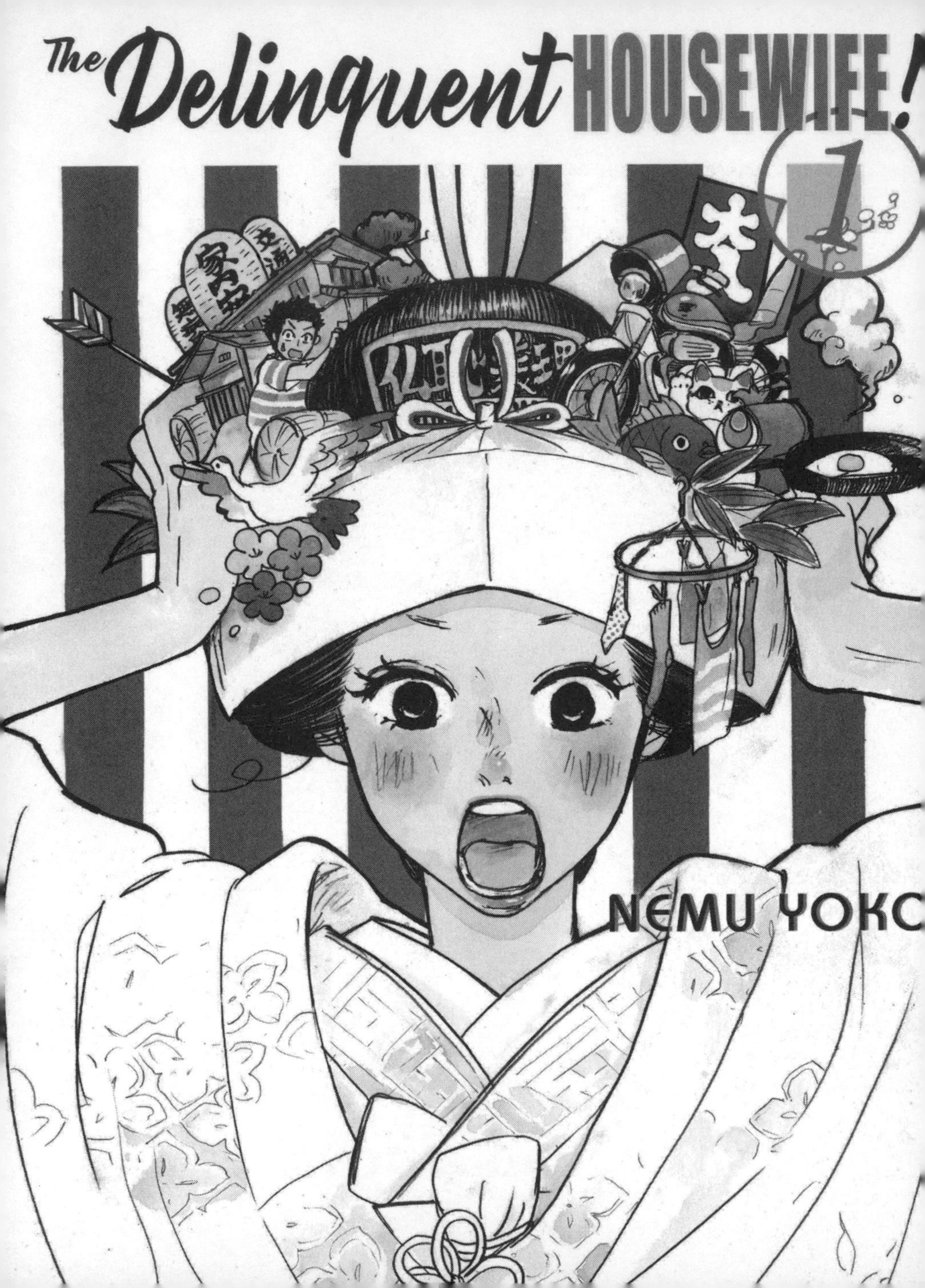
The Delinquent HOUSEWIFE!
1
NEMU YOKO

define "ordinary"

in this just-surreal-enough take on the "school genre" of manga, a group of friends (which includes a robot built by a child professor) grapples with all sorts of unexpected situations in their daily lives as high schoolers.

the gags, jokes, puns and random haiku keep this series off-kilter even as the characters grow and change. check out this new take on a storied genre and meet the new ordinary.

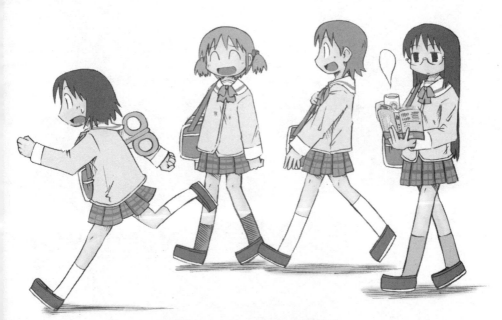

all volumes
available now!

nichijou

my ordinary life

keiichi
arawi

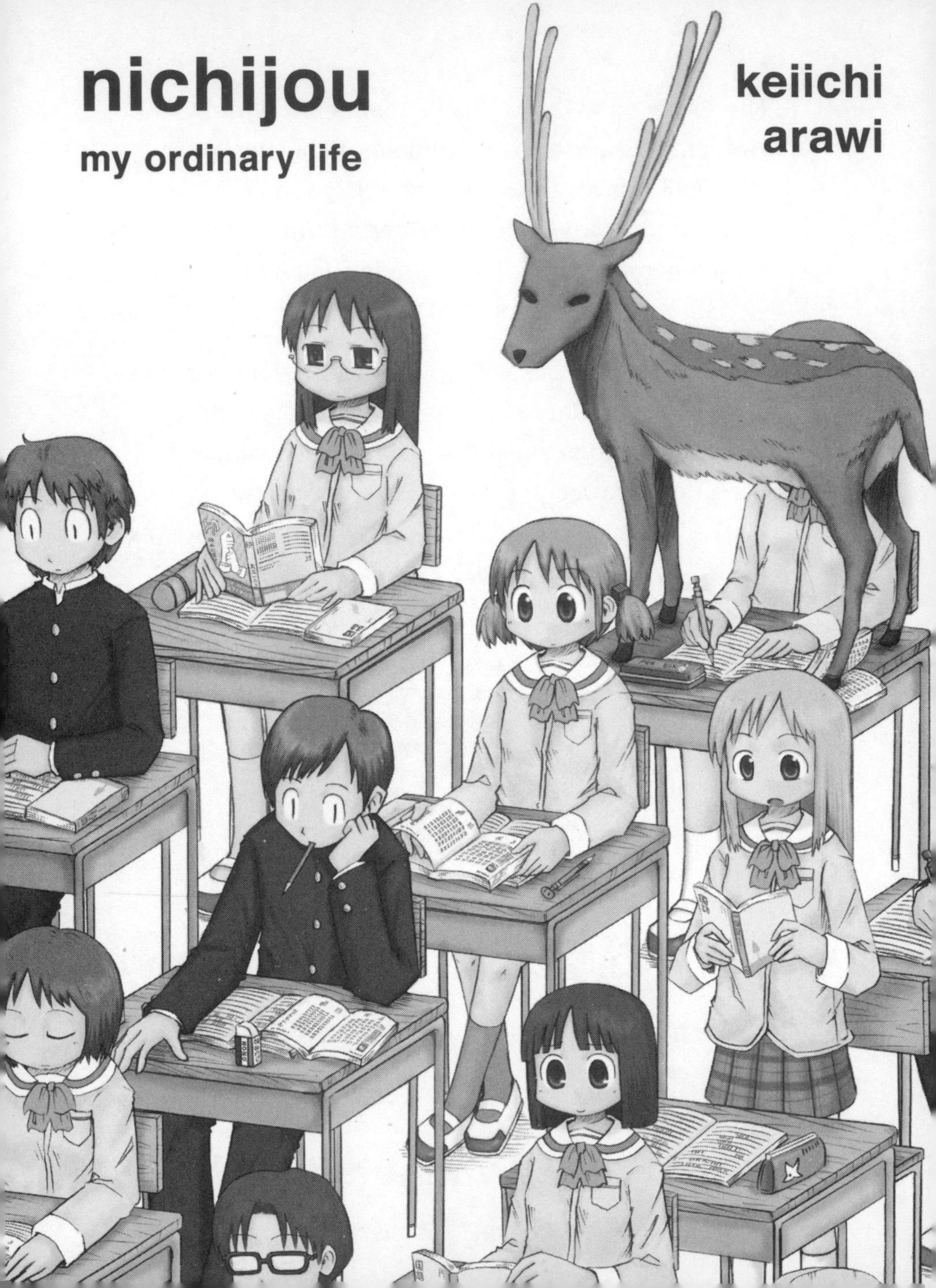

The follow up to the hit manga series *nichijou*, **Helvetica Standard** is a full-color anthology of Keiichi Arawi's comic art and design work. Funny and heartwarming, **Helvetica Standard** is a humorous look at modern day Japanese design in comic form.

Helvetica Standard is a deep dive into the artistic and creative world of Keiichi Arawi. Part comic, part diary, part art and design book, **Helvetica Standard** is a deconstruction of the world of *nichijou*.

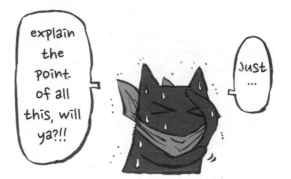

Helvetica Standard BOLD

Helvetica Standard ITALIC

Both Parts Available Now!

keiichi
Arawi

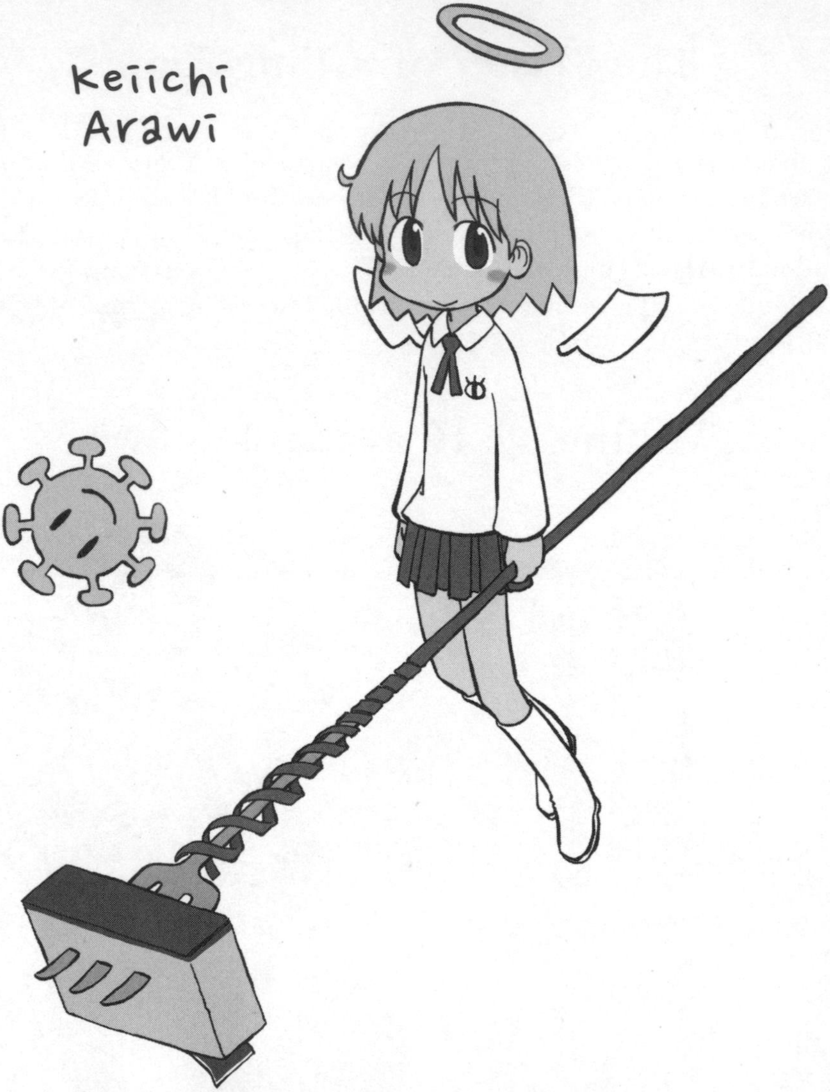

Helvetica Standard

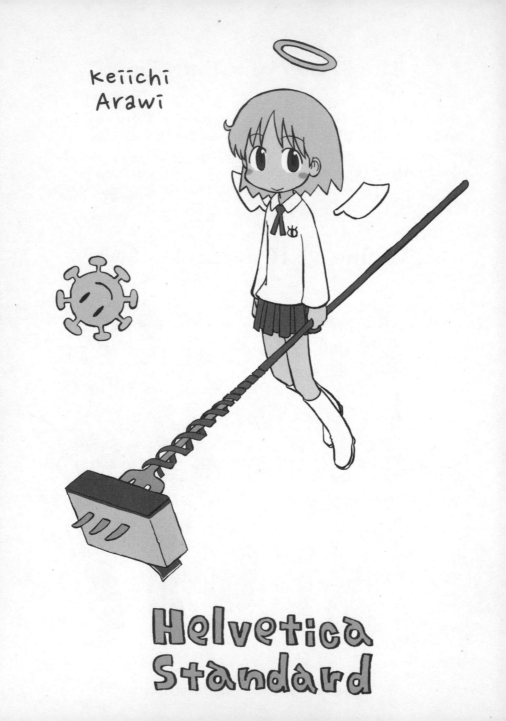

The Master of Killing Time

Toshinari Seki takes goofing off to new heights. Every day, on or around his school desk, he masterfully creates his own little worlds of wonder, often hidden to most of his classmates. Unfortunately for Rumi Yokoi, his neighbor at the back of the room, his many games, dioramas, and projects are often way too interesting to ignore; even when they are hurting her grades.

Volumes 1-10 available now!

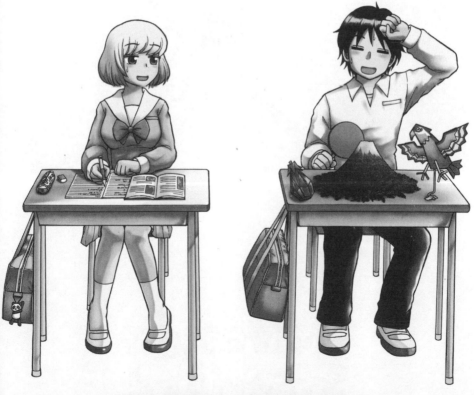

My Neighbor Seki

Tonari no Seki-kun

Takuma Morishige

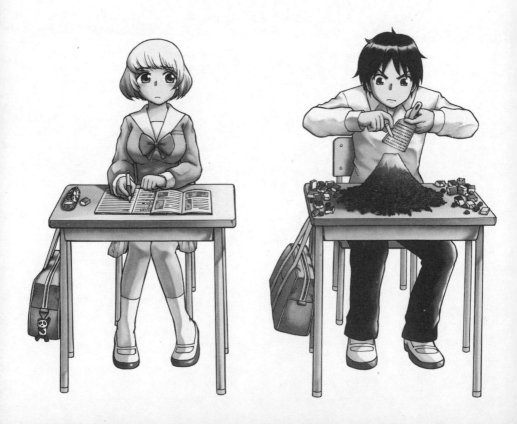

OWN THE *&#@
MANGA THAT
INSPIRED
THE ANIME!

Get volumes
1 and 2 NOW!

© bkub OKAWA / Takeshobo Co. Ltd.

POP TEAM EPIC

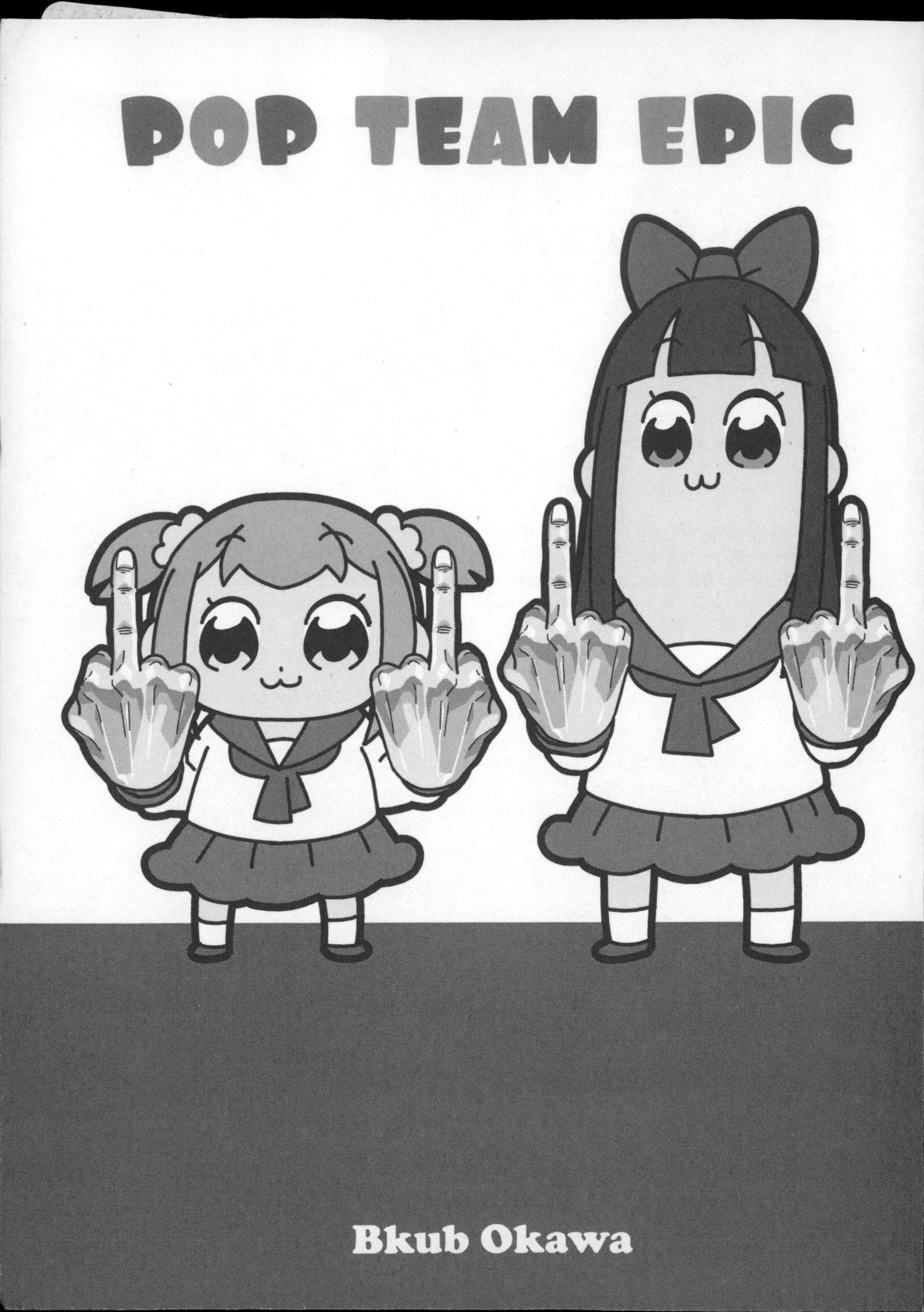

Bkub Okawa

THE DAILY LIVES OF HIGH SCHOOL BOYS 1

Yasunobu Yamauchi

A Vertical Comics Edition

Editor: Kristi Fernandez
Translation: David Musto
Production: Grace Lu
        Anthony Quintessenza

© 2010 Yasunobu Yamauchi / SQUARE ENIX CO., LTD.
First published in Japan in 2010 by SQUARE ENIX CO., LTD.
English translation rights arranged with SQUARE ENIX CO., LTD.
and Kodansha USA Publishing, LLC through Tuttle-Mori Agency, Inc.
Translation © 2020 by SQUARE ENIX CO., LTD.

Translation provided by Vertical Comics, 2020
Published by Vertical Comics, an imprint of Kodansha USA Publishing, LLC.,
New York

Originally published in Japanese as *Danshi Kokosei no Nichijo 1*
by SQUARE ENIX Co., Ltd., 2010
Danshi Kokosei no Nichijo first serialized in *Gangan Online*, SQUARE ENIX Co.,
Ltd., 2009-2012

This is a work of fiction.

ISBN: 978-1-949980-21-9

Manufactured in the United States of America

First Edition

Kodansha USA Publishing, LLC.
451 Park Avenue South
7th Floor
New York, NY 10016
www.readvertical.com

Vertical books are distributed through Penguin-Random House Publisher Services.